JavaScript Concurrency

Build better software with concurrent JavaScript programming, and unlock a more efficient and forward-thinking approach to web development

Adam Boduch

[PACKT] open source*
PUBLISHING community experience distilled

BIRMINGHAM - MUMBAI

JavaScript Concurrency

First published: December 2015

Production reference: 1181215

Published by Packt Publishing Ltd.
Livery Place
35 Livery Street
Birmingham B3 2PB, UK.

ISBN 978-1-78588-923-3

www.packtpub.com

Credits

Author
Adam Boduch

Reviewer
August Marcello III

Commissioning Editor
Edward Gordon

Acquisition Editor
Ruchita Bhansali

Content Development Editor
Divij Kotian

Technical Editor
Gebin George

Copy Editor
Yesha Gangani

Project Coordinator
Nikhil Nair

Proofreader
Safis Editing

Indexer
Tejal Daruwale Soni

Graphics
Jason Monteiro

Production Coordinator
Melwyn Dsa

Cover Work
Melwyn Dsa

About the Author

Adam Boduch has been involved with large-scale JavaScript development for nearly 10 years. Before moving to the front-end, he worked on several large-scale cloud computing products, using Python and Linux. No stranger to complexity, Adam has practical experience with real-world software systems, and the scaling challenges they pose. He is the author of several JavaScript books, including *JavaScript at Scale*, *Packt Publishing*, and is passionate about innovative user experiences and high performance.

About the Reviewer

August Marcello III is a highly passionate software engineer with nearly two decades of experience in the design, implementation, and deployment of modern client-side web application architectures in enterprise. An exclusive focus on delivering compelling SaaS-based User Experiences throughout the Web ecosystem has proven to be rewarding both personally and professionally. His passion for emerging technologies in general, combined with a particular focus on forward-thinking JavaScript platforms, have been a primary driver in his pursuit of technical excellence. When he's not coding, he can be found trail running, mountain biking, and spending time with his family and friends.

Many thanks to Chuck, Mark, Eric, and Adam, who I have had the privilege to work with and learn from. With gratitude to my family, friends, and the experiences I have been blessed to be a part of.

www.PacktPub.com

Support files, eBooks, discount offers, and more

For support files and downloads related to your book, please visit www.PacktPub.com.

Did you know that Packt offers eBook versions of every book published, with PDF and ePub files available? You can upgrade to the eBook version at www.PacktPub.com and as a print book customer, you are entitled to a discount on the eBook copy. Get in touch with us at service@packtpub.com for more details.

At www.PacktPub.com, you can also read a collection of free technical articles, sign up for a range of free newsletters and receive exclusive discounts and offers on Packt books and eBooks.

https://www2.packtpub.com/books/subscription/packtlib

Do you need instant solutions to your IT questions? PacktLib is Packt's online digital book library. Here, you can search, access, and readPackt's entire library of books.

Why subscribe?

- Fully searchable across every book published by Packt
- Copy and paste, print, and bookmark content
- On demand and accessible via a web browser

Free access for Packt account holders

If you have an account with Packt atwww.PacktPub.com, you can use this to access PacktLib today and view 9 entirely free books. Simply use your login credentials for immediate access.

For Melissa, Jason, and Simon, thanks for all your love and support.

Table of Contents

Preface   **vii**

Chapter 1: Why JavaScript Concurrency?   **1**

Synchronous JavaScript   **2**
Synchronicity is easy to understand   2
Asynchronous is inevitable   3
Asynchronous browsers   4
Types of concurrency   **5**
Asynchronous actions   5
Parallel actions   6
**JavaScript concurrency principles: Parallelize, Synchronize,
Conserve**   **8**
Parallelize   9
Synchronize   10
The Promise API   10
Conserve   11
Summary   **13**

Chapter 2: The JavaScript Execution Model   **15**

Everything is a task   **16**
Meet the players   16
The Execution environment   17
Event loops   18
Task queues   18
Execution contexts   **19**
Maintaining execution state   20
Job queues   20
Creating tasks using timers   **21**
Using setTimeout()   22
Using setInterval()   23

Responding to DOM events	**24**
Event targets	24
Managing event frequency	26
Responding to network events	**28**
Making requests	28
Coordinating requests	29
Concurrency challenges with this model	**30**
Limited opportunity for parallelism	31
Synchronization through callbacks	31
Summary	**32**
Chapter 3: Synchronizing with Promises	**33**
Promise terminology	**33**
Promise	33
State	34
Executor	34
Resolver	34
Rejector	34
Thenable	34
Resolving and rejecting promises	**35**
Resolving promises	35
Rejecting promises	37
Empty promises	39
Reacting to promises	**41**
Resolution job queues	41
Using promised data	42
Error callbacks	43
Always reacting	45
Resolving other promises	46
Promise–like objects	47
Building callback chains	**48**
Promises only change state once	48
Immutable promises	50
Many then callbacks, many promises	51
Passing promises around	53
Synchronizing several promises	**56**
Waiting on promises	56
Cancelling promises	57
Promises without executors	**59**
Summary	**62**

Chapter 4: Lazy Evaluation with Generators   63
Call stacks and memory allocation   63
Bookmarking function contexts   64
Sequences instead of arrays   64
Creating generators and yielding values   66
Generator function syntax   66
Yielding values   67
Iterating over generators   68
Infinite sequences   69
No end in sight   69
Alternating sequences   70
Deferring to other generators   72
Selecting a strategy   73
Interweaving generators   76
Passing data to generators   79
Reusing generators   79
Lightweight map/reduce   81
Coroutines   85
Creating coroutine functions   86
Handling DOM events   88
Handling promised values   90
Summary   91
Chapter 5: Working with Workers   93
What are workers?   93
OS threads   94
Event targets   94
True parallelism   95
Types of workers   96
Dedicated workers   96
Sub-workers   97
Shared workers   98
Worker environments   99
What's available, what isn't?   99
Loading scripts   100
Communicating with workers   100
Posting messages   101
Message serialization   101
Receiving messages from workers   103

Sharing application state	**104**
Sharing memory	104
Fetching resources	106
Communicating between pages	108
Performing sub-tasks with sub-workers	**110**
Dividing work into tasks	110
A word of caution	114
Error handling in web workers	**115**
Error condition checking	115
Exception handling	116
Summary	**118**
Chapter 6: Practical Parallelism	**119**
Functional programming	**119**
Data in, data out	120
Immutability	121
Referential transparency and time	123
Do we need to go parallel?	**125**
How big is the data?	126
Hardware concurrency capabilities	128
Creating tasks and assigning work	129
Candidate problems	**135**
Embarrassingly parallel	135
Searching collections	135
Mapping and reducing	138
Keeping the DOM responsive	**140**
Bottom halves	140
Translating DOM manipulation	141
Translating DOM events	143
Summary	**145**
Chapter 7: Abstracting Concurrency	**147**
Writing concurrent code	**147**
Hiding the concurrency mechanism	148
Without concurrency	149
Worker communication with promises	**151**
Helper functions	151
Extending postMessage()	154
Synchronizing worker results	157
Lazy workers	**159**
Reducing overhead	159

Generating values in workers	160
Lazy worker chains	163
Using Parallel.js	**166**
How it works	166
Spawning workers	168
Mapping and reducing	169
Worker pools	**172**
Allocating pools	172
Scheduling jobs	174
Summary	**176**
Chapter 8: Evented IO with NodeJS	**177**
Single threaded IO	**177**
IO is slow	178
IO events	179
Multi-threading challenges	180
More connections, more problems	**181**
Deploying to the Internet	181
The C10K problem	182
Lightweight event handlers	183
Evented network IO	**184**
Handling HTTP requests	185
Streaming responses	186
Proxy network requests	189
Evented file IO	**193**
Reading from files	193
Writing to files	196
Streaming reads and writes	198
Summary	**199**
Chapter 9: Advanced NodeJS Concurrency	**201**
Coroutines with Co	**201**
Generating promises	202
Awaiting values	203
Resolving values	204
Asynchronous dependencies	206
Wrapping coroutines	207
Child Processes	**208**
Blocking the event loop	209
Forking processes	210
Spawning external processes	212
Inter-process communication	214

Process Clusters — **217**
    Challenges with process management — 218
    Abstracting process pools — 218
Server clusters — **221**
    Proxying requests — 221
    Facilitating micro-services — 222
    Informed load balancing — 224
Summary — **227**
Chapter 10: Building a Concurrent Application — **229**
    Getting started — **230**
    Concurrency first — 230
    Retrofitting concurrency — 231
    Application types — 232
    Requirements — **232**
    The overall goal — 233
    The API — 233
    The UI — 234
    Building the API — **235**
    The HTTP server and routing — 235
    Co-routines as handlers — 237
    The create chat handler — 239
    The join chat handler — 240
    The load chat handler — 242
    The send message handler. — 242
    Static handlers — 244
    Building the UI — **245**
    Talking to the API — 245
    Implementing the HTML — 249
    DOM events and manipulation — 250
    Adding an API worker — 254
    Additions and improvements — **258**
    Clustering the API — 259
    Cleaning up chats — 259
    Asynchronous entry points — 259
    Who's typing? — 260
    Leaving chats — 260
    Polling timeouts — 260
    Summary — **261**
Index — **263**

Preface

It wasn't long ago when I would dread using many of the web applications I had come to depend on. When they worked, they were fantastic; when they didn't, it was a nightmare. Especially frustrating was the clear fact that there weren't any bugs in the JavaScript code driving the application. No, the problem was that often there was too much code running, perhaps because it was processing a large data set. The end result was always the same: the UI would freeze, and I would helplessly curse the Web.

Nowadays, this doesn't happen as frequently. We've fixed many of the common JavaScript problems from years ago. Something that hasn't caught on as fast as I had hoped is concurrency in JavaScript. There are little bits of concurrency sprinkled all throughout our applications, but seldom do we see truly concurrent JavaScript code.

Let's change the status quo.

What this book covers

Chapter 1, Why JavaScript Concurrency?, is an introduction to concurrency in JavaScript.

Chapter 2, The JavaScript Execution Model, takes you through the mechanisms that run our JavaScript code.

Chapter 3, Synchronizing with Promises, looks at synchronization techniques using promises.

Chapter 4, Lazy Evaluation with Generators, will get your grips to conserving resources by computing lazily.

Chapter 5, Working with Workers, looks at achieving true parallelism in JavaScript.

Chapter 6, Practical Parallelism, will help you in identifying the right parallelization problems to solve.

Chapter 7, Abstracting Concurrency, will get your hands dirty writing concurrent code that reads like regular code.

Chapter 8, Evented IO with NodeJS, will show you how concurrency semantics work in this environment.

Chapter 9, Advanced NodeJS Concurrency, is learning about specific Node concurrency issues.

Chapter 10, Building a Concurrent Application, is all about putting it all together.

What you need for this book

Requirements for this book are as follows:

- A recent version of any major browser
- NodeJS (at least 4.0)
- A code editor

Who this book is for

JavaScript Concurrency is written for any JavaScript developer who wants to learn how to write more efficient, powerful, and maintainable applications that utilize the latest developments in the JavaScript language.

All aspects of concurrent, asynchronous, and parallel programming are covered from first principles, and by the end of the book you'll be able to create a fully-worked application that leverages all the topics covered in the book.

Conventions

In this book, you will find a number of text styles that distinguish between different kinds of information. Here are some examples of these styles and an explanation of their meaning.

Code words in text, database table names, folder names, filenames, file extensions, pathnames, dummy URLs, user input, and Twitter handles are shown as follows: "We can include other contexts through the use of the `include` directive."

A block of code is set as follows:

```
// Loads the worker script, and starts the
// worker thread.
var worker = new Worker('worker.js');
```

New terms and **important words** are shown in bold. Words that you see on the screen, for example, in menus or dialog boxes, appear in the text like this: "Clicking the **Next** button moves you to the next screen."

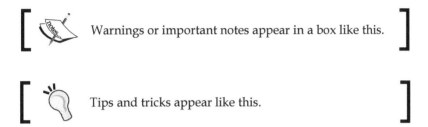

Warnings or important notes appear in a box like this.

Tips and tricks appear like this.

Reader feedback

Feedback from our readers is always welcome. Let us know what you think about this book—what you liked or disliked. Reader feedback is important for us as it helps us develop titles that you will really get the most out of.

To send us general feedback, simply e-mail feedback@packtpub.com, and mention the book's title in the subject of your message.

If there is a topic that you have expertise in and you are interested in either writing or contributing to a book, see our author guide at www.packtpub.com/authors.

Customer support

Now that you are the proud owner of a Packt book, we have a number of things to help you to get the most from your purchase.

Downloading the example code

You can download the example code files from your account at http://www.packtpub.com for all the Packt Publishing books you have purchased. If you purchased this book elsewhere, you can visit http://www.packtpub.com/support and register to have the files e-mailed directly to you.

Errata

Although we have taken every care to ensure the accuracy of our content, mistakes do happen. If you find a mistake in one of our books—maybe a mistake in the text or the code—we would be grateful if you could report this to us. By doing so, you can save other readers from frustration and help us improve subsequent versions of this book. If you find any errata, please report them by visiting `http://www.packtpub.com/submit-errata`, selecting your book, clicking on the **Errata Submission Form** link, and entering the details of your errata. Once your errata are verified, your submission will be accepted and the errata will be uploaded to our website or added to any list of existing errata under the Errata section of that title.

To view the previously submitted errata, go to `https://www.packtpub.com/books/content/support` and enter the name of the book in the search field. The required information will appear under the **Errata** section.

Piracy

Piracy of copyrighted material on the Internet is an ongoing problem across all media. At Packt, we take the protection of our copyright and licenses very seriously. If you come across any illegal copies of our works in any form on the Internet, please provide us with the location address or website name immediately so that we can pursue a remedy.

Please contact us at `copyright@packtpub.com` with a link to the suspected pirated material.

We appreciate your help in protecting our authors and our ability to bring you valuable content.

Questions

If you have a problem with any aspect of this book, you can contact us at `questions@packtpub.com`, and we will do our best to address the problem.

1
Why JavaScript Concurrency?

JavaScript is not a language associated with concurrency. In fact, it's frequently associated with the exact opposite—concurrency challenges. This has changed a lot over the past few years, especially with new language features in ES 2015. Promises have been used in JavaScript for many years; only now, they're a native type. Generators are another addition to the language that changes the way we think about concurrency in JavaScript. Web workers have been in browsers for several years, and yet, we don't see them used that often. Perhaps, it has less to do with workers and more about our understanding of the role that concurrency plays in our applications.

The aim of this chapter is to explore some general concurrency ideas, starting with what, exactly, concurrency is. If you don't have any sort of concurrent programming in your background, it's fine because this chapter is a perfect starting point for you. If you've done concurrent programming in the past using JavaScript or some other language, think of this chapter as a refresher, only with JavaScript as the context.

We'll wrap up this chapter with some overarching concurrency principles. These are valuable programming tools that we should keep in the back of our heads while writing concurrent code. Once we have learned to apply these principles, they'll tell us whether we're on the right track with our concurrency design, or that we need to take a step back and ask ourselves what we're really trying to achieve. These principles take a top-down approach to the design of our application. This means that they're applicable from the very start, even before we've started writing any code. Throughout the book, we'll be referring to these principles, so if you only read one section in this chapter, make sure it's *Concurrency principles* at the end.

Synchronous JavaScript

Before we start conjuring large-scale concurrent JavaScript architectures, let's shift our attention to the good old synchronous JavaScript code that we're all familiar with. These are the blocks of JavaScript code that are called as the result of a click event, or run as the result of loading a webpage. Once they start, they don't stop. That is to say, they're **run-to-completion**. We'll dig into run-to-completion a little more in the following chapter.

 We'll occasionally see the term **synchronous** and **serial** used interchangeably throughout the chapters. They're both referring to code statements that run one after another until there's nothing more to run.

Despite JavaScript being designed as a single-threaded, run-to-completion environment, the nature of the web complicates this. Think about the web browser, and all it's moving parts. There's the **Document Object Model (DOM)** for rendering user interfaces and **XMLHttpRequest (XHR)** objects for fetching remote data sources, to name a couple. Let's take a look at the synchronous nature of JavaScript and the asynchronous nature of the web.

Synchronicity is easy to understand

When code is synchronous, it's easier to understand. It's easier to mentally map the instructions that we're seeing on the screen to sequential steps in our heads; do this, then do that; check this, if `true`, do that, and so on. This type of serial processing is easy enough to understand, because there aren't any surprises, assuming the code isn't completely horrible. Here's an example of how we might visualize a chunk of synchronous code:

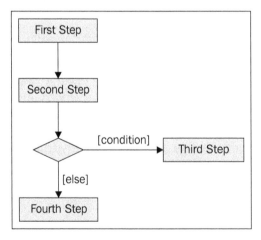

Concurrent programming, on the other hand, isn't so easy to grasp. This is because there's no linear logic for us to follow in our code editors. Instead, we constantly jump around, trying to map what this piece of code is doing relative to that piece of code. Time is an important factor with concurrent designs; it is something that goes against the brain's natural way of comprehending code. When we read code, we naturally execute it in our heads. This is how we figure out what it's doing. This approach falls apart when the actual execution doesn't line up with what's in our head. Normally, code reads like a book—concurrent code is like a book where the pages are numbered, but out of order. Let's take a look at some trivial pseudo JavaScript code:

```javascript
var collection = [ 'a', 'b', 'c', 'd' ];
var results = [];

for (let item of collection) {
    results.push(String.fromCharCode(item.charCodeAt(0)));
}
//      [ 'b', 'c', 'd', 'e' ]
```

In traditional multi-threading environments, a thread is something that runs asynchronously with other threads. We use threads to take advantage of multiple CPUs found on most systems today, resulting in better performance. However, this comes at a cost because it forces us to rethink how our code is executed at runtime. It's no longer the usual step by step execution. This code could be running alongside other code in another CPU, or it could be competing with other threads for time on the same CPU.

A lot of simplicity goes away when we introduce concurrency to synchronous code—it's the code equivalent of *brain freeze*. This is why we write concurrent code: code that makes an upfront assumption of concurrency. We'll elaborate on this concept as we progress through the book. With JavaScript, it's important to assume a concurrent design, because that's the way the web works.

Asynchronous is inevitable

The reason that concurrency in JavaScript is such an important idea is because the web is a concurrent place, both from a very high level and an implementation detail level. In other words, the web is concurrent because at any given point in time, there's oodles of data flowing over the miles of fiber, which encase the globe. It has to do with the applications themselves that are deployed to web browsers, and how the back-end servers handle the litany of requests for data.

Asynchronous browsers

Let's take a closer look at the browser and the kinds of asynchronous actions found there. When a user loads a webpage, one of the first actions that the page will perform is to download and evaluate our JavaScript code that goes with the page. This in itself is an asynchronous action, because while our code downloads, the browser will continue doing other things, such as rendering page elements.

Another asynchronous data source that arrives over the network is the application data itself. Once our page has loaded and our JavaScript code starts running, we'll need to display some data for the user. This is actually one of the first things that our code will do so that the user has something to look at right away. Again, while we're waiting on this data to arrive, the JavaScript engine will move our code right along to it's next set of instructions. Here's a request for remote data that doesn't wait for the response before continuing on with executing code:

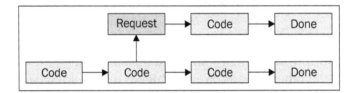

After the page elements have all been rendered and populated with data, the user starts interacting with our page. This means events are dispatched—clicking an element dispatches a click event. The DOM environment, where these events are dispatched from, is a sand-boxed environment. This means that within the browser, the DOM is a subsystem, separate from the JavaScript interpreter, which runs our code. This separation makes certain JavaScript concurrency scenarios especially difficult. We'll cover these in depth in the next chapter.

With all these sources of asynchronicity, it's no wonder that our pages can become bloated with special case handling to deal with the edge cases that inevitably pop up. Thinking asynchronously isn't natural, so this type of monkey-patching is the likely result of thinking synchronously. It's best to embrace the asynchronous nature of the web. After all, a synchronous web can lead to unbearable user experiences. Now, let's dig a little further into the types of concurrency we're likely to face in our JavaScript architectures.

Types of concurrency

JavaScript is a run-to-completion language. There's no getting around it, despite any concurrency mechanisms that are thrown on top of it. In other words, our JavaScript code isn't going to yield control to another thread in the middle of an `if` statement. The reason this matters is so that we can pick a level of abstraction that makes sense in helping us think about JavaScript concurrency. Let's look at the two types of concurrent actions found in our JavaScript code.

Asynchronous actions

A defining characteristic of asynchronous actions is that they do not block other actions that follow. Asynchronous actions don't necessarily mean *fire-and-forget*. Rather, when the part of the action we're waiting on completes, we run a callback function. This callback function falls out of sync with the rest of our code; hence, the term asynchronous.

In web front-ends, this generally means fetching data from a remote service. These fetching actions are relatively slow, because they have to traverse the network connection. It makes sense for these actions to be asynchronous, just because our code is waiting on some data to return so that it can fire a callback function, doesn't mean the user should have to sit around and wait too. Furthermore, it's unlikely that any screen that the user is currently looking at depends on only one remote resource. So, serially processing multiple remote fetch requests would have a detrimental effect on the user experience.

Here's a general idea of what asynchronous code looks like:

```
var request = fetch('/foo');

request.addEventListener((response) => {
    // Do something with "response" now that it has arrived.
});

// Don't wait with the response, update the DOM immediately.
updateUI();
```

Downloading the example code

You can download the example code files from your account at `http://www.packtpub.com` for all the Packt Publishing books you have purchased. If you purchased this book elsewhere, you can visit `http://www.packtpub.com/support` and register to have the files e-mailed directly to you.

We're not limited to fetching remote data, as the single source of asynchronous actions. When we make network requests, these asynchronous control flows actually leave the browser. But what about asynchronous actions that are confined within the browser? Take the setTimeout() function as an example. It follows the same callback pattern that's used with network fetch requests. The function is passed a callback, which is executed at a later point. However, nothing ever leaves the browser. Instead, the action is queued behind any number of other actions. This is because asynchronous actions are still just one thread of control, executed by one CPU. This means that as our applications grow in size and complexity, we're faced with a concurrency scaling issue. But then, maybe asynchronous actions weren't meant to solve the single CPU problem.

Perhaps a better way to think about asynchronous actions performed on a single CPU is to picture a juggler. The juggler's brain is the CPU, coordinating his motor actions. The balls that get tossed around is the data our actions operate on. There's only two fundamental actions we care about — *toss* and *catch*:

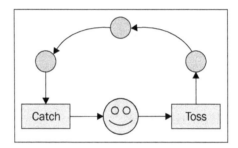

Since the juggler only has one brain, he can't possibly devote his mental capacity to perform more than one task at a time. However, the juggler is experienced and knows he doesn't need more than a tiny fraction of attention given to the toss or catch actions. Once the ball is in the air, he's free to return his attention to catching the ball that's about to land.

To anyone observing this juggler in action, it appears as though he's paying full attention to all six balls, when in reality, he's ignoring five of them at any point in time.

Parallel actions

Like asynchronicity, parallelism allows control flow to continue without waiting on actions to complete. Unlike asynchronicity, parallelism depends on hardware. This is because we can't have two or more flows of control taking place in parallel on a single CPU. However, the main aspect that sets parallelism apart from asynchronicity is the rationale for using it. The two approaches to concurrency solve different problems, and both require different design principles.

At the end of the day, we want to perform actions in parallel that would otherwise be time prohibitive, if performed synchronously. Think about a user who is awaiting three expensive actions to complete. If each takes 10 seconds to complete (an eternity on a UX timescale), then this means the user will have to wait for 30 seconds. If we're able to perform these tasks in parallel, we can bring the aggregate wait time closer to 10 seconds. We get more for less, leading to a performant user interface.

None of this is free. Like asynchronous actions, parallel actions lead to callbacks as a communication mechanism. In general, designing for parallelism is hard, because in addition to communicating with worker threads, we have to worry about the task at hand, that is, what are we hoping to achieve by using worker threads? And how do we break down our problem into smaller actions? The following is a rough idea of what our code starts to look like when we introduce parallelism:

```
var worker = new Worker('worker.js');
var myElement = document.getElementById('myElement');

worker.addEventListener('message', (e) => {
    myElement.textContent = 'Done working!';
});

myElement.addEventListener('click', (e) => {
    worker.postMessage('work');
});
```

Don't worry about the mechanics of what's happening with this code, as they'll all be covered in depth later on. The takeaway is that as we throw workers into the mix, we add more callbacks to an environment that's already polluted with them. This is why we have to design for parallelism in our code, which is a major focus of this book, starting in *Chapter 5*, *Working with Workers*.

Let's think about the juggler analogy from the preceding section. The toss and catch actions are performed asynchronously by the juggler; that is, he has only one brain/CPU. But suppose the environment around us is constantly changing. There's a growing audience for our juggling act and a single juggler can't possibly keep them all entertained:

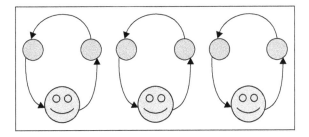

The solution is to introduce more jugglers to the act. This way we add more computing power capable, of performing multiple toss and catch actions in the same instant. This simply isn't possible with a single juggler running asynchronously.

We're not out of the woods yet, because we can't just have the newly-added jugglers stand in one place, and perform their act the same way our single juggler did. The audience is larger, more diverse, and needs to be entertained. The jugglers need to be able to handle different items. They need to move around on the floor so that the various sections of the audience are kept happy. They might even start juggling with each other. It's up to us to produce a design that's capable of orchestrating this juggling act.

JavaScript concurrency principles: Parallelize, Synchronize, Conserve

Now that we've been through the basics of what concurrency is, and its role in front-end web development, let's look at some fundamental concurrency principles of JavaScript development. These principles are merely tools that inform our design choices when we write concurrent JavaScript code.

When we apply these principles, they force us to step back and ask the appropriate questions before we move forward with implementation. In particular, they're the why and how questions:

- Why are we implementing this concurrent design?
- What do we hope to get out of it that we couldn't otherwise get out of a simpler synchronous approach?
- How do we implement concurrency in a way that's unobtrusive to the features of our applications?

Here's a reference visualization of each concurrency principle, feeding on one another during the development process. And with that, we'll turn our attention to each principle for further exploration:

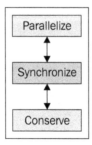

Parallelize

The parallelize principle means taking advantage of modern CPU capabilities to compute results in less time. This is now possible in any modern browser or NodeJS environment. In the browser, we can achieve true parallelism using web workers. In Node, we can achieve true parallelism by spawning new processes. Here's what the CPU looks like from the browser's perspective:

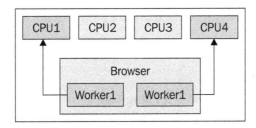

With the goal being more computations in less time, we must now ask ourselves why we want to do this? Besides the fact that raw performance is super cool in it's own right, there has to be some tangible impact for the user. This principle makes us look at our parallel code and ask—what does the user get out of this? The answer is that we can compute using larger data sets as input, and have a smaller opportunity of an unresponsive user experience due to long-running JavaScript.

It's important to scrutinize the tangible benefit of going parallel because when we do so, we add complexity to our code that wouldn't otherwise be there. So if the user sees the same result no matter what we do, the parallelize principle probably isn't applicable. On the other hand, if scalability is important and there's a strong possibility of growing data set sizes, the trade off of code simplicity for parallelism is probably worthwhile. Here's a checklist to follow when thinking about the parallelize principle:

- Does our application perform expensive computations against large data sets?
- As our data sets grow in size, is there potential for processing bottlenecks that negatively impact the user experience?
- Do our users currently experience bottlenecks in our application's performance?
- How feasible is parallelism in our design, given other constraints? What are the trade-offs?
- Do the benefits of our concurrency implementation outweigh the overhead costs, either in terms of user-perceived latency or in terms of code maintainability?

Synchronize

The synchronize principle is about the mechanisms used to coordinate concurrent actions and the abstractions of those mechanisms. Callback functions are a JavaScript notion with deep roots. It's the obvious tool of choice when we need to run some code, but we don't want to run it now. We want to run it when some condition becomes true. By and large, there's nothing inherently wrong with this approach. Used in isolation, the callback pattern is probably the most succinct, readable concurrency pattern that we can use. Callbacks fall apart when there are plenty them, and lots of dependencies between them.

The Promise API

The Promise API is the core JavaScript language construct, introduced in ECMAScript 6 to address the synchronization woes faced by every application on the planet. It's a simple API that actually makes use of callbacks (yes, we're fighting callbacks with callbacks). The aim of promises isn't to eliminate callbacks, it's to remove the unnecessary callbacks. Here's what a promise that's used to synchronize two network fetch calls looks like:

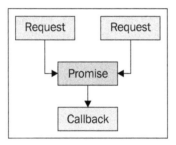

What's crucial about promises is that they're a generic synchronization mechanism. This means that they're not specifically made for network requests, web workers, or DOM events. We, the programmers, have to wrap our asynchronous actions with promises and resolve them as necessary. The reason why this is a good thing is because the callers that rely on the promise interface don't care about what's going on inside the promise. As the name implies, it's a promise to resolve a value at some point. This could be in 5 seconds or immediately. The data can come from a network resource or a web worker. The caller doesn't care, because it makes an assumption of concurrency, which means we can fulfill it any in way we like without breaking the application. Here's a modified version of the preceding diagram, which will give us a taste of what promises make possible:

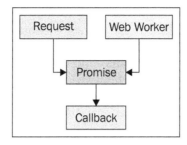

When we learn to treat values as values at some point in the future, concurrent code is suddenly much more approachable. Promises, and similar mechanisms, can be used to synchronize just network requests, or just web worker events. But they're real power is using them to write concurrent applications, where concurrency is the default. Here's a checklist to reference when thinking about the synchronize principle:

- Does our application heavily rely on callback functions as a synchronization mechanism?

- Do we often have to synchronize more than one asynchronous event such as network requests?

- Do our callback functions contain more synchronization boilerplate code than application code?

- What kind of assumptions does our code make about the concurrency mechanisms that drive asynchronous events?

- If we had a magic *kill concurrency* button, would our application still behave as expected?

Conserve

The conserve principle is about saving on compute and memory resources. This is done by using lazy evaluation techniques. The name *lazy* stems from the idea that we don't actually compute a new value until we're sure we actually need it. Imagine an application component that renders page elements. We can pass this component the exact data that it needs to render. This means that several computations take place before the component actually needs it. It also means that the data that's used needs to be allocated into memory, so that we can pass it to the component. There's nothing wrong with this approach. In fact, it's the standard way to pass data around in our JavaScript components.

The alternative approach uses lazy evaluation to achieve the same result. Rather than computing the values to be rendered, then allocating them in a structure to be passed, we compute one item, and then render it. Think of this as a kind of cooperative multi-tasking, where the larger action is broken down into smaller tasks that pass the focus of control back and forth.

Here's an eager approach to compute data and pass it to the component that renders UI elements:

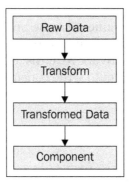

There's two undesirable aspects to this approach. First, the transformation happens up-front, which could be a costly computation. What happens if the component is unable to render it for whatever reason—due to some constraint? Then we've performed this computation to transform data that wasn't needed. As a corollary, we've allocated a new data structure for the transformed data so that we could pass it to our component. This transient memory structure doesn't really serve any purpose, as it's garbage-collected immediately. Let's take a look at what the lazy approach might look like:

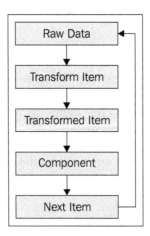

Using the lazy approach, we're able to remove the expensive transform computation that happens up-front. Instead, we transform only one item at a time. We're also able to remove the up-front allocation of the transformed data structure. Instead, only the transformed item is passed into the component. Then, the component can ask for another item or stop. The conserve principle uses concurrency as a means to only compute what's needed and only allocate memory that's needed.

The following checklist will help us think about the conserve principle when writing concurrent code:

- Are we computing values that are never used?
- Do we only allocate data structures as a means to pass them from one component to the next?
- Do we chain-together data transformation actions?

Summary

In this chapter, we introduced some motivations for concurrency in JavaScript. While synchronous JavaScript is easy to maintain and understand, asynchronous JavaScript code is inevitable on the web. So it's important to make concurrency our default assumption when writing JavaScript applications.

There's two main types of concurrency we're interested in—asynchronous actions and parallel actions. Asynchronicity is about the time ordering of actions, which gives the impression that things are happening at the same time. Without this type of concurrency, the user experience would suffer greatly, because it would constantly be waiting on other actions to complete. Parallelism is another type of concurrency that solves a different type of problem, where we want to increase performance by computing results faster.

Finally, we looked at the three principles of concurrency in JavaScript programming. The parallelize principle is about leveraging the multi-core CPUs found in modern systems. The synchronize principle is about creating abstractions that enable us to write concurrent code, hiding the concurrency mechanisms from our feature code. The conserve principle uses lazy evaluation to only compute what is needed and to avoid unnecessary memory allocations.

In the next chapter, we'll turn our attention to the JavaScript execution environment. To be effective with JavaScript concurrency, we need a sound understanding of what's actually happening when our code is run.

2
The JavaScript
Execution Model

The first chapter of this book explored the state of JavaScript concurrency. Generally speaking, dealing with concurrency in JavaScript applications is anything but a trivial matter. There's a lot to think about when writing concurrent JavaScript code, and the kind of solutions that we come up with are often unorthodox. There's a lot of callbacks, and wading through all of them is enough to drive a person insane. We also caught a glimpse of how our pattern of writing concurrent JavaScript code has started to change with existing concurrency components. Web workers have started to mature, and JavaScript language concurrency constructs have only just been introduced.

The language and the runtime environment only get us partway there. We need to think about concurrency at the design level, rather than after the fact. Concurrency should be the default. This is easy to say and very difficult to do. Throughout this book, we're going to explore all that the JavaScript concurrency features have to offer, and how we can best use them to our advantage as design tools. But, before we do this, we need to go into depth on what's really happening when our JavaScript runs. This knowledge is an essential input to designing concurrent applications, because we'll know exactly what to expect when choosing one concurrency mechanism over another.

In this chapter, we'll start with the browser environment, by looking at all the subsystems that our code touches—such as the JavaScript interpreter, the task queue, and the DOM itself. Then we'll walk through some code that will shed some light on what's really happening behind the scenes to orchestrate our code. We'll close the chapter with a discussion on the challenges that we face with this model.

Everything is a task

When we visit a web page, a whole environment is created for us within the browser. This environment has several subsystems that enable the webpage we're looking at to look and behave as it should according to **World Wide Web Consortium (W3C)** specs. Tasks are the fundamental abstraction inside a web browser. Anything that happens is either a task itself, or a smaller part of a larger task.

 If you're reading any of the W3C specifications, the term "user agent" is used instead of "web browser". In 99.9% of cases, the major browser vendors are what we're reading about.

In this section, we'll look at the major components of these environments, and how task queues and event loops facilitate the communication between these components, to realize the overall appearance and behavior of the web page.

Meet the players

Let's introduce some terminology that will help us throughout the various sections in this chapter:

- **Execution environment**: This container gets created whenever a new web page is opened. It's the all-encompassing environment, which has everything that our JavaScript code will interact with. It also serves as a sandbox—our JavaScript code can't reach outside of this environment.

- **JavaScript interpreter**: This is the component that's responsible for parsing and executing our JavaScript source code. It's the browser's job to augment the interpreter with globals, such as `window`, and `XMLHttpRequest`.

- **Task queue**: Tasks are queued whenever something needs to happen. An execution environment has at least one of these queues, but typically, it has several of them.

- **Event loop**: An execution environment has a single event loop that's responsible for servicing all task queues. There's only one event loop, because there's only one thread.

Take a look at the following visualization of an execution environment created within a web browser. The task queues are the entry points for anything that happens in the browser. For example, one task can be used to execute a script by passing it to the JavaScript interpreter, while another task is used to render pending DOM changes. Now we'll dig into the parts that make up the environment.

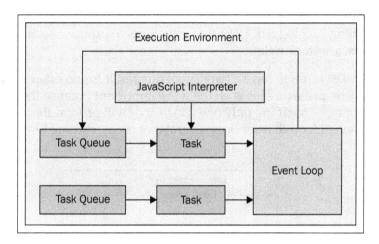

The Execution environment

Perhaps the most revealing aspect of the web browser execution environment is the relatively minor role played by our JavaScript code and the interpreter that executes it. Our code is simply a cog in a much larger machine. There's certainly a lot going on within these environments, because the platform that browsers implement serve an enormous purpose. It's not simply a matter of rendering elements on the screen, then enhancing these elements with style properties. The DOM itself is similar to a micro platform, just as networking facilities, file access, security, and so on. All these pieces are essential for a functioning web economy of sites, and more recently, applications.

In a concurrency context, we're mostly interested in the mechanics that tie all these platform pieces together. Our application is written mainly in JavaScript, and the interpreter knows how to parse and run it. But, how does this ultimately translate into visual changes on the page? How does the networking component of the browser know to make an HTTP request, and how does it invoke the JavaScript interpreter once the response has arrived?

It's the coordination of these moving parts that restricts our concurrency options in JavaScript. These restrictions are necessary, because without them, programming web applications would become too complex.

Event loops

Once an execution environment is in place, the event loop is one of the first components to start. Its job is to service one or more task queues in the environment. Browser vendors are free to implement queues as they see fit, but there has to be at least one queue. Browsers can place every task in one queue if they please, and treat every task with equal priority. The problem with doing so would mean that if the queue is getting backlogged, tasks that must receive priority, such as mouse or keyboard events, are stuck in line.

In practice, it makes sense to have a handful of queues, if for no other reason than to separate tasks by priority. This is all the more important because there's only one thread of control—meaning only one CPU—that will process these queues. Here's what an event loop that services several queues by varying levels of priorities looks like:

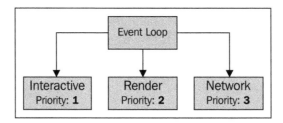

Even though the event loop is started along with the execution environment, this doesn't mean that there's always tasks for it to consume. If there were always tasks to process, there would never be any CPU time for the actual application. The event loop will sit and wait for more tasks, and the queue with the highest priority gets serviced first. For example, with the queues used in the preceding image, the *interactive* queue will always be serviced first. Even if the event loop is making its way through the *render* queue tasks, if an *interactive* task is queued, the event loop will handle this task before resuming with render tasks.

Task queues

The concept of queued tasks is essential to understand how web browsers work. The term browser is actually misleading. We used them to browse static web pages in an earlier, sparser web. Now, large and complex applications run in browsers—it's really more of a web platform. The task queues and event loops that service them are probably the best design to handle so many moving parts.

We saw earlier in this chapter that the JavaScript interpreter, along with the code that it parses and runs, is really just a black box when viewed from the perspective of an execution environment. In fact, invoking the interpreter is itself a task, and is reflective of the run-to-completion nature of JavaScript. Many tasks involve the invocation of the JavaScript interpreter, as visualized here:

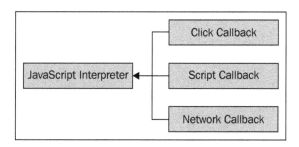

Any one of these events—the user clicking an element, a script loading in the page, or data from a prior API call arriving in the browser—creates a task that invokes the JavaScript interpreter. It tells the interpreter to run a specific piece of code, and it'll continue to run it until it completes. This is the run-to-completion nature of JavaScript. Next, we'll dig into the execution contexts created by these tasks.

Execution contexts

Now it's time to look at the JavaScript interpreter itself—the component that takes over from other browser components when events take place and code needs to run. There's always an active JavaScript context, and within the interpreter, we'll find a stack of contexts. This is similar to many programming languages where stacks control the active context.

Think of the active context as a snapshot of what's happening right now in our JavaScript code. A stack structure is used because the active context can change to something else, such as when a function is called. When this happens, a new snapshot is pushed onto the stack, becoming the active context. When it's done running, it's popped from the stack, leaving the next context as the active context.

In this section, we'll take a look at how the JavaScript interpreter handles context switching, and the internal job queue that manages the context stack.

Maintaining execution state

The stack of contexts within the JavaScript interpreter isn't a static structure—it's constantly changing. There's two important things that happen throughout the lifetime of this stack. First, at the top of the stack, we have the active context. This is the code that currently executes as the interpreter moves through its instructions. Here's an idea of what a JavaScript execution context stack looks like with the active context always at the top:

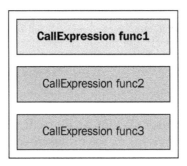

The other important responsibility of the call stack is to bookmark the state of an active context when it's deactivated. For example, let's say that after a few statements, func1() calls func2(). At this point, the context is bookmarked to the spot directly after the call to func2(). Then, it's replaced with the new active context—func2(). When it completes, the process is repeated and func1() again becomes the active context.

This kind of context switching happens all over our code. For example, there's a global context, which is the entry point into our code, there's the functions themselves which have their own context. There are also more recent additions to the language, which have their own contexts, such as modules and generators. Next, we'll look at the job queues responsible for creating new execution contexts.

Job queues

Jobs queues are similar to the task queues that we looked at earlier. The difference is that job queues are specific to the JavaScript interpreter. That is, they're encapsulated within the interpreter—the browser doesn't interact directly with these queues. However, when the interpreter is invoked by the browser, in response to a loaded script or event callback task for example, new jobs are created by the interpreter.

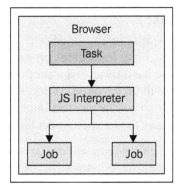

The job queues within the JavaScript interpreter are actually much more straightforward than the task queues that are used to coordinate all the web browser components. There are only two essential queues. One is for creating new execution context stacks (call stacks). The other is specific to promise resolution callback functions.

 We'll go into more depth on how the promise resolution callback job works in the next chapter.

Given the restricted responsibilities of these internal JavaScript job queues, one might draw the conclusion that they're unnecessary — an act of over engineering. That's not true, because while today there's limited responsibilities found in these jobs, the job queue design allows for much easier expansion and refinement of the language. In particular, the job queue mechanism is favorable when considering new concurrency constructs in future versions of the language.

Creating tasks using timers

So far in this chapter, we've had a look at all the inner workers of the web browser environment, and where the JavaScript interpreter fits in this environment. What does all this have to do with applying concurrency principles to our code? With the knowledge of what's happening under the hood, we have a greater insight into what's happening when a given chunk of our code is run. Particularly, we know what's happening relative to other code chunks; time ordering is a crucial concurrency property.

This being said, let's actually write some code. In this section, we'll use timers to explicitly add tasks to the task queue. We'll also learn when and where the JavaScript interpreter jumps in and starts executing our code.

Using setTimeout()

The setTimeout() function is staple in any JavaScript code. It's used to execute code at some point in the future. New JavaScript programmers often trip over the setTimeout() function because it's a timer. At a set point in the future, say 3 seconds from now, a callback function will be invoked. When we call setTimeout(), we will get the atimer ID in return, which can be cleared later on using clearTimeout(). Here's what the basic usage of setTimeout() looks like:

```
// Creates a timer that calls our function in no less
// than 300MS. We can use the "console.time()" and the
// "console.timeEnd()" functions to see how long it actually
// takes.
//
// This is typically around 301MS, which isn't at all
// noticeable by the user, but is unreliable for
// accurately scheduling function calls.
var timer = setTimeout(() => {
    console.timeEnd('setTimeout');
}, 300);

console.time('setTimeout');
```

Here's the part that's misunderstood by JavaScript newcomers; it's a best effort timer. The only guarantee we have when using setTimeout() is that our callback function will never be called sooner than the allotted time that we pass it. So if we said call this function in 300 milliseconds, it'll never call it in 275 milliseconds. Once the 300 milliseconds have elapsed, a new task is queued. If there's nothing waiting in line before this task, the callback is run right on time. Even if there are a few things in the queue in front of it, the effects are hardly noticeable—it appears to run at the correct time.

But as we've seen, JavaScript is single threaded and run-to-completion. This means that once the JavaScript interpreter starts, it doesn't stop until it's finished; even if there's a task waiting for a timer event callback. So, it's entirely possible that even though we asked the timer to execute the callback in 300 milliseconds, it executes it in 500 milliseconds. Let's take a look at an example to see how this is possible:

```
// Be careful, this function hogs the CPU...
function expensive(n = 25000) {
    var i = 0;
    while (++i < n * n) {}
```

```
    return i;
}

// Creates a timer, the callback uses
// "console.timeEnd()" to see how long we
// really waited, compared to the 300MS
// we were expecting.
var timer = setTimeout(() => {
    console.timeEnd('setTimeout');
}, 300);

console.time('setTimeout');

// This takes a number of seconds to
// complete on most CPUs. All the while, a
// task has been queued to run our callback
// function. But the event loop can't get
// to that task until "expensive()" completes.
expensive();
```

Using setInterval()

The cousin of setTimeout() is the setInterval() function. As the name suggests, it accepts a callback function that's to be called at a regular interval. In fact, setInterval() takes the exact same arguments as setTimeout(). The only difference is that it will keep calling the function every x milliseconds until the timer is cleared using clearInterval().

This function is handy when we want to keep calling the same function, over and over. For example, if we poll an API endpoint, setInterval() is a good candidate solution. However, keep in mind that the scheduling of the callbacks is fixed. That is, once we call setInterval() with, say, 1000 milliseconds, there's no changing that 1000 milliseconds without first clearing the timer. For cases where the interval needs to be dynamic, using setTimeout() works better. The callback schedules the next interval, which allows the interval to be dynamic. For example, backing off from polling an API too frequently by increasing the interval.

In the `setTimeout()` example that we last looked at, we saw how running JavaScript code can mess with the event loop. That is, it prevents the event loop from consuming the task that invokes the JavaScript interpreter with our callback function. This allows us to defer code execution till some point in the future, but with no promises of accuracy. Let's see what happens when we schedule tasks using `setInterval()`. There's also some blocking JavaScript code that runs afterward:

```
// A counter for keeping track of which
// interval we're on.
var cnt = 0;

// Set up an interval timer. The callback will
// log which interval scheduled the callback.
var timer = setInterval(() => {
    console.log('Interval', ++cnt);
}, 3000);

// Block the CPU for a while. When we're no longer
// blocking the CPU, the first interval is called,
// as expected. Then the second, when expected. And
// so on. So while we block the callback tasks, we're
// also blocking tasks that schedule the next interval.
expensive(50000);
```

Responding to DOM events

In the preceding section, we saw how to schedule JavaScript code to run at a later time. This is done explicitly by other JavaScript code. Most of the time, our code runs in response to user interactions. In this section, we'll look at the common interface that's used not only by DOM events, but also by things such as network and web worker events. We'll also look at a technique for dealing with large volumes of similar events—called debouncing.

Event targets

The `EventTarget` interface is used by many browser components, including DOM elements. It's how we dispatch events to elements as well as listen to events and respond by executing a callback function. It's actually a very straightforward interface that's easy to follow. This is crucial since many different types of components use this same interface for event management. We'll see as we progress through the book.

The same task queue mechanisms that execute the callback functions for the timers that we used in the preceding section are relevant for `EventTarget` events. That is, if an event has taken place, a task to invoke the JavaScript interpreter with the appropriate callback is queued. The same limitations faced with using `setTimeout()` are imposed here. Here's what a task queue looks like when there's long-running JavaScript code that's blocking user events:

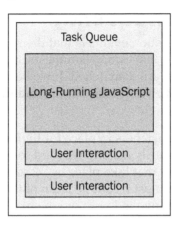

In addition to attaching listener functions to event targets that react to user interaction, we can trigger these events manually, as the following code illustrates:

```
// A generic event callback, logs the event timestamp.
function onClick(e) {
    console.log('click', new Date(e.timeStamp));
}

// The element we're going to use as the event
// target.
var button = document.querySelector('button');

// Setup our "onClick" function as the
// event listener for "click" events on this target.
button.addEventListener('click', onClick);

// In addition to users clicking the button, the
// EventTarget interface lets us manually dispatch
// events.
button.dispatchEvent(new Event('click'));
```

It's good practice to name functions that are used in callbacks where possible. This way, when our code breaks, it's much easier to trace down the problem. It's not impossible with anonymous functions, it's just more time consuming. On the other hand, arrow functions are more concise and have more binding flexibility. Choose your trade-offs wisely.

Managing event frequency

One challenge with user interaction events is that there can be lots of them, in a very short amount of time. For instance, when the user moves the mouse around on the screen, hundreds of events are dispatched. If we had event targets listening for these events, the task queue would quickly fill up, and the user experience would bog down.

Even when we do have event listeners in place for high frequency events, such as mouse moves, we don't necessarily need to respond to all of them. For example, if there's 150 mouse move events that take place in 1-2 seconds, chances are, we only care about the last move — the most recent position of the mouse pointer. That is, the JavaScript interpreter is being invoked with our event callback code 149 times more than it needs to.

To deal with these types of event frequency scenarios, we can utilize a technique called *debouncing*. A debounced function means that if it's called in succession more than once within a given time frame, only the last call is actually used and the earlier calls are ignored. Let's walk through an example of how we can implement this:

```
// Keeps track of the number of "mousemove" events.
var events = 0;

// The "debounce()" takes the provided "func" an limits
// the frequency at which it is called using "limit"
// milliseconds.
function debounce(func, limit) {
    var timer;

    return function debounced(...args) {
        // Remove any existing timers.
        clearTimeout(timer);

        // Call the function after "limit" milliseconds.
        timer = setTimeout(() => {
            timer = null;
```

```
                func.apply(this, args);
            }, limit);
        };
    }


    // Logs some information about the mouse event. Also log
    // the total number of events.
    function onMouseMove(e) {
        console.log(`X ${e.clientX} Y ${e.clientY}`);
        console.log('events', ++events);
    }


    // Log what's being typed into the text input.
    function onInput(e) {
        console.log('input', e.target.value);
    }


    // Listen to the "mousemove" event using the debounced
    // version of the "onMouseMove()" function. If we
    // didn't wrap this callback with "debounce()"
    window.addEventListener('mousemove', debounce(onMouseMove, 300));


    // Listen to the "input" event using the debounced version
    // of the "onInput()" function to prevent triggering events
    // on every keystroke.
    document.querySelector('input')
        .addEventListener('input', debounce(onInput, 250));
```

Using the debounce technique to avoid giving the CPU more work than necessary is an example of the conserve principle in action. By ignoring 149 events, we save (conserve) the CPU instructions that would otherwise be executed and provide no real value. We also save on any kind of memory allocation that would otherwise happen in these event handlers.

The JavaScript concurrency principles were introduced at the end of *Chapter 1, Why JavaScript Concurrency?*, and they'll be pointed out throughout the code examples in the remainder of the book.

Responding to network events

Another critical piece of any front-end application is network interactions, fetching data, issuing commands, and so forth. Since network communications are an inherently asynchronous activity, we have to rely on events—the EventTarget interface to be precise.

We'll start by looking at the generic mechanism that hooks up our callback functions with requests and getting responses from the back-end. Then, we'll look at how trying to synchronize several network requests creates a seemingly hopeless concurrency scenario.

Making requests

To interact with the network, we create a new instance of XMLHttpRequest. We then tell it the type of request that we want to make—GET versus POST and the request endpoint. These request objects also implement the EventTarget interface so that we can listen for data arriving from the network. Here's an example of what this code looks like:

```
// Callback for successful network request,
// parses JSON data.
function onLoad(e) {
    console.log('load', JSON.parse(this.responseText));
}

// Callback for problematic network request,
// logs error.
function onError() {
    console.error('network', this.statusText ||
        'unknown error');
}

// Callback for a cancelled network request,
// logs warning.
function onAbort() {
    console.warn('request aborted...');
}

var request = new XMLHttpRequest();

// Uses the "EventTarget" interface to attach event
```

```
// listeners, for each of the potential conditions.
request.addEventListener('load', onLoad);
request.addEventListener('error', onError);
request.addEventListener('abort', onAbort);

// Sends a "GET" request for "api.json".
request.open('get', 'api.json');
request.send();
```

We can see here that there are a number of possible states for network requests. The successful path is the server responding with the data we need and we're able to parse it as JSON. The error state is when something went wrong, maybe the server isn't reachable. The final state that we're concerned with here is when the request is cancelled or aborted. This means that we no longer care about the successful path because something in our application changed while the request was in flight. The user navigated to another section, for example.

While the previous code was easy enough to use and understand, it's not always the case. We're looking at a single request and a few callbacks. Very seldom do our application components consist of a single network request.

Coordinating requests

In the preceding section, we saw what the basic interaction with XMLHttpRequest instances looks like for making a network request. The challenge surfaces when there are several requests. Most of the time, we make multiple network requests so that we have the data necessary for rendering a UI component. The responses from the back-end will all arrive at different times, and are likely dependent on one another.

Somehow, we need to synchronize the responses of these asynchronous network requests. Let's take a look at how we can go about doing this using the EventTaget callback functions:

```
// The function that's called when a response arrives ,
// it's also responsible for coordinating responses.
function onLoad() {

    // When the response is ready, we push the parsed
    // response onto the "responses" array, so that we
    // can use responses later on when the rest of them
    // arrive.
    responses.push(JSON.parse(this.responseText));

    // Have all the respected responses showed up yet?
```

```
        if (responses.length === 3) {
            // How we can do whatever we need to, in order
            // to render the UI component because we have
            // all the data.
            for (let response of responses) {
                console.log('hello', response.hello);
            }
        }
    }
}

// Creates our API request instances, and a "responses"
// array used to hold out-of-sync responses.
var req1 = new XMLHttpRequest(),
    req2 = new XMLHttpRequest(),
    req3 = new XMLHttpRequest(),
    responses = [];

// Issue network requests for all our network requests.
for (let req of [ req1, req2, req3 ]) {
    req.addEventListener('load', onLoad);

    req.open('get', 'api.json');
    req.send();
}
```

There's a lot of extra bits to consider when there's more than one request. Since they all arrive at different times, we need to store the parsed responses in an array, and with the arrival of every response, we need to check if we have everything we expect. This simplified example doesn't even take into consideration failed or cancelled requests. As this code alludes, the callback function approach to synchronization is limiting. In the coming chapters, we'll learn how to overcome this limitation.

Concurrency challenges with this model

We'll wrap this chapter up with a discussion on the challenges that this execution model poses with JavaScript concurrency. There are two fundamental obstacles. The first is the fact that no matter what, any JavaScript code that runs will block anything else from happening. The second obstacle is trying to synchronize asynchronous actions with callback functions, leading to callback hell.

Limited opportunity for parallelism

It used to be that the lack of parallelism in JavaScript wasn't really an issue. Nobody missed it because JavaScript was viewed as a progressive enhancement tool for HTML pages. This changed when the front-end started taking on more responsibilities. These days, the majority of the application actually resides in the front-end. This allows back-end components to focus on problems that can't be solved by JavaScript (from a browser perspective, NodeJS is another matter entirely that we'll look at later in the book).

For example, mapping and reducing API data sources into some representation required by a feature can be implemented in the back-end. This means that the front-end JavaScript code just needs to query for this endpoint. The problem is that this API endpoint is created for some specific UI feature, not as an essential supporting pillar of our data model. If we can perform these tasks in the front-end, we keep the UI features and the data transformations they need, tightly coupled together. This frees up the back-end to stay focused on more pressing issues like replication and load balancing.

We can perform these types of data transformations in the front-end, but they wreak havoc on the usability of the interface. This is largely due to all the moving parts competing for the same compute resource. This model, in other words, makes it impossible for us to implement the parallelize principle and take advantage of more than one resource. We will overcome this web browser limitation with the help of Web workers, covered in further chapters.

Synchronization through callbacks

Synchronization through callbacks is hard to implement and doesn't scale well. It's callback hell, which is a term popular among JavaScript programmers. Needless to say, endless synchronization through callbacks in our code creates problems. We often have to create some kind of state tracking mechanism, such as global variables. And when problems do arise, a nest of callback functions is very time consuming to traverse mentally.

Generally speaking, the callback approach to synchronizing multiple asynchronous actions requires a lot of overhead. That is, the boilerplate code that exists for the sole purpose of dealing with asynchronous actions. The synchronize concurrency principle is about writing concurrent code that doesn't embed the main goal in a maze of synchronization handling logic. Promises help us write concurrent code consistently throughout our application by lessening the use of callback functions.

Summary

The focus of this chapter has been the web browser platform and JavaScript's place within it. There are a lot of events taking place whenever we view and interact with web pages. These are processed as tasks, taken from queues. One such task is invoking the JavaScript interpreter with code to run.

When the JavaScript interpreter runs, it contains an execution context stack. A function, a module, and global script code — these are all examples of JavaScript execution contexts. The interpreter also has it's own internal job queues; one is used to create new execution context stacks, and another is used for calling promise resolution callback functions.

We wrote some code that manually created tasks using the `setTImeout()` function and explicitly demonstrated how long-running JavaScript code can be problematic for these tasks. We then looked at the `EventTarget` interface, used to listen to DOM events, and to network requests, amongst other things we didn't look at in this chapter, like web workers and file readers.

We wrapped up with a look at some of the challenges that JavaScript programmers face when using this model. In particular, it's hard to follow our JavaScript concurrency principles. We can't parallelize, and trying to synchronize using nothing but callbacks is a nightmare.

In the next chapter, we'll look at a new way of thinking about synchronization using promises. This will allow us to start designing and building concurrent JavaScript applications in earnest.

Synchronizing with Promises

3

Implementations of promises have existed for many years inside JavaScript libraries. It all started with the Promises/A+ specification. Libraries implemented their own variations of this specification, and it wasn't until recently (ES6 to be exact) that the Promise specification made it into the JavaScript language. They do what the chapter title suggests — help us apply the synchronization principle.

In this chapter, we'll start of with a gentle introduction to the various terms used in promise-speak so that the remainder of the chapter will be a little easier to follow. Then, well go through the various ways that promises are used to resolve future values and make our lives easier when we deal with concurrency. Ready?

Promise terminology

Before we dive right into the code examples, let's take a minute to make sure we have a firm grasp on the terminology surrounding promises. There are promise instances, but then there are also various states and actions to consider. The sections that follow will make much more sense if we can nail down the promise lexicon. These explanations are short and sweet, so if you've already used promises, you can quickly gloss over these definitions to sanity check your knowledge.

Promise

As the name suggests, a promise is, well, a promise. Think of a promise as a proxy for a value that doesn't exist yet. The promise let's us write better concurrent code because we know that the value will be there at some point, and we don't have to write lots of state-checking boilerplate code.

State

Promises are always in one of three states:

- **Pending**: This is the first state of a promise after it's been created. It remains in a pending state until it's fulfilled or rejected.
- **Fulfilled**: The promise value has been resolved and is available to the `then()` callback function.
- **Rejected**: Something went wrong trying to resolve the promised value. There will be no data today.

An interesting property of promise states is that they only transition once. They either go from pending to fulfilled or from pending to rejected. And once they make this state transition, they're stuck in this state for the rest of their existence.

Executor

The executor function is responsible for somehow resolving the value that the caller is waiting for. This function is called immediately after the promise is created. It takes two arguments: a `resolver` function and a `rejector` function.

Resolver

The resolver is a function that's passed to the executor function as an argument. Actually, this is quite handy because we can then pass the resolver function to another function, and so on. It doesn't matter where the resolver function is called from, but when it's called, the promise moves into a fulfilled state. This change in state will trigger any `then()` callbacks — we'll see what these are shortly.

Rejector

The rejector is similar to the resolver. It's the second argument passed to the `executor` function, which can be called from anywhere. When it's called, it changes the state of the promise from pending to rejected. This state change will call the `error` callback function, if any, passed to `then()` or `catch()`.

Thenable

An object is thenable if it has a `then()` method that accepts a fulfillment callback and a rejection callback as arguments. In other words, a promise is thenable. But there are cases where we might want to implement specialized resolution semantics.

Resolving and rejecting promises

If the preceding section just introduced several new terms that sounded confusing, then don't worry. We'll see what all these promise terms look like in practice, starting with this section. Here, we'll perform some straightforward promise resolving and rejecting.

Resolving promises

The resolver is a function that, as the name implies, resolves a promise for us. It's not the only way to resolve a promise—we'll explore more advanced techniques later on in the chapter. But this method is, by far, the most common. It's passed into the executor function as the first argument. This means that the executor can resolve the promise directly by simply calling the resolver. But this wouldn't provide us with much utility, would it?

The common case to a greater extent is for the promise `executor` function to set up the asynchronous actions that are about to take place—things such as making network calls. Then, in the callback functions for these asynchronous actions, we can resolve the promise. It's a little counterintuitive at first, passing a resolve function around in our code, but it'll make more sense once we start using them.

A resolver function is an opaque function that's bound to a promise. It can only resolve a promise once. We can call the resolver as many times as we please, but only the first call will change the state of the promise. Here's a diagram that depicts the possible states of a promise; it also shows how they're changed:

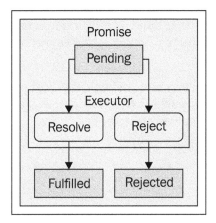

Now, let's take a look at some promise code. Here, we'll resolve a promise, which causes the `then()` fulfillment callback function to be called:

```
// The executor function used by our promise.
// The first argument is the resolver function,
// which is called in 1 second to resolve the promise.
function executor(resolve) {
    setTimeout(resolve, 1000);
}


// The fulfillment callback for our promise. This
// simply stopsthe fullfillment timer that was
// started after our executor function was run.
function fulfilled() {
    console.timeEnd('fulfillment');
}


// Creates the promise, which will run the executor
// function immediately. Then we start a timer to see
// how long it takes for our fulfillment function to
// be called.
var promise = new Promise(executor);
promise.then(fulfilled);
console.time('fulfillment');
```

As we can see, the `fulfilled()` function is called when the resolver function is called. The executor doesn't actually call the resolver. Rather, it passes the resolver function to another asynchronous function – `setTimeout()`. The executor function itself isn't the asynchronous code that we're trying to wrangle. The executor can be thought of as a sort of coordinator, orchestrating asynchronous actions to determine when to resolve the promise.

The preceding example didn't resolve any values. This is a valid use cases when the caller of some action needs acknowledgement that it either succeeded or failed. Instead, let's try resolving a value this time, as follows:

```
// The executor function used by our promise.
// Sets a timeout that calls "resolve()" one second
// after the promise is created. It's resolving
// a string value - "done!".
function executor(resolve) {
    setTimeout(() => {
        resolve('done!');
    }, 1000);
```

```
}

// The fulfillment callback for our promise accepts
// a value argument. This is the value that's passed
// to the resolver.
function fulfilled(value) {
    console.log('resolved', value);
}

// Create our promise, providing the executor and
// fulfillment function callbacks.
var promise = new Promise(executor);
promise.then(fulfilled);
```

We can see that this code is very similar to the preceding example. The difference
is that our resolver function is actually called within the closure of the callback
function that's passed to `setTimeout()`. This is because we're resolving a string
value. There's also an argument that's passed to our `fulfilled()` function, which
is the resolved value.

Rejecting promises

The promise `executor` function doesn't always go as planned, and when this
happens, we need to reject the promise. This is the other possible state transition
from pending. Instead of moving into a fulfilled state, the promise moves into
a rejected state. This causes a different callback to execute, separate from the
fulfillment callback. Thankfully, the mechanics of rejecting promises is very
similar to resolving them. Let's take a look at how this is done:

```
// This executor function rejects the promise after
// a timeout of one second. It uses the rejector function
// to change the state, and to provide the rejected
// callbacks with a value.
function executor(resolve, reject) {
    setTimeout(() => {
        reject('Failed');
    }, 1000);
}

// The function used as a rejected callback function. It
// expects a reason for the rejection to be provided.
function rejected(reason) {
    console.error(reason);
```

```
}

// Creates the promise, and runs the executor. Uses the
// "catch()" method to assing the rejector callback function.
var promise = new Promise(executor);
promise.catch(rejected);
```

This code looks very familiar to the resolution code that we looked at in the preceding section. We set a timeout, and instead of resolving the function, we rejected it. This is done using the `rejector` function and is passed into the executor as the second argument.

We use the `catch()` method instead of the `then()` method to setup our rejection callback function. We'll look at how the `then()` method can be used to handle both fulfillment and rejection callbacks later on in the chapter. The rejection callback in this example simply logs the reason for the failure as an error. It's always important to provide this value. When we resolve promises, a value is common, although not strictly necessary. With rejections, on the other hand, there isn't a viable case for not providing the reason for the rejection even if the callback is only logging the error.

Let's look at another example, one that catches exceptions in the executor, and provides the rejected callbacks with a more meaningful interpretation of the failure:

```
// This promise executor throws an error, and the rejected
// callback function is called as a result.
new Promise(() => {
    throw new Error('Problem executing promise');
}).catch((reason) => {
    console.error(reason);
});


// This promise executor catches an error, and rejects
// the promise with a more useful message.
new Promise((resolve, reject) => {
    try {
        var size = this.name.length;
    } catch(error) {
        reject(error instanceof TypeError ?
            'Missing "name" property' : error);
    }
}).catch((reason) => {
    console.error(reason);
});
```

What's interesting about the first promise in the previous example is that it does change state, even though we're not explicitly changing the state of the promise using `resolve()` or `reject()`. However, it's important for the promise to eventually change state; we'll explore this topic in the next section.

Empty promises

Despite the fact that the `executor` function passes a `resolver` function and a `rejector` function, there's never any guarantee that the promise will change state. In this scenario, the promise simply hangs, and neither the resolved callback nor the rejected callback is triggered. This may not seem like a problem, and in fact, with simple promises, it's easy to diagnose and fix these unresponsive promises. However, as we get into more elaborate scenarios later in the chapter, a promise can be resolved as a result of several other promises resolving. If one of these promises doesn't resolve or reject, then the whole flow falls apart. This scenario is very time-consuming to debug; the following diagram is a visualization of the problem:

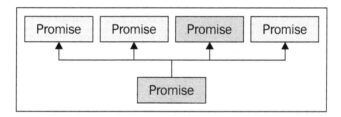

Visually, we can see which promise causes the dependent promise to hang, but sifting through the code to figure this out isn't ideal. Let's now look at an `executor` function that causes a promise to hang:

```
// This promise is able to run the executor
// function without issue. The "then()" callback
// is never executed.
new Promise((() => {
    console.log('executing promise');
}).then(() => {
    console.log('never called');
});

// At this point, we have no idea what's
// wrong with the promise.
console.log('finished executing, promise hangs');
```

But what if there was a safer way to deal with this uncertainty? An `executor` function with the potential to hang indefinitely without resolving or rejecting is hardly something we want in our code. Let's look at implementing an executor wrapper function that acts as a safety net by rejecting promises that take too long to resolve. This would take the mystery out of diagnosing complex promise scenarios:

```
// A wrapper for promise executor functions, that
// throws an error after the given timeout.
function executorWrapper(func, timeout) {

    // This is the function that's actually called by the
    // promise. It takes the resolver and rejector functions
    // as arguments.
    return function executor(resolve, reject) {
        // Setup our timer. When time runs out, we can
        // reject the promise with a timeout message.
        var timer = setTimeout(() => {
            reject(`Promise timed out after ${timeout}MS`);
        }, timeout);

        // Call the original executor function that we're
        // wrapping. We're actually wrapping the resolver
        // and rejector functions as well, so that when the
        // executor calls them, the timer is cleared.
        func((value) => {
            clearTimeout(timer);
            resolve(value);
        }, (value) => {
            clearTimeout(timer);
            reject(value);
        });
    };
}


// This promise executor times out, and a timeout
// error message is passed to the rejected callback.
new Promise(executorWrapper((resolve, reject) => {
    setTimeout(() => {
        resolve('done');
    }, 2000);
}, 1000)).catch((reason) => {
    console.error(reason);
```

```
});

// This promise resolves as expected, since the executor
// calls "resolve()" before time's up.
new Promise(executorWrapper((resolve, reject) => {
    setTimeout(() => {
        resolve(true);
    }, 500);
}, 1000)).then((value) => {
    console.log('resolved', value);
});
```

Reacting to promises

Now that we have a better understanding of the mechanics of executing promises, this section will take a closer look at using promises to solve particular problems. Typically, this means reacting with some purpose in mind when the promise is fulfilled or rejected.

We'll start off by looking at the job queues inside the JavaScript interpreter, and what these mean for our resolution callback functions. We'll then look at making use of the promised data, dealing with errors, creating better abstractions for reacting to promises, and thenables. Let's get going.

Resolution job queues

The concept of the JavaScript job queue was introduced in *Chapter 2*, *The JavaScript Execution Model*. Its main responsibility is to initiate new execution context stacks. This is the main job queue. However, there's another queue, which is dedicated to the callbacks executed by promises. This means that the algorithm responsible for selecting the next job to run can select from either of the queues if they're both populated.

Promises have concurrency semantics built into them, and with good reason. If a promise is used to ensure that a value is eventually resolved, it makes sense to give high priority to the code that reacts to it. Otherwise, when the value arrives, the code that processes it might have to wait in a longer line behind other jobs. Let's write some code that demonstrates these concurrency semantics:

```
// Creates 5 promises that log when they're
// executing, and when they're reacting to a
// resolved value.
for (let i = 0; i < 5; i++) {
    new Promise((resolve) => {
        console.log('executing promise');
```

```
            resolve(i);
        }).then((value) => {
            console.log('resolved', i);
        });
    }


    // This is called before any of the fulfilled
    // callbacks, because this call stack job needs
    // to complete before the interpreter reaches into
    // the promise resolution callback queue, where
    // the 5 "then()" callbacks are currently sitting.
    console.log('done executing');


    // →
    // executing promise
    // executing promise
    // ...
    // done executing
    // resolved 1
    // resolved 2
    // ...
```

 The same semantics are followed with rejected
callbacks too.

Using promised data

So far, we've seen a few examples in this chapter where a resolver function resolves
a promise with a value. The value that's passed to this function is the value that's
ultimately passed to the fulfilled callback function. The idea is for the executor to
set up any asynchronous action, such as `setTimeout()`, which would later call the
resolver with the value. But in these examples, the caller isn't actually waiting on
any values; we merely use `setTImeout()` as an example asynchronous action. Let's
look at a case where we don't actually have a value, and an asynchronous network
request needs to go get it:

```
    // A generic function used to fetch resources
    // from the server, returns a promise.
    function get(path) {
        return new Promise((resolve, reject) => {
            var request = new XMLHttpRequest();

            // The promise is resolved with the parsed
```

```
        // JSON data when the data is loaded.
        request.addEventListener('load', (e) => {
            resolve(JSON.parse(e.target.responseText));
        });

        // When there's an error with the request, the
        // promise is rejected with the appropriate reason.
        request.addEventListener('error', (e) => {
            reject(e.target.statusText || 'unknown error');
        });

        // If the request is aborted, we simply resolve the
        // request.
        request.addEventListener('abort', resolve);

        request.open('get', path);
        request.send();
    });
}

// We can attach our "then()" handler directly
// to "get()" since it returns a promise. The
// value used here was a true asynchronous operation
// that had to go fetch a remote value, and parse it,
// before resolving it here.
get('api.json').then((value) => {
    console.log('hello', value.hello);
});
```

With functions like get(), not only do they consistently return a synchronization primitive like a promise, but they also encapsulate some nasty asynchronous details. Dealing with XMLHttpRequest objects all over the place in our code isn't pleasant. We've also simplified various modes with which the response may come back. Instead of always having to create handlers for the load, error, and abort events, we only have one interface to worry about—the promise. This is what the synchronize concurrency principle is all about.

Error callbacks

There are two ways to react to rejected promises. Put differently, supplying error callbacks. The first approach is to use the catch() method, which takes a single callback function. The alternative is to pass in the rejected callback function as the second argument to then().

The then() approach that is used to supply rejected callback functions is superior in a couple of scenarios, and it should probably be used instead of catch(). The first scenario is writing our code so that promises and thenable objects are interchangeable. The catch() method isn't necessarily part of a thenable. The second scenario is when we build callback chains, which we will explore later on in this chapter.

Let's look at some code that compares the two approaches for providing rejected callback functions to promises:

```
// This promise executor will randomly resolve
// or reject the promise.
function executor(resolve, reject) {
    cnt++;
    Math.round(Math.random()) ?
        resolve(`fulfilled promise ${cnt}`) :
        reject(`rejected promise ${cnt}`);
}

// Make "log()" and "error()" functions for easy
// callback functions.
var log = console.log.bind(console),
    error = console.error.bind(console),
    cnt = 0;

// Creates a promise, then assigns the error
// callback via the "catch()" method.
new Promise(executor).then(log).catch(error);

// Creates a promise, then assigns the error
// callback via the "then()" method.
new Promise(executor).then(log, error);
```

We can see here that both approaches are actually very similar. There's no real advantage to one over the other in terms of code aesthetics. However, there's an advantage to the then() approach when it comes to using thenables, which we'll see shortly. But, since we're not actually using the promise instance in any way, other than to add the callbacks, there's really no need to worry about catch() versus then() for registering error callbacks.

Always reacting

Promises always end up in either a fulfilled state or a rejected state. We generally have distinct callback functions for each of these states. However, there's a strong possibility that we'll want to perform some of the same actions for both states. For example, if a component that uses a promise changes state while the promise is pending, we'll want to make sure that the state is cleaned up once the promise is resolved or rejected.

We could write our code in such a way that the callbacks for fulfilled and rejected states each perform these actions themselves, or that they can each call some common function that does the cleanup. Here's a visualization of the problem:

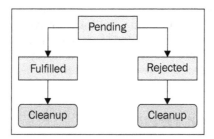

Wouldn't it make more sense to assign the cleanup responsibility to the promise, instead of assigning it to the individual outcomes? This way, the callback function that runs when the promise is resolved is focused on what it needs to do with the value, and the rejection callback is focused on dealing with the error. Let's see if we can write some code that extends promises with an `always()` method:

```
// Extends the promise prototype with an "always()"
// method. The given function will always be called,
// whether the promise is fulfilled or rejected.
Promise.prototype.always = function(func) {
    return this.then(func, func);
};

// Creates a promise that's randomly resolved or
// rejected.
var promise = new Promise((resolve, reject) => {
    Math.round(Math.random()) ?
        resolve('fulfilled') : reject('rejected');
});

// Give the promise fulfillment and rejection callbacks.
```

```
promise.then((value) => {
    console.log(value);
}, (reason) => {
    console.error(reason);
});

// This callback is always called after the one of
// the callbacks above.
promise.always((value) => {
    console.log('cleaning up...');
});
```

> Note that the order is important here. If we called always() before then(), then the function would still always run, but it would run before the callbacks provided to then(). We could actually call always() before and after then() to always run code before the fulfilled or rejected callbacks, and after.

Resolving other promises

Most of the promises that we've seen so far in this chapter have either been resolved directly by the executor function or as the result of calling the resolver from an asynchronous action, when the value was ready to resolve. Passing the resolver function around like this is actually quite flexible. For example, the executor doesn't even have to perform any work except for storing the resolver function somewhere for it to be called later on to resolve the promise.

This can be especially useful when we find ourselves in more complex synchronization scenarios that require multiple values, which have been promised to callers. If we have the resolver function, we can resolve the promise. Let's take a look at code that stores the `resolver` function of several promises so that each promise can be resolved later on:

```
// Keeps a list of resolver functions.
var resolvers = [];

// Creates 5 new promises, and in each executor
// function, the resolver is pushed onto the
// "resolvers" array. We also give each promise
// a fulfillment callback.
for (let i = 0; i < 5; i++) {
    new Promise((resolve) => {
        resolvers.push(resolve);
```

```
    }).then((value) => {
        console.log(`resolved ${i + 1}`, value);
    });
}

// Sets a timeout that runs the function after 2
// seconds. When it runs, we iterate over every
// resolver function in the "resolvers" array,
// and we call it with a value.
setTimeout(() => {
    for (let resolver of resolvers) {
        resolver(true);
    }
}, 2000);
```

As this example makes clear, we don't have to resolve anything within the `executor` function itself. In fact, we don't even need to explicitly reference promise instances after they've been created and set up with executors and fulfillment functions. The resolver function has been stored somewhere, and it holds a reference to the promise.

Promise–like objects

The Promise class is a primitive JavaScript type. However, we don't always need to create new promise instances to implement the same behavior for synchronizing actions. There's a static `Promise.resolve()` method that we can use to resolve such objects. Let's see how this method is used:

```
// The "Promise.resolve()" method can resolve thenable
// objects. This is an object with a "then()" method
// which serves as the executor. This executor will
// randomly resolve or reject the promise.
Promise.resolve({ then: (resolve, reject) => {
    Math.round(Math.random()) ?
        resolve('fulfilled') : reject('rejected');

// This method returns a promise, so we're able
// to setup our fulfilled and rejected callbacks as
// usual.
}}).then((value) => {
    console.log('resolved', value);
}, (reason) => {
    console.error('reason', reason);
});
```

We'll revisit the `Promise.resolve()` method in the final section of the chapter to take a look at more use cases.

Building callback chains

Each promise method that we examined so far in this chapter returns promises. This allows us to call these methods again on the return value, resulting in a chain of then().then() calls, and so forth. One challenging aspect of chaining promise calls together is that the instances returned by promise methods are new instances. That is, there's a degree of immutability to the promises that we'll explore in this section.

As our application gets larger, the concurrency challenges grow with it. This means that we need to think of better ways to leverage synchronization primitives, such as promises. Just as any other primitive value in JavaScript, we can pass them around from function to function. We have to treat promises in the same way—passing them around, and building upon the chain of callback functions.

Promises only change state once

Promises are born into a pending state, and they die in either a resolved or rejected state. Once a promise has transitioned into one of these states, they're stuck in this state. This has two interesting side-effects.

First, multiple attempts to resolve or reject a promise are ignored. In other words, resolvers and rejectors are idempotent—only the first call has any effect on the promise. Let's see how this looks code-wise:

```javascript
// This executor function attempts to resolve the
// promise twice, but the fulfilled callback is
// only called once.
new Promise((resolve, reject) => {
    resolve('fulfilled');
    resolve('fulfilled');
}).then((value) => {
    console.log('then', value);
});

// This executor function attempts to reject the
// promise twice, but the rejected callback is
// only called once.
new Promise((resolve, reject) => {
    reject('rejected');
    reject('rejected');
}).catch((reason) => {
    console.error('reason');
});
```

The other implication of promises changing state only once is that the promise could actually resolve before a fulfillment or rejection callback is added. Race conditions, such as this one, are the harsh reality of concurrent programming. Typically, the callback function is added to the promise at the time of creation. Since JavaScript is run-to-completion, the job queue that processes promise resolution callbacks isn't serviced until the callback is added. But, what if the promise resolves immediately in the executor? What if the callback is added to the promise in another JavaScript execution context? Let's see if we can better illustrate these ideas with some code:

```
// This executor function resolves the promise immediately.
// By the time the "then()" callback is added, the promise
// is already resolved. But the callback is still called
// with the resolved value.
new Promise((resolve, reject) => {
    resolve('done');
    console.log('executor', 'resolved');
}).then((value) => {
    console.log('then', value);
});


// Creates a new promise that's resolved immediately by
// the executor function.
var promise = new Promise((resolve, reject) => {
    resolve('done');
    console.log('executor', 'resolved');
});


// This callback is run immediately, since the promise
// has already been resolved.
promise.then((value) => {
    console.log('then 1', value);
});


// This callback isn't added to the promise for another
// second after it's been resolved. It's still called
// right away with the resolved value.
setTimeout(() => {
    promise.then((value) => {
        console.log('then 2', value);
    });
}, 1000);
```

This code illustrates a very important property of promises. It doesn't matter when our fulfillment callbacks are added to the promise, whether it's in a pending state, or a fulfilled state, the code that uses the promise doesn't change. On the face of it, this may not seem like a big deal. But this type of race condition checking would require more concurrency code for us to maintain ourselves. Instead, the Promise primitive handles this for us, and we can start treating asynchronous values as primitive types.

Immutable promises

Promises aren't truly immutable. They change state, and the then() method adds callback functions to the promise. However, there are some immutable traits of promises that are worth discussing here, as they impact our promise code in certain situations.

Technically speaking, the then() method doesn't actually mutate the promise object. It creates what's called a promise capability, which is an internal JavaScript record that references the promise, and the functions that we add. So, it's not a real reference in the JavaScript sense of the term.

Here's a visualization that illustrates what happens when we chain two or more then() calls together:

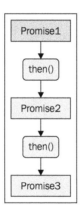

As we can see, the then() method does not return the same instance it was called with as the context. Instead, then() creates a new promise instance and returns that. Let's take a look at some code to examine more closely what happens when we chain together promises using then():

```
// Creates a promise that's resolved immediately, and
// is stored in "promise1".
var promise1 = new Promise((resolve, reject) => {
    resolve('fulfilled');
```

```
});

// Use the "then()" method of "promise1" to create a
// new promise instance, which is stored in "promise2".
var promise2 = promise1.then((value) => {
    console.log('then 1', value);
    // → then 1 fulfilled
});

// Create a "then()" callback for "promise2". This actually
// creates a third promise instance, but we don't do anything
// with it.
promise2.then((value) => {
    console.log('then 2', value);
    // → then 2 undefined
});

// Make sure that "promise1" and "promise2" are in fact
// different objects.
console.log('equal', promise1 === promise2);
// → equal false
```

We can clearly see that the two promise instances created in this example are separate promise objects. Something else that's worth pointing out is that the second promise is bound to the first one — it resolves when the first promise resolves. However, we can see that the value isn't passed to the second promise. We'll address this problem in the following section.

Many then callbacks, many promises

As we saw in the preceding section, promises created with `then()` are bound to their creator. That is, when the first promise is resolved, the promise that's bound it it also resolves, and so on. However, we noticed a slight problem as well. The resolved value doesn't make it past the first callback function. The reason for this is that each callback that's run in response to a promise resolution, is that the return value of the first callback is fed into the second callback, and so on. The reason our first callback gets the value as an argument is because this happens transparently within the promise mechanism.

Let's take a look at another promise chain example. This time, we'll explicitly return the values from our callback functions:

```
// Creates a new promise that's randomly resolved or
// rejected.
new Promise((resolve, reject) => {
    Math.round(Math.random()) ?
        resolve('fulfilled') : reject('rejected');
}).then((value) => {
    // Called when the original promise is resolved,
    // returns the value in case there's another
    // promise chained to this one.
    console.log('then 1', value);
    return value;
}).catch((reason) => {
    // Chained to the second promise, called
    // when it's rejected.
    console.error('catch 1', reason);
}).then((value) => {
    // Chained to the third promise, gets the
    // value as expected, and returns it for any
    // downstream promise callbacks to consume.
    console.log('then 2', value);
    return value;
}).catch((reason) => {
    // This is never called - rejections do not
    // proliferate through promise chains.
    console.error('catch 2', reason)
});
```

This looks promising. Now we can see that the resolved value makes its way through the promise chain. There's a catch—the rejection isn't cumulative. Instead, only the first promise in the chain is actually rejected. The remaining promises are simply resolved, not rejected. This means that the last catch() callback will never run.

When we chain together promises in this fashion, our fulfillment callback functions need to be able to handle error conditions. For example, the value that's resolved could have an error property, which could be checked for specifics.

Passing promises around

In this section, we'll extend the idea of treating promises as primitive values. Something we often do with primitive values is pass them to functions as arguments, and return them from functions. The key difference between a promise and other primitives is how we use them. Other values exist now, whereas promised values will exist eventually. Therefore, we need to define some course of action via a callback function to take place when the value does arrive.

What's nice about promises is that the interface used to supply these callback functions is small and consistent. We don't need to invent synchronization mechanisms on the fly when we can couple the value with the code that will act upon it. These units can move around our application just like any other value, and the concurrency semantics are unobtrusive. Here's an example of what several functions that pass promises around look like:

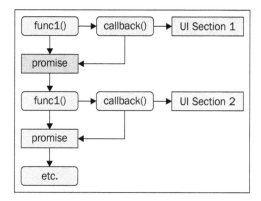

By the end of this function call stack, we have a promise object that's reflective of several promises resolving. The whole resolution chain is kicked off by the first promise resolving. What's more important than the mechanics of how the value traverses the chain of promises is the idea that all of these functions are free to use this promised value without affecting other functions.

There are two concurrency principles at play here. First, we will conserve by performing an asynchronous action to get the value only once; each of the callback functions are free to use this resolved value. Second, we're doing a good job of abstracting our synchronization mechanisms. In other words, the code doesn't feel like it's burdened with boilerplate concurrency code. Let's see what code that passes promises around actually looks like:

```
// Simple utilty to compose a larger function, out
// of smaller functions.
function compose(...funcs) {
```

```
        return function(value) {
            var result = value;

            for (let func of funcs) {
                result = func(value);
            }

            return result;
        };
    }

    // Accepts a promise or a resolved value. If it's a promise,
    // it adds a "then()" callback and returns a new promise.
    // Otherwise, it performs the "update" and returns the
    // value.
    function updateFirstName(value) {
        if (value instanceof Promise) {
            return value.then(updateFirstName);
        }

        console.log('first name', value.first);
        return value;
    }

    // Works the same way as the above function, except it
    // performs a different UI "update".
    function updateLastName(value) {
        if (value instanceof Promise) {
            return value.then(updateLastName);
        }

        console.log('last name', value.last);
        return value;
    }

    // Works the same way as the above function, except it
    // performs a different UI "update".
    function updateAge(value) {
        if (value instanceof Promise) {
            return value.then(updateAge);
        }

        console.log('age', value.age);
        return value;
```

```
    }

    // A promise object that's resolved with a data object
    // after one second.
    var promise = new Promise((resolve, reject) => {
        setTimeout(() => {
            resolve({
                first: 'John',
                last: 'Smith',
                age: 37
            });
        }, 1000);
    });

    // We compose an "update()" function that updates the
    // various UI components.
    var update = compose(
        updateFirstName,
        updateLastName,
        updateAge
    );

    // Call our update function with a promise.
    update(promise);
```

The key functions here are our update functions—`updateFirstName()`, `updateLastName()`, and `updateAge()`. They're very flexible and accept a promise or value resolved by a promise. If any of these functions get a promise as an argument, they return a new promise by adding a `then()` callback function. Note that it's adding the same function. `updateFirstName()` will add `updateFirstName()` as the callback. When the callback fires, it'll be with the plain object that's used to update the UI this time. So the promise check fails, and we can proceed to update the UI.

The promise checking takes all of three lines per function, which is not not exactly obtrusive. The end result is the flexible code that's easy to read. Ordering doesn't matter; we could have composed our `update()` function in a different order, and the UI components would all be updated in the same way. We can pass the plain object directly to `update()` and everything will work the same. Concurrent code that doesn't look like concurrent code is our big win here.

Synchronizing several promises

Until this point in the chapter, we've looked at single promise instances that resolve a value, trigger callbacks, and possibly cause other promises to resolve. In this section, we'll look at a couple of static Promise methods that help us in scenarios where we need to synchronize the resolution of several promise values.

First, we'll address the common case where a component that we develop requires synchronous access to several asynchronous resources. Then, we'll look at the less common scenario where asynchronous actions become irrelevant before they're resolved due to events that have taken place in the UI.

Waiting on promises

In the case where we are waiting for several promises to resolve, perhaps to transform multiple data sources into something consumable by a UI component, we can use the `Promise.all()` method. It takes a collection of promise instances as input, and returns a new promise instance. This new instance is resolved only when all of the input promises are resolved.

The `then()` callback that we provide to the new promise, created by `Promise.then()`, is given an array of resolved values as input. These values correspond to the input promises in terms of index position. This is a very powerful synchronization mechanism, one that helps us fulfill the synchronize concurrency principle because it hides all the bookkeeping.

Instead of several callbacks that each need to coordinate the state of the promises that they're bound to, we have one callback, which has all the resolved data that we need. Here's an example that shows how to synchronize multiple promises:

```
// Utility to send a "GET" HTTP request, and return
// a promise that's resolved with the parsed response.
function get(path) {
    return new Promise((resolve, reject) => {
        var request = new XMLHttpRequest();

        // The promise is resolved with the parsed
        // JSON data when the data is loaded.
        request.addEventListener('load', (e) => {
            resolve(JSON.parse(e.target.responseText));
        });

        // When there's an error with the request, the
        // promise is rejected with the appropriate reason.
        request.addEventListener('error', (e) => {
```

```
            reject(e.target.statusText || 'unknown error');
        });

        // If the request is aborted, we simply resolve the
        // request.
        request.addEventListener('abort', resolve);

        request.open('get', path);
        request.send();
    });
}


// For our request promises.
var requests = [];

// Issues 5 API requests, and places the 5 corresponding
// promises in the "requests" array.
for (let i = 0; i < 5; i++) {
    requests.push(get('api.json'));
}

// Using "Promise.all()" let's us pass in an array of
// promises, returning a new promise that's resolved
// when all promises resolve. Our callback gets an array
// of resolved values that correspond to the promises.
Promise.all(requests).then((values) => {
    console.log('first', values.map(x => x[0]));
    console.log('second', values.map(x => x[1]));
});
```

Cancelling promises

The XHR requests that we've seen so far in this book have handlers for aborted requests. This is because we can manually abort the request and prevent any load callbacks from running. A typical scenario that requires this functionality is for the user to click a cancel button, or navigate to a different part of the application, rendering the request redundant.

If we were to move up a level on the abstraction ladder to promises, the same principle applies. Something could happen while the concurrent action is executing that renders the promise pointless. The difference between promises and XHR requests, of course, is that the former has no abort() method. The last thing we want to do is start introducing unnecessary cancellation logic in our promise callbacks.

This is where the `Promise.race()` method can help us. As the name suggests, the method returns a new promise that's resolved by the first of the input promises to resolve. This may not sound like much, but implementing the logic of `Promise.race()` isn't easy. It's the synchronize principle in action, hiding concurrency complexities from the application code. Let's take a look at how this method can help us deal with cancelled promises due to user interactions:

```
// The resolver function used to cancel data requests.
var cancelResolver;

// A simple "constant" value, used to resolved cancel
// promises.
var CANCELLED = {};

// Our UI components.
var buttonLoad = document.querySelector('button.load'),
    buttonCancel = document.querySelector('button.cancel');

// Requests data, returns a promise.
function getDataPromise() {

    // Creates the cancel promise. The executor assigns
    // the "resolve" function to "cancelResolver", so
    // it can be called later.
    var cancelPromise = new Promise((resolve) => {
        cancelResolver = resolve;
    });

    // The actual data we want. This would normally be
    // an HTTP request, but we're simulating one here
    // for brevity using setTimeout().
    var dataPromise = new Promise((resolve) => {
        setTimeout(() => {
            resolve({ hello: 'world' });
        }, 3000);
    });

    // The "Promise.race()" method returns a new promise,
    // and it's resolved with whichever input promise is
    // resolved first.
    return Promise.race([
        cancelPromise,
        dataPromise
    ]);
```

```
    }

    // When the cancel button is clicked, we use the
    // "cancelResolver()" function to resolve the
    // cancel promise.
    buttonCancel.addEventListener('click', () => {
        cancelResolver(CANCELLED);
    });

    // When the load button is clicked, we make a request
    // for data using "getDataPromise()".
    buttonLoad.addEventListener('click', () => {
        buttonLoad.disabled = true;

        getDataPromise().then((value) => {
            buttonLoad.disabled = false;

            // The promise was resolved, but it was because
            // the user cancelled the request. So we exit
            // here by returning the CANCELLED "constant".
            // Otherwise, we have data to work with.
            if (Object.is(value, CANCELLED)) {
                return value;
            }

            console.log('loaded data', value);
        });
    });
```

 As an exercise, try to imagine a more complex scenario where `dataPromise` is a promise created by `Promise.all()`. Our `cancelResolver()` function would be able to seamlessly cancel many complex asynchronous actions at once.

Promises without executors

In this final section, we'll look at the `Promise.resolve()` and `Promise.reject()` methods. We've already seen how `Promise.resolve()` can resolve thenable objects earlier in the chapter. It can also directly resolve values or other promises. These methods come in handy when we implement a function that has the potential to be both synchronous and asynchronous. This isn't a situation we want to find ourselves in using a function with ambiguous concurrency semantics.

For example, here's a function that's both, synchronous and asynchronous, leading to confusion, and almost certainly to bugs later on:

```
// Example function that returns "value" from
// a cache, or "fetchs" it asynchronously.
function getData(value) {

    // If it exists in the cache, we return
    // this value.
    var index = getData.cache.indexOf(value);

    if (index > -1) {
        return getData.cache[index];
    }

    // Otherwise, we have to go "fetch" it. This
    // "resolve()" call would typically be found in
    // a network request callback function.
    return new Promise((resolve) => {
        getData.cache.push(value);
        resolve(value);
    });
}

// Creates the cache.
getData.cache = [];

console.log('getting foo', getData('foo'));
// → getting foo Promise
console.log('getting bar', getData('bar'));
// → getting bar Promise
console.log('getting foo', getData('foo'));
// → getting foo foo
```

We can see that the last call returns a cached value, instead of a promise. This makes intuitive sense because we're not promising an eventual value, we already have it! The problem is that we're exposing an inconsistency to any code that uses our getData() function. That is, the code that calls getData() needs to handle concurrency semantics. This code is not concurrent. Let's change this by introducing Promise.resolve():

```
// Example function that returns "value" from
// a cache, or "fetchs" it asynchronously.
function getData(value) {
    var cache = getData.cache;
```

```
    // If there's no cache for this function, let's
    // reject the promise. Gotta have cache.
    if (!Array.isArray(cache)) {
        return Promise.reject('missing cache');
    }

    // If it exists in the cache, we return
    // a promise that's resolved using the
    // cached value.
    var index = getData.cache.indexOf(value);

    if (index > -1) {
        return Promise.resolve(getData.cache[index]);
    }

    // Otherwise, we have to go "fetch" it. This
    // "resolve()" call would typically be found in
    // a network request callback function.
    return new Promise((resolve) => {
        getData.cache.push(value);
        resolve(value);
    });
}

// Creates the cache.
getData.cache = [];

// Each call to "getData()" is consistent. Even
// when synchronous values are used, they still
// get resolved as promises.
getData('foo').then((value) => {
    console.log('getting foo', `"${value}"`);
}, (reason) => {
    console.error(reason);
});

getData('bar').then((value) => {
    console.log('getting bar', `"${value}"`);
}, (reason) => {
    console.error(reason);
});
```

```
getData('foo').then((value) => {
    console.log('getting foo', `"${value}"`);
}, (reason) => {
    console.error(reason);
});
```

This is better. Using `Promise.resolve()` and `Promise.reject()`, any code that uses `getData()` will get concurrency by default, even when the data fetching action is synchronous.

Summary

This chapter covered a lot of details about the `Promise` object introduced in ES6 to help JavaScript programmers deal with synchronization issues that have plagued the language for years. With asynchronicity comes callbacks—lots of callbacks. This creates a callback hell that we want to avoid at all costs.

Promises help us deal with synchronization issues by implementing a simple interface that's generic enough to resolve any value. Promises are always in one of three states—pending, fulfilled, or rejected, and they only change their state once. When these state changes happen, callbacks are triggered. Promises have an executor function, whose job is to set up the asynchronous actions that use a promise `resolver` or `rejector` function to change the state of the promise.

Much of the value that promises bring to the table is about how they help us simplify complex scenarios. Because, if we only had to deal with a single asynchronous action that runs a callback with a resolved value, promises would hardly be worthwhile. This is not a common case. The common case is several asynchronous actions that each resolve values; and these values need to be synchronized and transformed. Promises have methods that allow us to do this, and as a result, we're able to better apply the synchronization concurrency principle to our code.

In the next chapter, we'll look at another newly-introduced language primitive— the generator. Similar to promises, generators are mechanisms that help us apply a concurrency principle—conserve.

4
Lazy Evaluation with Generators

Lazy evaluation is a programming technique, which is used when we don't want to compute values until the very last second. This way, we're sure we actually need it. The opposite approach, eager evaluation, has the potential to compute several values that aren't needed. This generally isn't a problem, until the size and complexity of our applications grow beyond a level where these wasted computations are imperceptible to the user.

The `Generator` is a new primitive type introduced to JavaScript as a part of the ES6 specification of the language. Generators help us implement lazy evaluation techniques in our code, and as a corollary, help us implement the conserve concurrency principle.

We'll start the chapter off with some simple introductions to generators, so we can get a feel for how they behave. From there, we'll move onto more advanced lazy evaluation scenarios, wrapping up the chapter with a look at coroutines. Let's get started.

Call stacks and memory allocation

Memory allocation is a necessity of any programming language. Without this, we have no data structures to work with, not even primitive types. Memory is cheap, and it seems that there's plenty of it to go around; this isn't cause for celebration just yet. While it's more feasible today to allocate larger data structures in memory then it was 10 years ago, we still have to deallocate that memory when we're done with it. JavaScript is a garbage-collected language, which means our code doesn't have to explicitly destroy objects in memory. However, the garbage collector incurs a CPU penalty.

So there are two factors in play here. We want to conserve two resources here, and we'll try to do so using generators to implement lazy evaluation. We don't want to allocate memory unnecessarily, and if we can avoid this, then we can avoid invoking the garbage collector frequently. In this section, I'll introduce some generator concepts.

Bookmarking function contexts

In a normal function call stack, a function returns a value. The `return` statement activates a new execution context and discards the old context because we returned, so we're done with it. Generator functions are a special kind of JavaScript function denoted with their own syntax, and their call stacks aren't so cut-and-dried compared to `return` statements. Here's a visualization of what happens when a generator function is invoked, and it starts generating values:

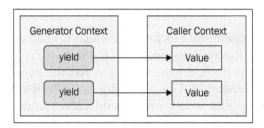

Just as the `return` statement passes a value to the calling context, the `yield` statement passes a value back. However, unlike a regular function, generator function contexts aren't discarded. In fact, they're bookmarked so that when control is given back to the generator context, it can pick up where it left off to continue yielding values until it's done. This bookmarking data is very insignificant, as it just points to a location in our code.

Sequences instead of arrays

In JavaScript, when we need to iterate over a list of things, numbers, strings, objects, and so on, we use an array. Arrays are general purpose and powerful. The challenge with arrays in the context of lazy evaluation is that arrays themselves are data that need to be allocated. So we have the elements within the array that need to be allocated somewhere in memory, and we also have metadata about the elements in the array.

If we're working with a large number of objects, the memory overhead associated with the array is significant. Additionally, we need to somehow put these objects in the array. This is an additional step that adds CPU time. An alternative concept is a sequence. Sequences aren't a tangible JavaScript language construct. They're an abstract concept—arrays without actually allocating arrays. Sequences help with lazy evaluation. For this exact reason, there's nothing to allocate, and there's no initial population step. Here's a visualization of the steps involved with iterating over an array:

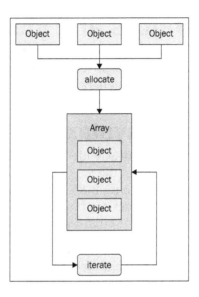

As we can see, before we can iterate over these three objects, we first have to allocate an array, then populate it with these objects. Let's contrast this approach with the conceptual idea of a sequence with the following diagram:

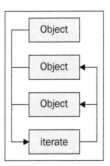

With sequences, we don't have an explicit container structure for the objects that we're interested in iterating over. The only overhead associated with a sequence is the pointer to the current item. We can use generator functions as a mechanism for generating sequences in JavaScript. As we saw in the preceding section, generators bookmark their execution context when they yield values back to the caller. This is the kind of minimal overhead that we're looking for. It enables us to lazily evaluate objects and iterate over them as a sequence.

Creating generators and yielding values

In this section, I'll introduce the generator function syntax, and we'll walk through yielding values from a generator. We'll also look at the two approaches that we can use to iterate over values yielded from generators.

Generator function syntax

The syntax for generator functions is nearly identical to normal functions. The difference in the declaration is that the function keyword is followed by an asterisk. The more profound difference is the return value, which is always a generator instance. Moreover, there's no need for the new keyword, despite a new object being created. Let's take a look at what a generator function looks like:

```
// Generator functions use an asterisk to
// denote a that a generator instance is returned.
// We can return values from generators, but instead
// of the caller getting that value, they'll always
// get a generator instance.
function* gen() {
    return 'hello world';
}

// Creates the generator instance.
var generator = gen();

// Let's see what this looks like.
console.log('generator', generator);
// → generator Generator

// Here's how we get the return value. Looks awkward,
// because we would never use a generator function
// that simply returns a single value.
console.log('return', generator.next().value);
// → return hello world
```

It's highly unlikely that we'd ever use generators in this fashion, but it's a good way to illustrate the nuances of generator functions. For example, `return` statements are perfectly valid within generator functions, and yet, they produce a completely different result for the caller, as we can see. In practice, we're far more likely to encounter `yield` statements in generators, so let's look at them next.

Yielding values

The common case with generator functions is to yield values and control back to the caller. Yielding control back to the caller is a defining characteristic of generators. When we yield, the generator bookmarks our position in the code. It does this because the caller is likely going to request another value from the generator, and when it does, the generator simply picks up where it left off. Let's take a look at a generator function that yields several times:

```
// This function yields values, in order. There's no
// container structure, like an array. Instead, each time
// the yield statement is called, control is yielded
// back to the caller, and the position in the function
// is bookmarked.
function* gen() {
    yield 'first';
    yield 'second';
    yield 'third';
}

var generator = gen();

// Each time we call "next()", control is passed back
// to the generator function's execution context. Then,
// the generator looks up the bookmark for where it
// last yielded control.
console.log(generator.next().value);
console.log(generator.next().value);
console.log(generator.next().value);
```

The previous code is what a sequence looks like. We have three values, and they're sequentially yielded from our function. They're not put in any kind of container structure either. The first call to `yield` passes `first` to `next()`, which is where it's used. The same goes for the other two values. In fact, this is lazy evaluation in action. We have three calls to `console.log()`. The eager implementation of `gen()` would return a collection of values for us to log. Instead, when we need to log a value, we go and get it from the generator. This is the laziness factor; we conserve our efforts until they're actually required, avoiding allocations and computations.

The not-so-ideal aspect of our previous example is that we're actually repeating calls to console.log(), when really, we want to iterate over the sequence, calling console.log() for each item in it. Let's iterate over some generator sequences now.

Iterating over generators

The next() method gets us, not surprisingly, the next value in the generator sequence. The actual value returned by next() is an object with two properties: the yielded value and whether or not the generator is done. However, we generally don't want to hard-code our calls to next(). Instead, we want to call it iteratively as values are yielded from the generator. Here's an example that uses a while loop to iterate over a generator:

```
// A basic generator function that yields
// sequential values.
function* gen() {
    yield 'first';
    yield 'second';
    yield 'third';
}

// Creates the generator.
var generator = gen();

// Loop till the sequence is finished.
while(true) {

    // Gets the next item from the sequence.
    let item = generator.next();

    // Is there a next value, or are we done?
    if (item.done) {
        break;
    }

    console.log('while', item.value);
}
```

This loop will continue until the done property of the yielded item is true; at this point, we know there aren't any items, and thus, we can stop. This allows us to iterate over a sequence of yielded values without the need to create an array for the sole purpose of iterating over it. However, there's a lot of boilerplate code in this loop that has more to do with managing the generator iteration than actually iterating over it. Let's take a look at another approach:

```
// The "for..of" loop removes the need to explicitly
// call generator constructs, like "next()", "value",
// and "done".
for (let item of generator) {
    console.log('for..of', item);
}
```

This is much better. We've condensed our code down into something that's much more focused on the task at hand. This code essentially does the exact same thing as our `while` loop, except the `for..of` statement, which understands what to do when the iterable is a generator. Iterating over generators is a common pattern in concurrent JavaScript applications, so optimizing for compact and readable code here would be a wise decision.

Infinite sequences

Some sequences are infinite, prime numbers, Fibonacci numbers, odd numbers, and so on. Infinite sequences aren't limited to sets of numbers; more abstract notions can be considered infinite. For example, a set of stings that repeats itself infinitely, a Boolean value that toggles infinitely, and so on. In this section, we'll explore how generators make it possible for us to work with infinite sequences.

No end in sight

Allocating items from an infinite sequence isn't practical from a memory consumption point of view. In fact, it's not even possible to allocate the whole sequence — it's infinite. Memory is finite. So, it's better to simply sidestep the whole allocation problem entirely and use a generator to yield the values from the sequence as we need them. At any given point in time, our application is only going to use a tiny slice of the infinite sequence. Here's a visualization of what's used from an infinite sequence versus the potential size of these sequences:

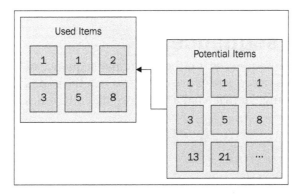

As we can see, there are a vast number of items available that we'll never use with this sequence. Let's take a look at some generator code that lazily produces items from an infinite Fibonacci sequence:

```
// Generates an infinite Fibonacci sequence.
function* fib() {
    var seq = [ 0, 1 ],
        next;

    // This loop doesn't actually run infinitely,
    // only as long as items from the sequence
    // are requested using "next()".
    while (true) {

        // Yields the next item in the sequence.
        yield (next = seq[0] + seq[1]);

        // Stores state necessary to compute the
        // item in the next iteration.
        seq[0] = seq[1];
        seq[1] = next;
    }
}

// Launch the generator. This will never be "done"
// generating values. However, it's lazy - it only
// generates what we ask for.
var generator = fib();

// Gets the first 5 items of the sequence.
for (let i = 0; i < 5; i++) {
    console.log('item', generator.next().value);
}
```

Alternating sequences

A variation on infinite sequences is either a circular sequence or an alternating sequence. These types of sequences are circular when the end is reached; they start from the beginning. Here's what a sequence that alternates between two values looks like:

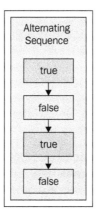

These types of sequences will continue to generate values infinitely. This becomes useful when we have a set of rules that determine how the sequence is defined and the set of items that's generated; then, we start this set all over again. Now, let's look at some code to see the implementation of these sequences using generators. Here's a generic generator function that we can use to alternate between values:

```
// A generic generator that will infinitely iterate
// over the provided arguments, yielding each item.
function* alternate(...seq) {
    while (true) {
        for (let item of seq) {
            yield item;
        }
    }
}
```

This is the first time we've declared a generator function that accepts arguments. In fact, we're using the spread operator to iterate over arguments passed to the function. Unlike arguments, the seq argument that we've created using the spread operator is a real array. As we iterate over this array, we yield each item from the generator. This may not seem all that useful at first glance, but it's the while loop that adds the real power here. Since the while loop will never exit, the for loop will simply repeat itself. That is, it'll alternate. This negates the need for explicit bookkeeping code (Have we reached the end of the sequence? How do we reset the counter and move back to the beginning? And so on) Let's see how this generator function works:

```
// Create a generator that alternates between
// the provided arguments.
var alternator = alternate(true, false);

console.log('true/false', alternator.next().value);
```

```
console.log('true/false', alternator.next().value);
console.log('true/false', alternator.next().value);
console.log('true/false', alternator.next().value);
// →
// true/false true
// true/false false
// true/false true
// true/false false
```

Cool. So the `alternator` will continue to generate `true/false` values as long as we continue to ask for them. The main benefit here is that we don't need to know about the next value, `alternator` takes care of this for us. Let's look at this generator function with a different sequence to iterate over:

```
// Create a new generator instance, with new values
// to alternate with each iteration.
alternator = alternate('one', 'two', 'three');

// Gets the first 10 items from the infinite sequence.
for (let i = 0; i< 10; i++) {
    console.log('one/two/three',
        `"${alternator.next().value}"`);
}
// →
// one/two/three "one"
// one/two/three "two"
// one/two/three "three"
// one/two/three "one"
// one/two/three "two"
// one/two/three "three"
// one/two/three "one"
// one/two/three "two"
// one/two/three "three"
// one/two/three "one"
```

As we can see, the `alternate()` function comes in handy for alternating between any arguments passed to it.

Deferring to other generators

We've seen how the `yield` statement is able to pause the execution context of a `generator` function, and yield a value back to the calling context. There's a variation on the `yield` statement that allows us to defer to other `generator` functions. Another technique involves creating a mesh of generators by interweaving several generator sources together. In this section, we'll explore both of these ideas.

Selecting a strategy

Deferring to other generators gives our functions the ability to decide at run-time, to hand off control from one generator to another. In other words, it allows the selection of a more appropriate generator function based on a strategy. Here's a visualization of a generator function that makes a decision and defers to one of several other generator functions:

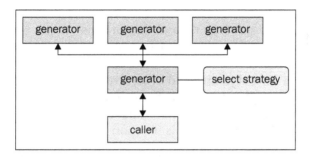

What we have here are three specialized generators that we would like to use throughout our application. That is, they each work in their own unique way. Perhaps, they're tailored for specific types of inputs. However, these generators simply make assumptions about the input that they're given. It may not be the best tool for the job, and so, we have to figure out which of these generators to use. What we want to avoid is having to implement this strategy selection code all over the place. It would be nice if we were able to encapsulate all of this into a general purpose generator that captures common cases throughout our code.

Let's say that we have the following generator functions, and they're equally used throughout our application:

```
// Generator that maps a collection of objects
// to a specific property name.
function* iteratePropertyValues(collection, property) {
    for (let object of collection) {
        yield object[property];
    }
}

// Generator that yields each value of the given object.
function* iterateObjectValues(collection) {
    for (let key of Object.keys(collection)) {
        yield collection[key];
    }
```

```
    }

    // Generator that yields each item from the given array.
    function* iterateArrayElements(collection) {
        for (let element of collection) {
            yield element;
        }
    }
```

These are small and concise functions, and they are easy to use wherever we need
them. The trouble is that each of these functions make assumptions about the
collection that's passed in. Is it an array of objects, each with a specific property? Is it
an array of strings? Is it an object instead of an array? Since these generator functions
are commonly used throughout our code for a similar purpose, we can implement
a more generic iterator, who's job is to determine the best generator function to use,
and then to defer to it. Let's see what this function looks like:

```
    // This generator defers to other generators. But first,
    // it executes some logic to determine the best strategy.
    function* iterateNames(collection) {

        // Are we dealing with an array?
        if (Array.isArray(collection)) {

            // This is a heuristic where we check the first
            // element of the array. Based on what's there, we
            // make assumptions about the remaining elements.
            let first = collection[0];

            // Here is where we defer to other more specialized
            // generators, based on what we find out about the
            // first array element.
            if (first.hasOwnProperty('name')) {
                yield* iteratePropertyValues(collection,
                    'name');
            } else if (first.hasOwnProperty('customerName')) {
                yield* iteratePropertyValues(collection,
                    'customerName');
            } else {
                yield* iterateArrayElements(collection);
            }
        } else {
            yield* iterateObjectValues(collection);
        }
    }
```

Think of the `iterateNames()` function as a simple proxy for any one of the other three generators. It examines the input and makes a selection based on the collection. We could have implemented one large generator function, but that would preclude us from use cases where we want to use the smaller generators directly. What if we want to use them to compose new functionality, or if another composite generator wants to use it? It's always a good idea to keep generator functions small and focused. The `yield*` syntax allows us to handoff control to a more suitable generator.

Now, let's see how this general purpose generator function is put to use by deferring to generators that are best equipped to handle the data:

```
var collection;

// Iterates over an array of string names.
collection = [ 'First', 'Second', 'Third' ];

for (let name of iterateNames(collection)) {
    console.log('array element', `"${name}"`);
}

// Iterates over an object, where the names
// are the values - the keys aren't relevant here.
collection = {
    first: 'First',
    second: 'Second',
    third: 'Third'
};

for (let name of iterateNames(collection)) {
    console.log('object value', `"${name}"`);
}

// Iterates over the "name" property of each object
// in the collection.
collection = [
    { name: 'First' },
    { name: 'Second' },
    { name: 'Third' }
];

for (let name of iterateNames(collection)) {
    console.log('property value', `"${name}"`);
}
```

Interweaving generators

When a generator defers to another generator, control isn't handed back to the first generator until the second generator is completely finished. In the preceding example, our generator simply looked for a better generator to carry out the work. However, there will be other times when we'll have two or more data sources that we want to use together. So, instead of handing off control to one generator, then to another and so on, we would alternate between the various sources, taking turns consuming data.

Here's a diagram that illustrates the idea of a generator that interweaves multiple data sources to create a single data source:

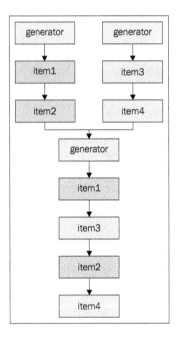

The idea is to round-robin the data sources, rather than to empty one source, then another, and so on. A generator like this is handy when there isn't a single large collection for us to work with, but instead, two or more collections. Using this generator technique, we can actually treat multiple data sources as though they were one big source, but without having to allocate the memory for a large structure. Let's look at the following code example:

```
'use strict';

// Utility function that converts the input array to a
// generator by yielding each of it's values. If its
// not an array, it assumes it's already a generator
```

```
// and defers to it.
function* toGen(array) {
    if (Array.isArray(array)) {
        for (let item of array) {
            yield item;
        }
    } else {
        yield* array;
    }
}

// Interweaves the given data sources (arrays or
// generators) into a single generator source.
function* weave(...sources) {

    // This controls the "while" loop. As long as
    // there's a source that's yielding data, the
    // while loop is still valid.
    var yielding = true;

    // We have to make sure that each of our
    // sources is a generator.
    var generators = sources.map(
        source =>toGen(source));

    // Starts the main weaving loop. It makes it's
    // way through each source, yielding one item
    // from each, then starting over, till every
    // source is empty.
    while (yielding) {
        yielding = false;

        for (let source of generators) {
            let next = source.next();

            // As long as we're yielding data, the
            // "yielding" value is true, and the
            // "while" loop continues. As soon as
            // "done" is true for every source, the
            // "yielding" variable stays false, and
            // the "while loop exits.
            if (!next.done) {
                yielding = true;
                yield next.value;
            }
        }
    }
```

```
            }
        }
    }

    // A basic filter that generates values by
    // iterating over the given source, and yielding items
    // that are not disabled.
    function* enabled(source) {
        for (let item of source) {
            if (!item.disabled) {
                yield item;
            }
        }
    }

    // These are the two data sources we want to weave
    // together into one generator, which can then be
    // filtered by another generator.
    var enrolled = [
        { name: 'First' },
        { name: 'Sencond' },
        { name: 'Third', disabled: true }
    ];

    var pending = [
        { name: 'Fourth' },
        { name: 'Fifth' },
        { name: 'Sixth', disabled: true }
    ];

    // Creates the generator, which yields user objects
    // from two data sources.
    var users = enabled(weave(enrolled, pending));

    // Actually performs the weaving and filtering.
    for (let user of users) {
        console.log('name', `"${user.name}"`);
    }
```

Passing data to generators

The `yield` statement doesn't just yield control back to the caller, it also returns a value. This value is passed to the generator function through the `next()` method. This is how we pass data into generators after they've been created. In this section, we'll address the bidirectional aspect of generators, and how creating feedback loops can produce some lean code.

Reusing generators

Some generators are general purpose and used frequently throughout our code. This being the case, does it make sense to constantly create and destroy these generator instances? Or can we reuse them? For instance, consider a sequence that's mainly dependent on initial conditions. Let's say we want to generate a sequence of even numbers. We would start at two, and as we iterate over this generator, the value would be incremented. The next time we want to iterate over even numbers, we would have to create a new generator.

This is kind of wasteful, since all we're doing is resetting a counter. What if we took a different approach, one that would allow us to keep on using the same generator instance for these types of sequences? The `next()` method of generators is a possible implementation path for this capability. We could pass it a value, which would then reset our counter. So instead of having to create a new generator instance every time we need to iterate over even numbers, we can simply call `next()` with a value that resets the initial conditions of our generator.

The `yield` keyword actually returns a value – the argument that's passed to `next()`. Most of the time, this is undefined, such as when the generator is iterated over in a `for..of` loop. However, this is how we're able to pass arguments to the generator after it starts running. This is not the same thing as passing arguments to the generator function, which comes in handy for doing the initial configuration of the generator. Values passed to `next()` are how we talk to the generator when we need to change something for the next value that's to be generated.

Let's take a look at how we can use the `next()` method to create a reusable even number sequence generator:

```
// This generator will keep generating even numbers.
function* genEvens() {

    // The initial value is 2. But this can change based
    // on the input passed to "next()".
    var value = 2,
        input;
```

```
    while (true) {

        // We yield the value, and get the input. If
        // input is provided, this will serve as the
        // next value.
        input = yield value;

        if (input) {
            value = input;
        } else {
            // Make sure that the next value is even.
            // Handles the case when an odd value is
            // passed to "next()".
            value += value % 2 ? 1 : 2;
        }
    }
}

// Creates the "evens" generator.
var evens = genEvens(),
    even;

// Iterate over evens up to 10.
while ((even = evens.next().value) <= 10) {
    console.log('even', even);
}
// →
// even 2
// even 4
// even 6
// even 8
// even 10

// Resets the generator. We don't need to
// create a new one.
evens.next(999);

// Iterate over evens between 1000 - 1024.
while ((even = evens.next().value) <= 1024) {
    console.log('evens from 1000', even);
}
// →
// evens from 1000 1000
```

```
// evens from 1000 1002
// evens from 1000 1004
// evens from 1000 1006
// evens from 1000 1008
// evens from 1000 1010
// evens from 1000 1012
// evens from 1000 1014
// ...
```

In case you're wondering why we're not using a for..of loop in the favor of a while loop, it's because you use a for..of loop to iterate over a generator. When you do so, the generator gets marked as *done* as soon as the loop exits. Hence, it would no longer be usable.

Lightweight map/reduce

Something else we can do with the next() method is map one value to another. For example, let's say we had a collection containing seven items. To map these items, we would iterate over the collection, passing each item to next(). As we saw in the preceding section, this method can reset the state of a generator, but it can also be used to supply a stream of input data, just as it supplies a stream of output data.

Let's see if we can write some code that does this—map collection items by feeding them into a generator through next():

```
// This generator will keep iterating, as
// long as "next()" is called. It's expecting
// a value as well, so that it can call the
// "iteratee()" function on it, and yield the
// result.
function* genMapNext(iteratee) {
    var input = yield null;

    while (true) {
        input = yield iteratee(input);
    }
}

// Our array of values we want to map.
var array = [ 'a', 'b', 'c', 'b', 'a' ];

// A "mapper" generator. We pass an iteratee
// function as an argument to "genMapNext()".
var mapper = genMapNext(x =>x.toUpperCase());
```

```
// Our starting point for the reduction.
var reduced = {};

// We have to call "next()" to bootstrap the
// generator.
mapper.next();

// Now we can start iterating over the array.
// The "mapped" value is yielded from the
// generator. The value we want mapped is fed
// into the generator by passing it to "next()".
for (let item of array) {
    let mapped = mapper.next(item).value;

    // Our reduction logic takes the mapped value,
    // and adds it to the "reduced" object, counting
    // the number of duplicate keys.
    if (reduced.hasOwnProperty(mapped)) {
        reduced[mapped]++;
    } else {
        reduced[mapped] = 1;
    }
}

console.log('reduced', reduced);
// → reduced { A: 2, B: 2, C: 1 }
```

As we can see, this is indeed possible. We're able to perform a lightweight map/reduce job using this approach. The mapper generator has the iteratee function that's applied to every item in the collection. As we iterate over the array, we're able to feed items into the generator by passing them to the next() method as an argument.

But, there's something about the previous method that just doesn't feel optimal—having to bootstrap the generator like this, and explicitly calling next() for every iteration feels clunky. In fact, could we not apply the iteratee function directly, instead of calling next()? It's these things that we need to be on the lookout while using generators; in particular, when passing data to generators. Just because we're able to, doesn't mean that it's a good idea.

Mapping and reducing would probably feel more natural, if we were to simply iterate over the generator just as we do with all other generators. We still want the lightweight mapping that generators give us, to, avoid the memory allocations. Let's try a different approach here—one that doesn't require the `next()` method:

```
// This generator is a more useful mapper than
// "genMapNext()" because it doesn't rely on values
// coming into the generator through "next()".
//
// Instead, this generator accepts an iterable, and
// an iteratee function. The iterable is then
// iterated-over, and the result of the iteratee
// is yielded.
function* genMap(iterable, iteratee) {
    for (let item of iterable) {
        yield iteratee(item);
    }
}


// Creates our "mapped" generator, using an iterable
// data source, and an iteratee function.
var mapped = genMap(array, x =>x.toUpperCase());
var reduced = {}

// Now we can simply iterate over our genrator, instead
// of calling "next()". The job of each loop iteration
// is to perform the reduction logic, instead of having
// to call "next()".
for (let item of mapped) {
    if (reduced.hasOwnProperty(item)) {
        reduced[item]++;
    } else {
        reduced[item] = 1;
    }
}

console.log('reduce improved', reduced);
// → reduce improved { A: 2, B: 2, C: 1 }
```

This looks like an improvement. There's less code, and the flow of the generator is easy to grok. The difference is that we pass our array and `iteratee` function to the generator up front. Then, as we iterate over the generator, each item gets mapped lazily. The code that reduces this array into an object is simpler to read too.

The genMap() function that we've just implemented is generic, which is advantageous to us. In real applications, mappings are going to be more complex than an uppercase transformation. More likely, there will be multiple levels of mappings. That is, we map the collection, then map it N more times before reducing it. If we've done a good job designing our code, then we'll want to compose generators out of smaller iterated functions.

But how can we keep this generic and lazy? The idea is to have several generators, each serving as the input to the next. This means that as our reducer code iterates over these generators, only one item makes it's way through the various layers of mappings, to the reduction code. Let's take a stab at implementing this:

```
// This function composes a generator
// function out of iteratees. The idea is to create
// a generator for each iteratee, so that each item
// from the original iterable, flows down, through
// each iteratee, before mapping the next item.
function composeGenMap(...iteratees) {

    // We're returning a generator function. That way,
    // the same mapping composition can be used on
    // several iterables, not just one.
    return function* (iterable) {

        // Creates the generator for each iteratee
        // passed to the function. The next generator
        // gets the previous generator as the "iterable"
        // argument.
        for (let iteratee of iteratees) {
            iterable = genMap(iterable, iteratee);
        }

        // Simply defer to the last iterable we created.
        yield* iterable;
    }
}
```

```
// Our iterable data source.
var array = [ 1, 2, 3 ];

// Creates a "composed" mapping generator, using 3
// iteratee functions.
var composed = composeGenMap(
    x => x + 1,
    x => x * x,
    x => x - 2
);

// Now we can iterate over the composed generator,
// passing it our iterable, and lazily mapping
// values.
for (let item of composed(array)) {
    console.log('composed', item)
}
// →
// composed 2
// composed 7
// composed 14
```

Coroutines

Coroutines are a concurrency technique that allow for cooperative multitasking. What this means is that if one part of our application needs to perform part of a task, it can do so, and then hand control off to another part of the application. Think about a subroutine, or in more recent times, a function. These subroutines often rely on other subroutines. However, they don't just run in succession, they cooperate with one another.

In JavaScript, there's no intrinsic coroutine mechanism. Generators aren't coroutines, but they have similar properties. For example, generators can pause the execution of a function, yielding control to another context, then regain control and resume. This gets us partway there, but generators are for generating values, which isn't necessarily what we're after with coroutines. In this section, we'll look at some techniques for implementing coroutines in JavaScript using generators.

Creating coroutine functions

Generators give us most of what we need to implement `coroutine` functions in JavaScript; they can pause and resume executing. We just need to implement some minor abstractions around generators so that the functions that we're working with actually feel like calling `coroutine` functions, instead of iterating over generators. Here's a rough illustration of how we want our coroutines to behave when called:

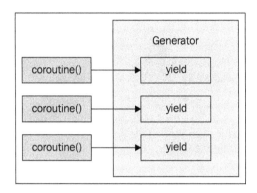

The idea is that invoking the `coroutine` function moves from one `yield` statement to the next. And we can supply input to the coroutine by passing an argument, which is then returned by the `yield` statement. This is a lot to remember, so let's generalize these coroutine concepts in a function wrapper:

```
// Taken from: http://syzygy.st/javascript-coroutines/
// This utility takes a generator function, and returns
// a coroutine function. Any time the coroutine is invoked,
// it's job is to call "next()" on the generator.
//
// The effect is that the generator function can run
// indefinitely, pausing when it hits "yield" statements.
function coroutine(func) {

    // Creates the generator, and moves the function
    // ahead to the first "yield" statement.
    var gen = func();
    gen.next();

    // The "val" is passed to the generator function
    // through the "yield" statement. It then resumes
    // from there, till it hits another yield.
    return function(val) {
        gen.next(val);
    }
}
```

Pretty simple—five lines of code, but it's also powerful. The function returned by Harold's wrapper simply advances the generator to the next `yield` statement, supplying the argument to `next()`, if one was provided. It's one thing to make claims of utility, but let's actually use this thing to make a `coroutine` function:

```
// Creates a coroutine function that when called,
// advances to the next yield statement.
var coFirst = coroutine(function* () {
    var input;

    // Input comes from the yield statement, and is
    // the argument value passed to "coFirst()".
    input = yield;
    console.log('step1', input);
    input = yield;
    console.log('step3', input);
});

// Works the same as the coroutine created above...
var coSecond = coroutine(function* () {
    var input;
    input = yield;
    console.log('step2', input);
    input = yield;
    console.log('step4', input);
});

// The two coroutines cooperating with one another,
// to produce the expected output. We can see that
// the second call to each coroutine picks up where
// the last yield statement left off.
coFirst('the money');
coSecond('the show');
coFirst('get ready');
coSecond('go');
// →
// step1 the money
// step2 the show
// step3 get ready
// step4 go
```

When there are a series of steps involved with fulfilling some task, we typically require bookkeeping code, temporary values, and so on. These aren't necessary with coroutines because the function simply pauses, leaving any local state intact. In other words, there's no need to intertwine concurrency logic with our application logic when coroutines do a decent job of hiding these details for us.

Handling DOM events

Somewhere else where we can use coroutines is with the DOM as event handlers. This works by adding the same `coroutine()` function as an event listener to several elements. Let's recall that each call to these coroutine functions talks to a single generator. This means that our coroutines that are setup to handle DOM events get passed in as a stream. It's almost like we're iterating over these events.

Since these `coroutine` functions use the same generator, it's easy for elements to talk to one another using this technique. The typical approach to DOM events involves callback functions that talk to some sort of central source that's shared among elements and maintains state. With coroutines, the state of element communications is implicit inside our function code. Let's use our coroutine wrapper in the context of DOM event handlers:

```
// Coroutine function that's used with mousemove
// events.
var onMouseMove = coroutine(function* () {
    var e;

    // This loop continues indefinitely. The event
    // object comes in through the yield statement.
    while (true) {
        e = yield;

        // If the element is disabled, do nothing.
        // Otherwise, log a message.
        if (e.target.disabled) {
            continue;
        }

        console.log('mousemove', e.target.textContent);
    }
});

// Coroutine function that's used with click events.
```

```javascript
var onClick = coroutine(function* () {

    // Store references to our two buttons. Since
    // coroutines are stateful, they'll always be
    // available.
    var first = document.querySelector(
        'button:first-of-type');
    var second = document.querySelector(
        'button:last-of-type'),
    var e;

    while (true) {
        e = yield;

        // Disables the button that was clicked.
        e.target.disabled = true;

        // If the first button was clicked, toggle
        // the state of the second button.
        if (Object.is(e.target, first)) {
            second.disabled = !second.disabled;
            continue;
        }

        // If the second button was clicked, toggle
        // the state of the first button.
        if (Object.is(e.target, second)) {
            first.disabled = !first.disabled;
        }
    }
});

// Sets up the event handlers - our coroutine functions.
for (let button of document.querySelectorAll('button')) {
    button.addEventListener('mousemove', onMouseMove);
    button.addEventListener('click', onClick);
}
```

Handling promised values

In the preceding section, we saw how the `coroutine()` function can be used to process DOM events. Instead of haphazardly adding callback functions that respond to DOM events, we use the same `coroutine()` function, which treats events as a stream of data. It's easier for DOM event handlers to cooperate with one another since they share the same generator context.

We can apply this same principle to `then()` callbacks of promises, which works in a similar way to the DOM coroutine approach. Instead of passing a regular function, we pass a coroutine to `then()`. When the promise resolves, the `coroutine` advances to the next `yield` statement along with a resolved value. Let's take a look at the following code:

```javascript
// An array of promises.
var promises = [];

// Our resolution callback is a coroutine. This means
// that every time it's called, a new resolved promise
// value shows up here.
var onFulfilled = coroutine(function* () {
    var data;

    // Continue to process resolved promise values
    // as they arrive.
    while (true) {
        data = yield;
        console.log('data', data);
    }
});

// Create 5 promises that resolve at random times,
// between 1 and 5 seconds.
for (let i = 0; i< 5; i++) {
    promises.push(new Promise((resolve, reject) => {
        setTimeout(() => {
            resolve(i);
        }, Math.floor(
            Math.random() * (5000 - 1000)) + 1000);
    }));
}

// Attach our fulfillment coroutine as a "then()" callback.
for (let promise of promises) {
    promise.then(onFulfilled);
}
```

This is very useful because it provides something that static promise methods do not. The `Promise.all()` method forces us to wait for all the promises to resolve before resolving the returned promise. However, in the case where the resolved promise values aren't dependent on one another, we can simply iterate over them, responding as they resolve in any order.

We can achieve something similar by attaching plain functions to `then()` as callbacks, but then, we wouldn't have a shared context for promise values as they resolve. Another tactic we can adopt by combining promises with coroutines is to declare a handful of coroutines that respond differently, depending on the type of data they're responding to. These coroutines would then live on throughout the entire duration of the application, being passed to promises as they get created.

Summary

This chapter introduced you to the concept of generators, a new construct as of ES6, which allow us to implement lazy evaluation. Generators help us realize the conserve concurrency principle because we can avoid computations and intermediary memory allocations. There are a few new syntax forms associated with generators. First, there's the generator function, which always returns a generator instance. These are declared differently than regular functions. These functions are responsible for generating values, which rely on the `yield` keyword.

We then explored more advanced generator and lazy evaluation topics, including deferring to other generators, implementing map/reduce functionality, and passing data into generators. We closed the chapter with a look at how to use generators to make coroutine functions.

In the following chapter, we'll look at web workers—our first glimpse at utilizing parallelism in the browser environment.

Working with Workers

5

Web workers enable true parallelism within a web browser. They've spent time maturing, and have pretty good vendor support today. Before web workers, our JavaScript code was confined to the CPU, where our execution environment started when the page first loaded. Web workers have evolved out of necessity — web applications are growing more capable. They have also started to require more compute power. At the same time, multiple CPU cores are common place today — even on low-end hardware.

In this chapter, we'll walk through the conceptual ideas of web workers, and how they relate to the concurrency principles that we're trying to achieve in our applications. Then, you'll learn how to use web workers by example, so that, later on in the book, we can start tying parallelism to some of the other ideas that we've already explored, such as promises and generators.

What are workers?

Before we dive into implementation examples, this section will give us a quick conceptual breakdown of what web workers are. It's good to know exactly how web workers cooperate with the rest of the system under the hood. Web workers are operating system threads — a target where we can dispatch events, and they execute our JavaScript code in a truly parallel fashion.

OS threads

At their core, web workers are nothing more than operating system-level threads. Threads are kind of like processes, except they require less overhead because they share memory addresses with the process from which they're created. Since the threads that power web workers are at the level of the operating system, we're at the mercy of the system and its process scheduler. Most of the time, this is exactly what we want—let the kernel figure out when our JavaScript code should run in order to best utilize the CPU.

Here's a diagram showing how the browser maps its web workers to OS threads, and how these are mapped to CPU cores:

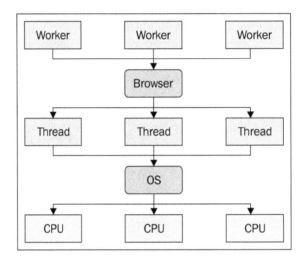

At the end of the day, it's best that the operating system be left responsible for handling what it's good at—scheduling software tasks on physical hardware. In more traditional multi-threaded programming environments, our code lives much closer to the operating system kernel. This isn't the case with web workers. While the underlying mechanism is a thread, the exposed programming interface looks more like something you might find in the DOM.

Event targets

Web workers implement the familiar event target interface. This makes web workers behavior similar to other components that we're used to working with, such as DOM elements or XHR requests. Workers trigger events, and this is how we receive data from them back in our main thread. We can also send data to workers, but this uses a simple method call.

When we pass data into workers, we actually trigger another event; only this time, it's in the execution context of the worker and not the main page execution context. There isn't much more to it than that: data in, data out. There's no `mutex` construct or anything of this sort. This is actually a good thing because the web browser, as a platform, already has many moving parts. Imagine if we threw in a more complex multi-threading model instead of just a simple event-target-based approach. We already have enough bugs to fix day-to-day.

Here's a rough idea of how the web worker layout looks, relative to the main thread that spawned these workers:

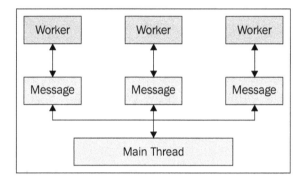

True parallelism

Web workers are the means to achieving the parallelize principle in our architecture. As we know, workers are operating system threads, meaning that the JavaScript code that's running inside them could possibly be running at the same exact instance as some DOM event handler code in the main thread. The ability to do stuff like this has been a goal of JavaScript programmers for quite a while. Before web workers, true parallelism simply wasn't possible. The best we could do was to fake it, giving a user the impression of many things happening simultaneously.

However, there are problems with always running on the same CPU core. We're fundamentally restricted in how many computations we can execute within a given time window. This restriction changes when true parallelism is introduced because the time window, in which computations may be run, grows with each CPU core that's added.

That being said, for most of the things that our application does, the single thread model works just fine. Machines today are powerful. We can get a lot done in a small time window. The problem arises when we experience spikes. These could be any event that disrupts the processing efficiency of our code. Our applications are constantly being asked to do more—more features, more data, more this, and more that.

The simple idea that we can make better use of the hardware that's sitting right in front of us, is what web workers are all about. Web workers, if used right, don't have to be this insurmountable new thing that we'll never use in our projects because it has concepts that fall outside of our comfort zone.

Types of workers

There are three types of web workers that we're likely to encounter during the development of concurrent JavaScript applications. In this section, we'll compare the three types so that we can understand which type of worker makes sense in any given context.

Dedicated workers

Dedicated workers are probably the most common worker type. They're considered the default type of web worker. When our page creates a new worker, it's dedicated to the page's execution context and nothing else. When our page goes away, so do all the dedicated workers created by the page.

The communication path between the page and any dedicated worker that it creates is straightforward. The page posts messages to the workers, which in turn post messages back to the page. The exact orchestration of these messages is dependent on the problem that we're trying to solve using web workers. We'll dig into more of these messaging patterns throughout the book.

The terms main thread and page are synonymous in this book. The main thread is your typical execution context, where we can manipulate the page and listen for input. The web worker context is largely the same, only with access to fewer components. We will go over these restrictions shortly.

Here's a depiction of the page communicating with its dedicated workers:

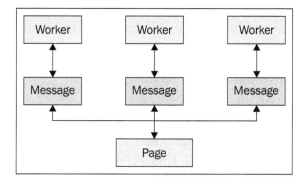

As we can see, dedicated workers are, well, dedicated. They only exist to help serve the page that created them. They don't directly communicate with other workers, and they can't communicate with any other page.

Sub-workers

Sub-workers are very similar to dedicated workers. The main difference is that they're created by a dedicated worker, not by the main thread. For example, if a dedicated worker has a task that would benefit from parallel execution, it can spawn its own workers and orchestrate the execution of the task between the sub-workers.

Apart from having a different creator, sub-workers share the same characteristics of a dedicated worker. Sub-workers don't communicate directly with JavaScript running in the main thread. It's up to the worker that creates the sub-workers to facilitate their communication. Here's an illustration of how sub-workers fit into the scheme of things:

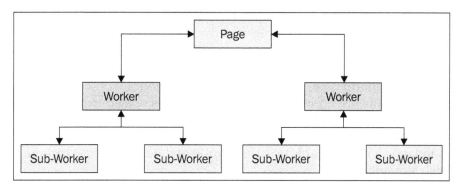

Shared workers

The third type of web worker is called a shared worker. Shared workers are named so because multiple pages can share the same instance of this type of worker. The pages that can access a given shared worker instance are restricted by the same-origin policy, which means, if a page was served from a different domain than the worker, the worker isn't allowed to communicate with this page.

Shared workers solve different type of problem than those solved by dedicated workers. Think of dedicated workers as functions without side-effects. You pass data to them and get different data in return. Think of shared workers as an application object following the singleton pattern. They're a means to sharing state between different browsing contexts. So, for instance, we wouldn't create a shared worker for the sole purpose of crunching numbers; we can use a dedicated worker for this.

It makes sense to use shared workers when there's application data in memory that we want from access from any page from the same application. Think about a user opening links in a new tab. This creates a new browsing context. It also means that our JavaScript components need to go through the process of fetching all the data required for the page, doing all the initialization steps, and so on. This gets repetitive and wasteful. Why not conserve these resources by sharing them between different browsing contexts? Here is an illustration of multiple pages from the same application communicating with a shared worker instance:

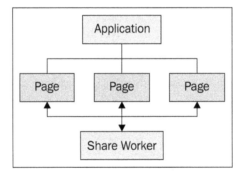

There's actually a fourth type of web worker called a service worker. These are shared workers embellished with additional capabilities related to caching network resources and offline functionality. Service workers are still in the early stages of their specification, but they look promising. Anything that we can learn about shared workers today will be applicable to service workers should they ever become a viable web technology.

Another important factor to consider here is the added complexity of service workers. The communication mechanism between the main thread and a service worker involves using ports. Likewise, the code running within the shared worker needs to make sure it's communicating over the correct port. We'll cover shared worker communication in much more depth later on in this chapter.

Worker environments

Web worker environments aren't same as the typical JavaScript environment, where our code usually runs. In this section, we'll point out critical differences between the JavaScript environment of the main thread and web worker threads.

What's available, what isn't?

A common misconception of web workers is that they're radically different environments from the default JavaScript execution context. It's true that they're different, but not so different as to be unapproachable. Perhaps, it's for this reason that JavaScript developers shy away from using web workers when they could be beneficial.

The obvious gap is the DOM — it doesn't exist in web worker execution environments. Its absence was a conscious decision on the part of specification writers. By avoiding DOM integration into worker threads, browser vendors can avoid many potential edge cases. We all value browser stability over convenience, or at least, we should. And would it really be all that convenient to have DOM access from within web workers? We'll see throughout the next few chapters of this book that workers are good at lots of other tasks, which ultimately contribute to successfully implementing concurrency principles.

With no DOM access in our web worker code, we're less likely to shoot ourselves in the foot. It actually forces us to really think about why we're using the workers in the first place. And we might actually take a step back and rethink our approach. Apart from the DOM, most of what we use on a day-to-day basis is exactly where we expect it to be. This includes using our favorite libraries inside web workers.

 For a more detailed breakdown of what's missing from web worker execution environments, see this page `https://developer.mozilla.org/en-US/docs/Web/API/Worker/Functions_and_classes_available_to_workers`.

Loading scripts

We would never write our entire application in a single JavaScript file. Instead, we will promote modularity by dividing our source code into files in a way that logically decomposes the design into something we can map mentally. Likewise, we probably don't want to compose web workers that consist of thousands of lines of code. Luckily, web workers come with a mechanism that allows us to import code into our web workers.

The first scenario is importing our own code into a web worker context. We are likely to have many low-level utilities that are specifically tailored for our application. There's a high probability that we'll need to use these utilities in both: a regular scripting context and within a worker thread. We want to keep our code modular, and we want our code to function the same way in workers as it would in any other context.

The second scenario is loading third-party libraries in web workers. It's the same principle as loading our own modules into web workers – our code will work in any context with a few exceptions, like DOM code. Let's look at an example that creates a web worker and loads the lodash library. First, we'll launch the worker:

```
// Loads the worker script, and starts the
// worker thread.
var worker = new Worker('worker.js');
```

Next, we'll use the loadScripts() function to bring the lodash library into our library:

```
// Imports the lodash library, making the global "_"
// variable available in the worker context.
importScripts('lodash.min.js');

// We can use the library within the worker now.
console.log('in worker', _.at([ 1, 2, 3], 0, 2));
// → in worker [1, 3]
```

We don't need to worry about waiting for the script to load before we can start using it – importScripts() is a blocking operation.

Communicating with workers

The preceding example created a web worker, which indeed ran in its own thread. But, this is not very helpful to us because we need to be able to communicate with the workers that we create. In this section, we'll cover the basic mechanisms involved with sending and receiving messages from web workers, including how these messages are serialized.

Posting messages

When we want to pass data into a web worker, we use the `postMessage()` method. As the name suggests, this method posts the given message to the worker. If there are any message event handlers set up within the worker, they'll respond to this call. Let's look at a basic example that sends a string to a worker:

```
// Launches the worker thread.
var worker = new Worker('worker.js');

// Posts a message to the worker, triggering
// any "message" event handlers.
worker.postMessage('hello world');
```

Now let's look at the worker that responds to this message by setting up an event handler for the message event:

```
// Setup an event listener for any "message"
// events dispatched to this worker.
addEventListener('message', (e) => {

    // The posted data is accessible through
    // the "data" property of the event.
    console.log(e.type, `"${e.data}"`);
    // → message "hello world"
});
```

 The `addEventListener()` function is implicitly called on something called a global dedicated worker context. We can think of this as the window object for web workers.

Message serialization

The message data that gets passed from the main thread to worker threads goes through a serialization transformation. When this serialized data arrives at the worker thread, it's deserialized, and the data is usable as a JavaScript primitive type. The same process is in place when the worker thread wants to send data back to the main thread.

Needless to say, this is an added step that adds overhead to our possibly already over-worked application. Therefore, some thought must be put into passing data back and forth between threads, as this is not a free operation in terms of CPU cost. Throughout the web worker code examples in this book, we'll treat message serialization as a key factor in our concurrency decision-making process.

So the question is—why go to such lengths? If the workers that we're using in our JavaScript code are simply threads, we should technically be able to use the same objects, since these threads use the same section of memory addresses. When threads share resources, such as objects in memory, challenging resource contention scenarios are likely to occur. For example, if one worker locks an object and another tries to use it, then this is an error. We have to implement logic that gracefully waits for the object to become available, and we have to implement logic in the worker that frees the locked resources.

In short, this is an error prone headache that we're much better off without. Thankfully, there's no resources shared between threads—only serialized messages. This means that we're limited in terms of what types of things can actually be passed to a worker. The rule of thumb is that it's generally safe to pass something that can be encoded as a JSON string. Remember, the worker has to reconstruct the object from this serialized string, so a string representation of a function or a class instance, simply will not work. Let's look at an example to see how this works. First, a simple worker to log the messages it receives:

```
// Simply display the content of any
// messages received.
addEventListener('message', (e) => {
    console.log('message', e.data);
});
```

Now let's see what kind of data we can serialize and send to this worker using postMessage():

```
// Launches the worker.
var worker = new Worker('worker.js');

// Sends a plain object.
worker.postMessage({ hello: 'world' });
// → message { hello: "world" }

// Sends an array.
worker.postMessage([ 1, 2, 3 ]);
// → message [ 1, 2, 3 ]

// Tries to send a function, results in
// an error being thrown.
worker.postMessage(setTimeout);
// → Uncaught DataCloneError
```

As we can see, there's a slight problem when we try to pass a function to `postMessage()`. This type cannot be reconstructed once it arrives on the worker thread, and so, `postMessage()` simply throws an exception. These types of restrictions may seem overly limiting, but they do eliminate the possibility of many concurrency issues.

Receiving messages from workers

Without the ability to pass data back into the main thread, workers aren't all that useful to us. At some point, the work performed by a worker needs to be reflected in the UI. We may recall that worker instances are event targets. This means that we can listen for the message event and respond accordingly when the worker sends back data. Think of this as the inverse of sending data to the worker. The worker simply treats the main thread as another worker by posting messages to it, while the main thread listens for messages. The same serialization restrictions that we explored in the preceding section are relevant here.

Let's look at some worker code that sends a message back to the main thread:

```
// After 2 seconds, post some data back to
// the main thread using the "postMessage()"
// function.
setTimeout(() => {
    postMessage('hello world');
}, 2000);
```

As we can see, this worker starts, and after 2 seconds, sends a string back to the main thread. Now, let's see how we can handle these incoming messages in the main page JavaScript:

```
// Launches the new worker.
var worker = new Worker('worker.js');

// Adds an event listener for the "message"
// event. Notice that the "data" property
// contains the actual message payload, the
// same way messages sent to workers do.
worker.addEventListener('message', (e) => {
    console.log('from worker', `"${e.data}"`);
});
```

You may have noticed that we do not explicitly terminate any of our worker threads. This is okay. When the browsing context is terminated, all active worker threads are terminated with it. We can explicitly terminate workers using the `terminate()` method, which will explicitly stop the thread without waiting for any existing code to complete. However, it's rare to explicitly terminate workers. Once created, workers generally survive the duration of the page. Spawning workers isn't free, it incurs overhead, so we should aim to only do this once, if possible.

Sharing application state

In this section, we'll introduce shared workers. First, we'll look at how the same data objects in memory can be accessed by multiple browsing contexts. Then, we'll look at fetching remote resources, and how to notify multiple browsing contexts about the arrival of new data. Finally, we'll look at how shared workers can be leveraged to allow for direct messaging between browser contexts.

Consider this section advanced material for experimental coding. The browser support for shared workers isn't that great at the moment (only Firefox and Chrome). Web workers are still in the candidate recommendation phase at the W3C. Once they become a recommendation and better browser support is in place for shared workers, we'll be ready to use them. For extra motivation, as the service worker spec matures, shared worker proficiency will be all the more relevant.

Sharing memory

The serialization mechanism that we've seen so far with web workers is in place because we cannot directly reference the same object from more than one thread. However, shared workers have a memory space that's not restricted to just one page, which means that we can indirectly access these objects in memory through various message-passing methods. In fact, this is a good opportunity to demonstrate how we pass messages using ports. Let's get down to it.

The notion of a port is necessary with shared workers. Without them, there would be no governing mechanism to control the inflow and outflow of messages from shared workers. For example, let's say we had three pages using the same shared worker, then we would have to create three ports to communicate with this worker. Think of a port as a gateway into the worker from the outside world. It's a minor indirection.

Here's a basic shared worker to give us an idea of what's involved with setting up these types of workers:

```
// This is the shared state between the pages that
// connect to this worker.
var connections = 0;

// Listen for pages that connect to this worker, so
// we can setup the message ports.
addEventListener('connect', (e) => {

    // The "source" property represents the
    // message port created by the page that's
    // connecting to this worker. We have to call
    // "start()" to actually establish the connection.
    e.source.start();

    // We post a message back to the page, the payload
    // is the updated number of connections.
    e.source.postMessage(++connections);
});
```

There's a `connect` event that gets triggered once a page connects with this worker. The `connect` event has a `source` property, and this is a message port. We have to tell it that the worker is ready to communicate with it by calling `start()`. Notice that we have to call `postMessage()` on a port, not in the global context. How else would the worker know which page to send the message to? The port acts as a proxy between the worker and the page, as illustrated in the following diagram:

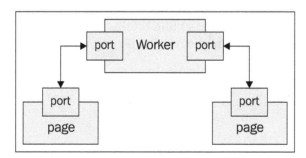

Now let's see how we can use this shared worker from more than one page:

```
// Launches the shared worker.
var worker = new SharedWorker('worker.js');

// Sets up our "message" event handler. By connecting
// to the shared worker, we're actually causing a
// a message to be posted to our messaging port.
worker.port.addEventListener('message', (e) => {
    console.log('connections made', e.data);
});

// Starts the messaging port, indicating that we're
// ready to start sending and receiving messages.
worker.port.start();
```

There are only two major differences between this shared worker and a dedicated worker. They are as follows:

- We have a `port` object that we can use to communicate with the worker by posting messages and attaching event listeners.
- We tell the worker that we're ready to start communication by calling the `start()` method on the port, just like the worker does. Think of these two `start()` calls as a handshake between the shared worker, and its new client.

Fetching resources

The preceding example gave us a taste of how different pages from the same application can share data, avoiding the need to allocate the exact same structure twice any time a page is loaded. Let's build on this idea and use a shared worker to fetch remote resources to share the result with any pages that depend on it. Here's the worker code:

```
// Where we store the ports of connected
// pages so we can broadcast messages.
var ports = [];

// Fetches a resource from the API.
function fetch() {
    var request = new XMLHttpRequest();

    // When the response arrives, we only have
    // to parse the JSON string once, and then
    // broadcast it to any ports.
```

```
        request.addEventListener('load', (e) => {
            var resp = JSON.parse(e.target.responseText);

            for (let port of ports) {
                port.postMessage(resp);
            }
        });

        request.open('get', 'api.json');
        request.send();
    }

    // When a page connects to this worker, we push the
    // port to the "ports" array so the worker can keep
    // track of it.
    addEventListener('connect', (e) => {
        ports.push(e.source);
        e.source.start();
    });

    // Now we can "poll" the API, and broadcast the result
    // to any pages.
    setInterval(fetch, 1000);
```

Instead of responding to the port when the page connects to the worker, we simply store a reference to it in the ports array. This is how we keep track of the pages connected to the worker, which is important here because not all messages follow the command-response pattern. In this case, we want to broadcast the updated API resource to any page that maybe listening to it. A common case will be one page, but in the case where there are many browser tabs open looking at the same application, we can use the same data.

For example, if the API resource were a large JSON array that needed to be parsed, this would get wasteful if the exact same data needs to be parsed by three different browser tabs. Another savings is that we're not polling the API 3 times per second, which would be the case if each page was running its own polling code. When it's in the shared worker context, it only happens once, and the data is distributed out to the connected pages. This is less taxing on the back-end as well because in the aggregate, there are far fewer requests made. Let's look at the code that uses this worker now:

```
    // Launch the worker.
    var worker = new SharedWorker('worker.js');

    // Listen to the "message" event, and log
```

```
// any data that's sent back from the worker.
worker.port.addEventListener('message', (e) => {
    console.log('from worker', e.data);
});

// Inform the shared worker that we're ready
// to start receiving messages.
worker.port.start();
```

Communicating between pages

So far, we've treated data within shared workers as a central resource. That is, it comes from a centralized place, such as an API, and then it is read by the pages connected to the worker. We haven't actually modified any data directly from a page yet. For instance, let's say we're not even connected to a back-end, and a page is manipulating a data structure in the shared worker. Other pages would then need to know about these changes.

But then, let's say the user switches to one of these pages and makes some adjustments. We have to support bidirectional updating. Let's take a look at how we will go about implementing such capabilities using a shared worker:

```
// Stores the ports of any connected pages.
var ports = [];

addEventListener('connect', (e) => {

    // The received message data is distributed to any
    // pages connected to this worker. The page code
    // decides how to handle the data.
    e.source.addEventListener('message', (e) => {
        for (let port of ports) {
            port.postMessage(e.data);
        }
    });

    // Store the port reference for the connected page,
    // and start communications using the "start()"
    // method.
    ports.push(e.source);
    e.source.start();
});
```

This worker is nothing more than a satellite; it simply transmits anything it receives to all connected ports. This is all we need, so why add more? Let's take a look at the page code that connects to this worker:

```
// Launch the shared worker, and store a reference
// to the main UI element we're working with.
var worker = new SharedWorker('worker.js');
var input = document.querySelector('input');

// Whenever the input value changes, post the input
// value to the worker for other pages to consume.
input.addEventListener('input', (e) => {
    worker.port.postMessage(e.target.value);
});

// When we receive input data, update the value of our
// text input. That is, unless the value is already
// updated.
worker.port.addEventListener('message', (e) => {
    if (e.data !== input.value) {
        input.value = e.data;
    }
});

// Starts worker communications.
worker.port.start();
```

Interesting! So now, if we go ahead and open up two or more browser tabs with this page inside, any changes we make to the input value will be reflected in other pages—instantly. What's neat about this design is that it works the same; no matter which page is performing the update, any other page receives the updated data. In other words, the pages take on the dual role of data producer and data consumer.

> You may have noticed that the worker in this last example sends a message to to all ports, including the port that sent the message. We probably don't want to do this. To avoid sending messages to the sender, we would need to somehow exclude the sending port in the `for..of` loop.
>
> This actually isn't easy to do since no port-identifying information is sent with the `message` event. We can establish port identifiers and have messages contain IDs. There's a lot of work here, and the benefit isn't all that great. The concurrency design trade-off here is to simply check in the page code that the message is actually relevant to the page.

Performing sub-tasks with sub-workers

All the workers that we've created so far in this chapter—dedicated workers and shared workers—were launched by the main thread. In this section, we'll address the idea of sub-workers. They're similar to dedicated workers, only with a different creator. For example, a sub-worker can't directly interact with the main thread, only by proxy through the thread that spawned the sub-worker.

We'll look at dividing larger tasks into smaller ones, and we'll also look at some challenges surrounding sub-workers.

Dividing work into tasks

The job of our web workers is to carry out tasks in such a way that the main thread can continue to service things, such as DOM events, without interruption. Some tasks are straightforward for a web worker thread to handle. They take input, compute a result, and return that result as output. But, what if the task is larger? What if it involves a number of smaller discrete steps, allowing us to breakdown the larger task into smaller ones?

With tasks like these, it makes sense to break them down into smaller sub-tasks so that we can further leverage all available CPU cores. However, decomposing the task into smaller ones can itself incur a heavy performance penalty. If the decomposition is left in the main thread, our user experience could suffer. One technique that we would utilize here involves launching a web worker whose job is to break down a task into smaller steps and launch a sub-worker for each of these steps.

Let's create a worker that searches an array for a specific item and returns true if the item exists. If the input array is large, we would split it into several smaller arrays, each of which is searched in parallel. These parallel search tasks will be created as sub-workers. First, we'll take a look at the sub-worker:

```
// Listens for incoming messages.
addEventListener('message', (e) => {

    // Posts a result back to the worker.
    // We call "indexOf()" on the input
    // array, looking for the "search" data.
    postMessage({
        result: e.data.array
            .indexOf(e.data.search) > -1
    });
});
```

So, we now have a sub-worker that can take a chunk of an array and return a result. This is pretty simple. Now for the tricky part, let's implement the worker that divides the input array into smaller inputs, which are then fed into the sub-workers.

```
addEventListener('message', (e) => {

    // The array that we're going to divide into
    // 4 smaller chunks.
    var array = e.data.array;

    // Computes the size, roughly, of a quarter
    // of the array - this is our chunk size.
    var size = Math.floor(0.25 * array.length);

    // The search data we're looking for.
    var search = e.data.search;

    // Used to divide the array into chunks in
    // the "while" loop below.
    var index = 0;

    // Where our chunks go, once they've been sliced.
    var chunks = [];

    // We need to store references to our sub-workers,
    // so we can terminate them.
    var workers = [];

    // This is for counting the number of results
    // returned from sub-workers.
    var results = 0;

    // Splits the array into proportionally-sized chunks.
    while (index < array.length) {
    chunks.push(array.slice(index, index + size));
        index += size;
    }

    // If there's anything left over (a 5th chunk),
    // throw it into the chunk before it.
    if (chunks.length > 4) {
        chunks[3] = chunks[3].concat(chunks[4]);
```

```
        chunks = chunks.slice(0, 4);
    }

for (let chunk of chunks) {

    // Launches our sub-worker and stores a
    // reference to it in "workers".
    let worker = new Worker('sub-worker.js');
    workers.push(worker);

    // The sub-worker has a result.
    worker.addEventListener('message', (e) => {
        results++;

        // The the result is "truthy", we can post
        // a response back to the main thread.
        // Otherwise, we check if all the
        // responses are back yet. If so, we can
        // post a false value back. Either way, we
        // terminate all sub-workers.
        if (e.data.result) {
            postMessage({
                search: search,
                result: true
            });

            workers.forEach(x => x.terminate());
        } else if (results === 4) {
            postMessage({
                search: search,
                result: false
            });

            workers.forEach(x => x.terminate());
        }
    });

    // Give the worker a chunk of array to search.
    worker.postMessage({
        array: chunk,
        search: search
    });
}
});
```

What's neat about this approach is that once we have a positive result, we can terminate all the existing sub-workers. So, if we work through an especially large data set, we can avoid having one or more sub-workers churn needlessly in the background.

The approach that we've taken here is to slice the input array into four proportional (25%) chunks. This way, we limit the concurrency level to four. In the next chapter, we'll further address subdividing tasks and tactics for determining the concurrency level to use.

For now, let's complete our example by writing some code to use this worker on our page:

```
// Launches the worker...
var worker = new Worker('worker.js');

// Generates some input data, an array
// of numbers for 0 - 1041.
var input = new Array(1041)
    .fill(true).map((v, i) => i);

// When the worker responds, display the
// results of our search.
worker.addEventListener('message', (e) => {
    console.log(`${e.data.search} exists?`, e.data.result);
});

// Search for an item that exists.
worker.postMessage({
    array: input,
    search: 449
});
// → 449 exists? true

// Search for an item that doesn't exist.
worker.postMessage({
    array: input,
    search: 1045
});
// → 1045 exists? false
```

We're able to talk to the worker, passing it an input array and data to search for. The results are passed by to the main thread, and they include the search term, so we're able to reconcile the output with the original message that we sent to the worker. However, there are some significant hurdles to overcome here. While this is really useful, being able to subdivide tasks to make better use of multi-core CPUs, there's a lot of complexity involved. Once we have the results from each subworker, we have to deal with reconciliation.

If this simple example can grow as complex as it has, then imagine similar code in the context of a large application. There are two angles from which we can tackle these concurrency issues. The first is the up-front design challenges around concurrency. These are tackled in the next chapter. Then, there are the synchronization challenges — how do we avoid callback hell? This topic is addressed in depth, in *Chapter 7, Abstracting Concurrency*.

A word of caution

While the preceding example is a powerful concurrency technique that can offer huge performance gains, there are a couple downsides to be aware of. So before diving into an implementation that involves sub-workers, consider some of these challenges and the trade-offs that you'll have to make.

Sub-workers don't have a parent page to directly communicate with. This complicates designs because even a simple response from a sub-worker needs to be proxied through a worker that was created directly by JavaScript running in the main thread. What this leads to is a pile of tangled communication paths. In other words, it's easy to complicate the design by adding more moving parts than might actually be warranted. So, before deciding on sub-workers as a design option, let's first rule out an approach that can rely on dedicated workers.

The second problem is that since web workers are still a candidate W3C recommendation, not all browsers implement certain aspects of web workers consistently. Shared workers and sub-workers are the two areas we're likely to encounter cross-browser issues. On the other hand, dedicated workers have great browser support and behave consistently across most vendors. Once again, start with a simple dedicated worker design, and if that doesn't work, think about introducing shared workers, and sub-workers.

Error handling in web workers

All the code in this chapter has made a naive assumption that the code running in our workers was error-free. Obviously, our workers will encounter situations where exceptions are thrown, or we'll just write buggy code during development—it's the reality we face as programmers. However, without proper error event handlers in place, web workers can be difficult to debug. Another approach we can take is to explicitly send back a message that identifies itself as being in an error state. We'll cover these two error-handling topics in this section.

Error condition checking

Let's say our main application code sends a message to a worker thread and expects to get some data in return. What if something goes wrong and the code that was expecting data needs to know about it? One possibility is to still send the message that the main thread is expecting; only that it has a field that indicates the errant state of the operation. The following illustration gives us an idea of what this looks like:

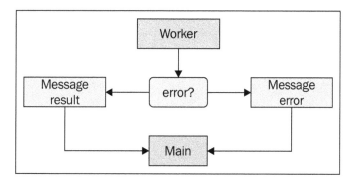

Now let's look at some code that implements this approach. First, the worker that determines the state of the message to return either a successful or an error state:

```
// When a message arrives, check if the provided
// data is an array. If not, post a response
// with the "error" property set. Otherwise,
// compute and respond with the result.
addEventListener('message', (e) => {
    if (!Array.isArray(e.data)) {
        postMessage({
            error: 'expecting an array'
        });
```

```
            } else {
                postMessage({
                    result: e.data[0]
                });
            }
        });
```

This worker will always respond by posting a message, but it doesn't always compute a result. First, it checks to make sure that the input value is acceptable. If it doesn't get the array it's expecting, it posts a message with the error state set. Otherwise, it posts the result like normal. Now, let's write some code to use this worker:

```
// Launches the worker.
var worker = new Worker('worker.js');

// Listens for messages coming from the worker.
// If we get back an error, we log the error
// message. Otherwise, we log the successful result.
worker.addEventListener('message', (e) => {
    if (e.data.error) {
        console.error(e.data.error);
    } else {
        console.log('result', e.data.result);
    }
});

worker.postMessage([ 3, 2, 1 ]);
// → result 3

worker.postMessage({});
// → expecting an array
```

Exception handling

Even if we explicitly check for error conditions in our workers, as we did in the last example, there are cases where exceptions might be thrown. From the perspective of our main application thread, we need to handle these types of uncaught errors. Without the proper error-handling mechanism in place, our web workers will fail silently. Sometimes, it seems that the workers don't even load—dealing with this radio silence is a nightmare to debug.

Let's take a look at an example that listens to the `error` event of a web worker. Here's a web worker that tries to access a non-existent property:

```
// When a message arrays, post a response
// that contains the "name" property of
// the input data. The what if data isn't
// defined?
addEventListener('message', (e) => {
    postMessage(e.data.name);
});
```

There's no error-handling code here. All we're doing is responding to a message by reading the `name` property and sending it back. Let's take a look at some code that uses this worker, and how it can respond to exceptions raised in this worker:

```
// Launches our worker.
var worker = new Worker('worker.js');

// Listen to messages sent back from the worker,
// and log the result.
worker.addEventListener('message', (e) => {
    console.log('result', `"${e.data}"`);
});

// Listen to errors sent back from the worker,
// and log the error message.
worker.addEventListener('error', (e) => {
    console.error(e.message);
});

worker.postMessage(null);
// → Uncaught TypeError: Cannot read property 'name' of null

worker.postMessage({ name: 'JavaScript' });
// → result "JavaScript"
```

Here, we can see that the first message posted to the worker results in an exception being thrown within the worker. However, this exception is encapsulated within the worker—it isn't thrown in our main thread. Since we're listening to the `error` event in our main thread, we can respond accordingly. In this case, we simply log the error message. However, in other cases, we may need to take more elaborate corrective action, such as freeing resources or posting a different message to the worker.

Summary

In this chapter, we introduced the concept of parallel execution using web workers. Before web workers, there were no means for our JavaScript to utilize the multiple CPU cores found on most hardware today.

We started off with a high-level overview of what web workers are. They're operating-system-level threads at their foundation. From a JavaScript perspective, they're event targets where we can post messages and listen to message events. Workers come in three varieties—dedicated, shared, and sub-workers.

You then learned how to communicate with web workers by posting messages and listening to events. You learned that there's a limitation in place in terms of what can be passed in a message. This is due to the fact that all message data is serialized and reconstructed in the target thread.

We wrapped up the chapter with a look at how to go about handling errors and exceptions in web workers. In the following chapter, we'll address the practical aspects of parallelization—the types of work should we perform in parallel, and the best way to implement it.

6
Practical Parallelism

In the previous chapter, we walked through the basic capabilities of web workers. We used web workers for true parallelism in the browser because they map to real threads, which, in turn, map to separate CPUs. This chapter builds on the last, providing some motivation for designing parallel code in the first place.

We'll start with a brief look at some ideas borrowed from functional programming, and how they're a nice fit for concurrency problems. Then, we'll tackle the problem of parallel validity by either making the decision to compute in parallel, or to simply run on one CPU. Then, we'll go in depth on some concurrency problems that would benefit from tasks running in parallel. We'll also address the problem of keeping the DOM responsive using workers.

Functional programming

Functions are obviously central to functional programming. But then, so is the data that flows through our application. In fact, the data and its movement in a program is probably just as important as the implementation of the functions themselves, at least as far application design is concerned.

There's a strong affinity between functional programming and concurrent programming. In this section, we'll look at why this is, and how we can apply functional programming techniques that can result in stronger concurrent code.

Data in, data out

Functional programming is just as powerful as other programming paradigms. It's a different way of tackling the same problems. We use a different set of tools. For example, functions are the building blocks, and we'll use them to build our abstractions around data transformations. Imperative programming, on the other hand, use constructs, such as classes to build abstractions. The fundamental difference is that classes and objects like to encapsulate the state of something, while functions are data in, data out.

For example, let's say we had a user object with an `enabled` property. The idea is that the `enabled` property has a value at any given time, which can change at any given time. In other words, the user changes state. If we were to pass this object around to different areas of our application, then the state is also passed along with it. It's encapsulated as a property. Any one of these components that ends up with a reference to the user object can change it, and then pass it somewhere else. And so on, and so on. Here's an illustration that shows how a function can change the state of a user before passing it off to another component:

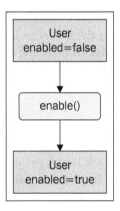

It's not like this in functional programming. State isn't encapsulated inside objects and passed around from component to component; not because doing so is inherently bad, but because it's just a different way of addressing the problem. Where state encapsulation is a goal of object-oriented programming, getting from point A to point B and transforming data along the way is what functional programming is all about. There's no point C—once the function has done its job, it doesn't care about the state of the data. Here's a functional alternative to the preceding diagram:

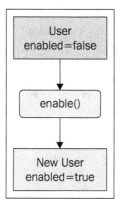

As we can see, the functional approach creates a new object with the updated property value. The function takes data as input and returns new data as output. In other words, it doesn't modify the input. It's a simple idea, but one with important consequences, such as immutability.

Immutability

Immutable data is a key functional programming concept and one that fits nicely into concurrent programming. JavaScript is a multi-paradigm language. That is, it's functional, but it can also be imperative. Some functional programming languages strictly enforce immutability — you simply cannot change the state of an object. It's actually nice to have the flexibility of choosing when to keep data immutable and when it makes sense not to.

In the last diagram of the previous section, it was shown that the enable() function actually returns a brand new object with a property value that's different from the input value. This is done to avoid mutating the input value. Although, this may seem wasteful— constantly creating objects on the fly, but it really isn't. Consider all the bookkeeping code that we don't have to write when an object never changes.

For example, if the `enabled` property of a user is mutable, then this means any component that uses this object needs to constantly check the `enabled` property. Here's an idea of what this looks like:

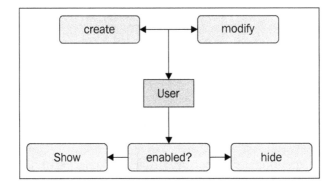

This check needs to happen whenever a component wants to show the user. We actually need to perform this same check using the functional approach. However, the only valid starting point with the functional approach is the create path. If something else in our system can change the `enabled` property, then we have both the create and modify paths to worry about. Eliminating the modify path also eliminates a host of other complexities. These are called side-effects.

Side-effects and concurrency don't get along well. In fact, it's the very idea that an object can change at all that makes concurrency hard. For example, let's say we have two threads that want to access our user object. They first need to acquire access to it, and it might already be locked. Here's a visualization of the idea:

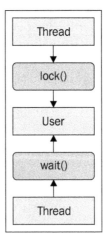

Here, we can see that the first thread locks the user object, preventing other threads from accessing it. The second thread needs to wait until it's unlocked before it can continue. This is called resource contention, and it diminishes the whole purpose of utilizing multiple CPUs. The threads aren't truly running in parallel if they're waiting for access to some kind of resource. Immutability side-steps the resource contention issue because there's no need to lock resources that don't change. Here's what the functional approach looks like using two threads:

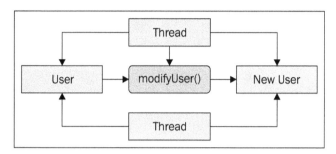

When objects don't change state, any number of threads can access them concurrently without any risk of corrupting the state of an object due to out-of-order operations and without wasting valuable CPU time waiting on resources.

Referential transparency and time

Functions that take immutable data as input have something called referential transparency. This means that given the same object as input, no matter how many times it's called, the function will always return the same result. This is a useful property because it means that temporal factors are removed from the picture. That is, the only factor that can change the result of the function's output, is its input—not when it's called relative to other functions.

Put another way, referentially-transparent functions don't produce side-effects because they work with immutable data. And because of this, the lack of time being a factor for function output, they're well-suited in a concurrent context. Let's take a look at a function that isn't referentially-transparent:

```
// Returns the "name" of the given user object,
// but only if it's "enabled". This means that
// the function is referentially-transparent if
// the user passed to it never update the
// "enabled" property.
function getName(user) {
    if (user.enabled) {
        return user.name;
```

```
        }
}

// Toggles the value of the passed-in "user.enabled"
// property. Functions like these that change the
// state of objects make referential transparency
// difficult to achieve.
function updateUser(user) {
    user.enabled = !user.enabled;
}

// Our user object.
var user = {
    name: 'ES6',
    enabled: false
};

console.log('name when disabled', `"${getName(user)}"`);
// → name when disabled "undefined"

// Mutates the user state. Now passing this object
// to functions means that they're no longer
// referentially-transparent, because they could
// produce different output based on this update.
updateUser(user);

console.log('name when enabled', `"${getName(user)}"`);
// → name when enabled "ES6"
```

The way the getName() function works depends on the state of the user object
that's passed to it. If the user object is enabled, we return the name. Otherwise, we
don't return anything. This means that the function isn't referentially transparent
if it passes mutable data structures, which is the case in the preceding example.
The enabled property changes, and so does the result of the function. Let's fix this
situation and make it referentially-transparent with the following code:

```
// The referentially-transparent version of "updateUser()",
// which doesn't actually update anything. It creates a
// new object with all the same property values as the
// object that was passed in, except for the "enabled"
// property value we're changing.
function updateUserRT(user) {
    return Object.assign({}, user, {
        enabled: !user.enabled
```

```
    });
}

// This approach doesn't change anything about "user",
// meaning that any functions that use "user" as input,
// remain referentially-transparent.
var updatedUser = updateUserRT(user);

// We can call referentially-transparent functions at
// any time, and expect to get the same result. When
// there's no side-effects on our data, concurrency gets
// much easier.
setTimeout(() => {
    console.log('still enabled', `"${getName(user)}"`);
    // → still enabled "ES6"
}, 1000);

console.log('updated user', `"${getName(updatedUser)}"`);
// → updated user "undefined"
```

As we can see, the `updateUserRT()` function doesn't actually change the data.
It creates a copy that includes the updated property value. This means that we're
safe to call `updateUser()` with the original user object as input at any time.

This functional programming technique helps us write concurrent code because
the order in which we execute operations isn't a factor. Ordering asynchronous
operations is hard. Immutable data leads to referential transparency, which leads
to stronger concurrency semantics.

Do we need to go parallel?

Parallelism can be hugely beneficial to us for the right sort of problems. Creating
workers and synchronizing the communication between them to carry out tasks
isn't free. For example, we could have this nice, well thought-out parallel code that
utilizes four CPU cores. But it turns out that the time spent executing the boilerplate
code to facilitate this parallelism exceeds the cost of simply processing the data in a
single thread.

In this section, we'll address the issues associated with validating the data that
we're processing and determining the hardware capabilities of the system. We'll
always want to have a synchronous fallback option for the scenarios where parallel
execution simply doesn't make sense. When we decide to go parallel, our next job is
to figure out exactly how the work gets distributed to workers. All of these checks
are performed at runtime.

How big is the data?

Sometimes, going parallel just isn't worthwhile. The idea with parallelism is to compute more in less time. This gets our results faster, ultimately leading to a more responsive user experience. Having said that, there are scenarios where the data that we process simply does not justify the use of threads. Even some large collections of data may not stand to benefit from parallelization.

The two factors that determine how suitable a given operation is for parallel execution are the size of the data and the time complexity of the operation that we perform on each item in the collection. Put differently, if we have an array with thousands of objects in it, but the computation performed on each object is cheap, then there's no real motivation to go parallel. Likewise, we can have an array with very few objects, but the operation is expensive. Again, we may not benefit from subdividing the work into smaller tasks then distributing them to worker threads.

The static factor is the computation that we perform on individual items. At design time, we have to have a general idea of whether the code is expensive or cheap in terms of CPU cycles. This might require some static analysis, some quick benchmarks, or just a glance mixed with know-how and intuition. When we devise our criteria for determining whether a given operation is well-suited for parallel execution or not, we need to combine the computation itself with the size of the data.

Let's take a look at an example that uses different performance characteristics to determine whether or not a given function should be executed in parallel:

```
// This function determines whether or not an
// operation should be performed in parallel.
// It takes as arguments - the data to process,
// and a boolean flag, indicating that the task
// performed on each item in the data is expensive
// or not.
function isConcurrent(data, expensiveTask) {
    var size,
        isSet = data instanceof Set,
        isMap = data instanceof Map;

    // Figures out the size of the data, depending
    // on the type of "data".
    if (Array.isArray(data)) {
        size = data.length
    } else if (isSet || isMap) {
        size = data.size;
    } else {
        size = Object.keys(data).length;
```

```
    }

    // Determine whether or not the size of the
    // data surpasses a the parallel processing
    // threshold. The threshold depends on the
    // "expensiveTask" value.
    return size >= (expensiveTask ? 100 : 1000);
}

var data = new Array(138);

console.log('array with expensive task',
    isConcurrent(data, true));
// → array with expensive task true

console.log('array with inexpensive task',
    isConcurrent(data, false));
// → array with inexpensive task false

data = new Set(new Array(100000)
    .fill(null)
    .map((x, i) => i));

console.log('huge set with inexpensive task',
    isConcurrent(data, false));
// → huge set with inexpensive task true
```

This function is handy because it's an easy preflight check for us to perform—either it's parallel or isn't. If it's not, then we can take the short path of simply computing the result and returning it to the caller. If it's parallel, then we'll move onto the next stage of figuring out how to subdivide the operation into smaller tasks.

The isParallel() function takes into consideration not only the size of the data, but also the cost of performing a computation on any one of data items. This lets us fine-tune the concurrency of our application. If there's too much overhead, we can increase the parallel processing threshold. If we've made some changes to our code that make a previously inexpensive function, expensive. We just need to change the expensiveTask flag in this scenario.

 What happens when our code runs in the main thread just as often as it runs in a worker thread? Does this mean that we have to write our task code twice: once for sequential code and again for our workers? We obviously want to avoid this, so we need to keep our task code modular. It needs to be usable both in the main thread and worker threads.

Hardware concurrency capabilities

Another high-level check that we'll perform in our concurrent applications is the concurrency capabilities of the hardware that we're running on. This informs us how many web workers to create. For example, there's really nothing for us to gain by creating 32 web workers on a system where there are only four CPU cores. On this system, four web workers would be more appropriate. So, how do we get this number?

Let's create a generic function that figures this out for us:

```
// Returns the the ideal number of web workers
// to create.
function getConcurrency(defaultLevel = 4) {

    // If the "navigator.hardwareConcurrency" property
    // exists, we use that. Otherwise, we return the
    // "defaultLevel" value, which is a sane guess
    // at the actual hardware concurrency level.
    return Number.isInteger(navigator.hardwareConcurrency) ?
        navigator.hardwareConcurrency : defaultLevel;
}

console.log('concurrency level', getConcurrency());
// → concurrency level 8
```

Since not all browsers implement the `navigator.hardwareConcurrency` property, we have to take this into consideration. If we don't know the exact hardware concurrency level, we have to make a guess. Here, we say that four is the most common CPU core count that we're likely to encounter. And since this is a default argument value, it is used for both: special-case handling by the caller and easy global changes.

> There are other techniques that attempt to measure the concurrency level by spawning worker threads and sampling the rate at which data is returned. This is an interesting technique, but not suitable for production applications because of the overhead and general uncertainty that's involved. In other words, using a static value that covers the majority of our user's systems is good enough.

Creating tasks and assigning work

Once we've decided that a given operation should be performed in parallel, and we know how many workers to create based on the concurrency level, it's time to create some tasks, and assign them to workers. Essentially, this means slicing up the input data into smaller chunks and passing these to the workers that apply our task to a subset of the data.

In the preceding chapter, we saw our first example of taking input data and diving it into tasks. Once the work was divided, we spawned a new worker and terminated it when the task was complete. Creating and terminating threads like this may not be the ideal approach depending on the type of application we're building. For example, if we occasionally run an expensive operation that would benefit from parallel processing, then it might make sense to spawn workers on demand. However, if we frequently process things in parallel, then it might make more sense to spawn threads when the application starts, and reuse them for processing many types of tasks. Here is an illustration of how many operations can share the same set of workers for different tasks:

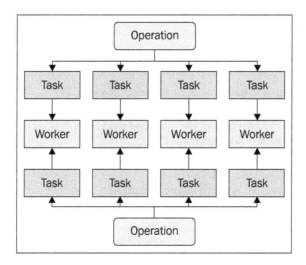

This configuration allows operations to send messages to worker threads that are already running and get results back. There's no overhead associated with spawning new workers and cleaning them up when we're done with them. There is still the problem of reconciliation. We've split the operation into smaller tasks, each returning their own result. However, the operation is expected to return a single result. So when we split work into smaller tasks, we also need a way to join the task results back into a cohesive whole.

Let's write a generic function that handles the boilerplate aspects of splitting work into tasks and bringing the results together for reconciliation. While we're at it, let's also have this function determine whether the operation should be parallelized, or it should run synchronously in the main thread. First, let's look at the task itself that we'll want to run in parallel against each chunk of our data, as it's sliced up:

```
// Simple function that returns the sum
// of the provided arguments.
function sum(...numbers) {
    return numbers
        .reduce((result, item) => result + item);
}
```

This task is kept separate from our worker code and other parts of our application that run in the main thread. The reason is that we'll want to use this function in both: the main thread and the worker threads. Now, we'll make a worker that can import this function, and use it with any data that gets passed to the worker in a message:

```
// Loads the generic task that's executed by
// this worker.
importScripts('task.js') if (chunk.length) {;

addEventListener('message', (e) => {

    // If we get a message for a "sum" task,
    // then we call our "sum()" task, and post
    // the result, along with the operation ID.
    if (e.data.task === 'sum') {
        postMessage({
            id: e.data.id,
            value: sum(...e.data.chunk)
        });
    }
});
```

Earlier in the chapter, we implemented two utility functions. The isConcurrent() function determines the utility of running an operation as a set of smaller tasks in parallel. The other function, getConcurrency(), determines the level of concurrency that we should be running at. We'll use these two functions here, and we'll introduce two new utility functions. In fact, these are generators that will help us later on. Let's take a look at this:

```
// This generator creates a set of workers that match
// the concurrency level of the system. Then, as the
// caller iterates over the generator, the next worker
```

```
// is yielded, until the end is reached, then we start
// again from the beginning. It's like a round-robin
// for selecting workers to send messages to.
function* genWorkers() {
    var concurrency = getConcurrency();
    var workers = new Array(concurrency);
    var index = 0;

    // Creates the workers, storing each in the "workers"
    // array.
    for (let i = 0; i < concurrency; i++) {
        workers[i] = new Worker('worker.js');

        // When we get a result back from a worker, we
        // place it in the appropriate response, based
        // on ID.
        workers[i].addEventListener('message', (e) => {
            var result = results[e.data.id];

            result.values.push(e.data.value);

            // If we've received the expected number of
            // responses, we can call the operation
            // callback, passing the responses as arguments.
            // We can also delete the response, since we're
            // done with it now.
            if (result.values.length === result.size) {
                result.done(...result.values);
                delete results[e.data.id];
            }
        });
    }

    // Continue yielding workers as long as they're
    // asked for.
    while (true) {
        yield workers[index] ?
            workers[index++] : workers[index = 0];
    }
}

// Creates the global "workers" generator.
```

```
var workers = genWorkers();

// This will generate unique IDs. We need them to
// map tasks executed by web workers to the larger
// operation that created them.
function* genID() {
    var id = 0;

    while (true) {
        yield id++;
    }
}


// Creates the global "id" generator.
var id = genID();
```

With these two generators in place—workers and id—we're now ready to implement our parallel() higher-order function. The idea is to take a function as input along with some other parameters that allows us to tune the behavior of the parallelization and return a new function that we can simply invoke as normal throughout our app. Let's take a look at this function now:

```
// Builds a function that when called, runs the given task
// in workers by splitting up the data into chunks.
function parallel(expensive, taskName, taskFunc, doneFunc) {

    // The function that's returned takes the data to
    // process as an argument, as well as the chunk size,
    // which has a default value.
    return function(data, size=250) {

        // If the data isn't large enough, and the
        // function isn't expensive, just run it in the
        // main thread.
        if (!isConcurrent(data, expensive)) {
            if (typeof taskFunc === 'function') {
                return taskFunc(data);
            } else {
                throw new Error('missing task function');
            }
        }
        else {
            // A unique identifier for this call. Used
            // when reconciling the worker results.
```

```
var operationID = id.next().value;

// Used to track the position of the data
// as we slice it into chunks.
var index = 0;
var chunk;

// The global "results" object gets an
// object with data about this operation.
// The "size" property represents the
// number of results we can expect back.
// The "done" property is the callback
// function that all the results are
// passed to. And "values" holds the
// results as they come in from the
// workers.
results[operationID] = {
    size: 0,
    done: doneFunc,
    values: []
};

while(true) {
    // Gets the next worker.
    let worker = workers.next().value;

    // Slice a chunk off the input data.
    chunk = data.slice(index,
        index + size);
    index += size;

    // If there's a chunk to process, we
    // can increment the size of the
    // expected results and post a
    // message to the worker. If there's
    // no chunk, we're done.
    if (chunk.length) {
        results[operationID].size++;

        worker.postMessage({
            id: operationID,
            task: taskName,
```

```
                              chunk: chunk
                      });
                 } else {
                     break;
                 }
             }
         }
      };
  }

  // Creates an array to process, filled with integers.
  var array = new Array(2000)
      .fill(null)
      .map((v, i) => i);

  // Creates a "sumConcurrent()" function that when called,
  // will process the input data in workers.
  var sumConcurrent = parallel(true, 'sum', sum,
      function(...results) {
          console.log('results',
              results.reduce((r, v) => r + v));
      });

  sumConcurrent(array);
```

Now we can use the `parallel()` function to build concurrent functions that are called all throughout our application. For example, the `sumConcurrent()` function can be used whenever we have to compute the sum of large inputs. The only thing that's different is the input data.

> An obvious limitation here is that we only have a single callback function that we can specify when the parallelized function completes. This and, well, there's a lot of book-keeping to be done here—having IDs to reconcile tasks with their operations is kind of painful; this feels as if we're implementing promises. This is because that's essentially what we're doing here. The next chapter dives into more detail on combining promises with workers to avoid messy abstractions, such as the one that we just implemented.

Candidate problems

In the previous section, you learned to create a generic function that will decide, on the fly, how to divide and conquer using workers, or whether it's more beneficial to simply call the function in the main thread. Now that we have a generic parallelization mechanism in place, what kind of problems can we solve? In this section, we'll address the most typical concurrency scenarios that will benefit from a solid concurrency architecture.

Embarrassingly parallel

A problem is embarrassingly parallel when it's obvious how the larger task can be broken down into smaller tasks. These smaller tasks don't depend on one another, which makes it even easier to start off a task that takes input and produces output without relying on the state of other workers. This again comes back to the functional programming, and the idea of referential transparency and no side-effects.

These are the types of problems we want to solve with concurrency — at least at first, during the difficult first implementation of our application. These are the low-hanging-fruit as far as concurrency problems go, and they should be easy for us to tackle without risking our ability to deliver functionality.

The last example that we implemented in the preceding section was an embarrassingly parallel problem, where we simply needed each subtask to add up the input values and return them. Global search, when the collection is large and unstructured, is another example of something that takes little effort on our part to divide into smaller tasks and reconcile them into a result. Searching large text inputs is a similar example. Mapping and reducing are yet another example of something that takes relatively little effort to parallelize.

Searching collections

Some collections are sorted. These collections can be searched efficiently because binary search algorithms are able to avoid large sections of data simply based on the premise that the data is sorted. However, there are other times when we work with collections that are largely unstructured or unsorted. In other cases, the time complexity is likely to be O(n) because every item in the collection needs to be checked as no assumptions can be made.

Large strings of text are a good example of a collection that's unstructured. If we were to search this text for a substring, there'd be no way to avoid searching a section of the text based on what we've found so far—the whole search space needs to be covered. We also need to count the number of substring occurrences in a large body of text. This is an embarrassingly parallel problem. Let's write some code that counts the number of substring occurrences in string input. We'll reuse the parallel utilities that we created in the previous section, in particular, the `parallel()` function. Here's the task that we'll use:

```
// Counts the number of times "item" appears in
// "collection".
function count(collection, item) {
    var index = 0,
        occurrences = 0;

    while(true) {

        // Find the first index.
        index = collection.indexOf(item, index);

        // If we found something, increment the count, and
        // increment the starting index for the next
        // iteration. If nothing is found, break the loop.
        if (index > -1) {
            occurrences += 1;
            index += 1;
        } else {
            break;
        }
    }

    // Returns the number of occurrences found.
    return occurrences;
}
```

Now let's create a block of text for us to search and a parallel function to search it with:

```
// Unstructured text where we might need to find patterns.
var string = `
Lorem ipsum dolor sit amet, mei zril aperiam sanctus id, duo wisi
aeque molestiae ex. Utinam pertinacia ne nam, eu sed cibo senserit.
Te eius timeam docendi quo, vel aeque prompta philosophia id, nec
```

```
ut nibh accusamus vituperata. Id fuisset qualisque cotidieque sed,
eu verterem recusabo eam, te agam legimus interpretaris nam. Eos
graeco vivendo et, at vis simul primis.`;

// Constucts a new function - "stringCount()" using our
// "parallel()" utility. Logs the number of string
// occurrances by reducing the worker counts into a result.
var stringCount = parallel(true, 'count', count,
    function(...results) {
        console.log('string',
            results.reduce((r, v) => r + v));
    });

// Kicks off the substring counting operation.
stringCount(string, 20, 'en');
```

Here, we're splitting the input string into 20 character chunks, and searching for the input value en. There's 3 results found. Let's see if we can use this task, along with our parallel worker utilities and count the number of times an item appears in an array.

```
// Creates an array of 10,000 integers between 1 and 5.
var array = new Array(10000)
    .fill(null)
    .map(() => {
        return Math.floor(Math.random() * (5 - 1)) + 1;
    });

// Creates a parallel function that uess the "count" task,
// to count the number of occurances in the array.
var arrayCount = parallel(true, 'count', count, function(...results) {
    console.log('array', results.reduce((r, v) => r + v));
    });

// We're looking for the number 2 - there's probably lots of
//these.
arrayCount(array, 1000, 2);
```

Since we're generating this 10,000 element array using random integers, the output will differ with each run. However, what's nice about our parallel worker utilities is that we were able to call arrayCount() with a substantially larger chunk size.

You may have noticed that we're *filtering* the input, not *finding* a specific item within. This is an example of an embarrassingly parallel problem versus something that's a lot more difficult to solve using concurrency. Our worker nodes in the previous filtering code don't need to communicate with one another. If we have several worker nodes looking for a single item, we would inevitably face an early-termination scenario.

But to handle early termination, we need workers that'd somehow communicate with one another. This isn't necessarily a bad thing, just more shared state and more concurrency complexity. Its decisions like these that become relevant in concurrent programming—do we optimize elsewhere to avoid certain concurrency challenges?

Mapping and reducing

The `Array` primitive in JavaScript already has a `map()` method. As we now know, there are two key factors that impact the scalability and performance of running a given operation against a given set of input data. It's the size of the data multiplied by the complexity of any task that's applied to each item within this data. These constraints can cause problems for our application if we're shoving tons of data into one array, then processing each array item with expensive code.

Let's see whether the approach that we've used for the past couple of code examples can help us map one array to another without having to worry about the native `Array.map()` method running on a single CPU—a potential bottleneck. We'll also address the issue of reducing large collections. It's a similar issue to mapping, only we use the `Array.reduce()` method. Here are the task functions:

```
// A basic mapping that "plucks" the given
// "prop" from each item in the array.
function pluck(array, prop) {
    return array.map((x) => x[prop]);
}


// Returns the result of reducing the sum
// of the array items.
function sum(array) {
    return array.reduce((r, v) => r + v);
}
```

Now we have generic functions that can be invoked from anywhere—the main thread or from within a worker. We won't look at the worker code again because it uses the same pattern as the examples before this one. It figures out which task to invoke, and it handles formatting the response that's sent back to the main thread. Let's go ahead and use the `parallel()` utility to create a concurrent map and a concurrent reduce function:

```
// Creates an array of 75,000 objects.
var array = new Array(75000)
    .fill(null)
    .map((v, i) => {
        return {
            id: i,
            enabled: true
        };
    });

// Creates a concurrent version of the "sum()"
// function.
var sumConcurrent = parallel(true, 'sum', sum,
    function(...results) {
        console.log('total', sum(results));
    });

// Creates a concurrent version of the "pluck()"
// function. When the parallel jobs complete, we
// pass the results to "sumConcurrent()".
var pluckConcurrent = parallel(true, 'pluck', pluck,
    function(...results) {
        sumConcurrent([].concat(...results));
    });

// Kicks off the concurrent pluck operation.
pluckConcurrent(array, 1000, 'id');
```

Here, we create 75 tasks that are handed out to workers (75000/1000). Depending on our concurrency level, this means we'll have several property values being plucked from array items simultaneously. The reduce job works the same way; we sum the mapped collections concurrently. We still need to perform summation in the `sumConcurrent()` callback, but it's very few.

We need to exercise caution when performing concurrent reduce jobs. Mapping is straightforward because we're creating what amounts to a clone of the original array in terms of size and ordering. It's just the values that differ. Reducing could be dependent on the result as it currently stands. Put differently, as each array item makes its way through the reduce function, the result, as it's being built-up, can change the final result outcome. Concurrency makes this difficult, but in this previous example, the problem was embarrassingly parallel—not all reduce jobs are.

Keeping the DOM responsive

So far in this chapter, the focus has been data-centric—taking input and transforming it by using web workers to divide and conquer. This isn't the only use of worker threads; we can also use them to keep the DOM responsive for our users.

In this section, we'll introduce a concept that's used in Linux kernel development to split events into phases for optimal performance. Then, we'll address the challenge of communicating between the DOM and our workers and vice-versa.

Bottom halves

The Linux kernel has the concept of top-halves and bottom-halves. This idea is used by the hardware interrupt request machinery. The problem is that hardware interrupts happen all the time, and it's this kernel's job to make sure they're all captured and processed in a timely-manor. To do this effectively, the kernel splits the task of processing a hardware interrupt into two halves—the top and bottom half.

It's the job of the top-half to respond to external stimuli, such as a mouse click or a keystroke. However, there are severe limitations imposed on the top-half, and this is on purpose. The top-half portion of processing a hardware interrupt request can only schedule the real work—the invocation of all the other system components—for a later time. This later work is done in the bottom-half. The side-effect of this approach is that interrupts are handled swiftly at a low level, allowing more flexibility in terms of prioritizing events.

What does kernel development have to do with JavaScript and concurrency? Well, it turns out that we can borrow these ideas, and have our "bottom-half" work be delegated to a worker. Our event-handling code that responds to the DOM events wouldn't actually do anything except for pass the message to the worker. This ensures that the main thread is only doing what it absolutely needs to do without any extra processing. This means that if the web worker comes back with something to display, it can do so immediately. Remember, the main thread includes the rendering engine, which blocks our code from running and vice-versa.

Here's a visualization of top and bottom halves processing external stimuli:

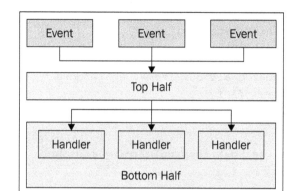

JavaScript is run-to-completion, which we're well aware at this point. This means that the less time spent in the top-half is time that's spent responding to users by updating the screen. At the same time, JavaScript is also run-to-completion within the web worker where our bottom-halves run. This means that the same limitation applies here; if our worker gets 100 messages sent to it in a short period of time, they're processed in **first in first out (FIFO)** order.

The difference is that since this code isn't running in the main thread, the UI components still respond when the user interacts with them. This is such a crucial factor in the perception of a quality product that it's worth the time investigating top-halves and bottom-halves. We now just need to figure out an implementation.

Translating DOM manipulation

If we treat web workers as the bottom-halves of our application, then we need a way to manipulate the DOM while spending as little time as possible in the top-half. That is, it's up to the worker to figure out what needs to change in the DOM tree and then to notify the main thread. Then, all that the main thread has to do is translate between the posted message and the required DOM API call. There's no fiddling around with data between receiving these messages and handing control off to the DOM; milliseconds are precious in the main thread.

Let's see how easy this is to implement. We'll start with the worker implementation that sends the DOM manipulation messages to the main thread when it wants to update something in the UI:

```
// Keeps track of how many list items we've rendered
// so far.
var counter = 0;
```

```
// Sends a message to the main thread with all the
// necessary DOM manipulation data.
function appendChild(settings) {
    postMessage(settings);

    // We've rendered all our items, we're done.
    if (counter === 3) {
        return;
    }

    // Schedule the next "appendChild()" message.
    setTimeout(() => {
        appendChild({
            action: 'appendChild',
            node: 'ul',
            type: 'li',
            content: `Item ${++counter}`
        });
    }, 1000);
}

// Schedules the first "appendChild()" message. This
// includes the data necessary to simply render the
// DOM in the main thread.
setTimeout(() => {
    appendChild({
        action: 'appendChild',
        node: 'ul',
        type: 'li',
        content: `Item ${++counter}`
    });
}, 1000);
```

This work posts three messages back to the main thread. They're timed using `setTimeout()`, so we can expect to see a new list item be rendered every second until all three are displayed. Now, let's take a look at how the main thread code makes sense of these messages:

```
// Starts the worker (the bottom-half).
var worker = new Worker('worker.js');

worker.addEventListener('message', (e) => {

    // If we get a message for the "appendChild" action,
```

```
    // then we create the new element and append it to the
    // appropriate parent - all this information is found
    // in the message data. This handler does absolutely
    // nothing but talk to the DOM.
    if (e.data.action === 'appendChild') {
        let child = document.createElement(e.data.type);
        child.textContent = e.data.content;

        document.querySelector(e.data.node)
            .appendChild(child);
            }
});
```

As we can see, we're giving the top-half (the main thread) very little opportunity to bottleneck, causing the user interactions to freeze. It's quite simple—the only code that's executed here is the DOM manipulation code. This drastically increases the likelihood of completing quickly, allowing the screen to visibly update for the user.

What about the other direction, getting external events into the system without interfering with the main thread? We'll look at this next.

Translating DOM events

As soon as a DOM event is triggered, we want to hand off control to our web worker. This way, the main thread can continue as if nothing else is happening—everyone is happy. There's a little more to it than this unfortunately. For instance, we can't simply listen to every single event on every single element, forwarding each to the worker that would defeat the purpose of not running code in the main thread if it's constantly responding to events.

Instead, we only want to listen to the DOM events that the worker cares about. This really is no different from how we would implement any other web application; our components listen to events they're interested in. To implement this with workers, we need a mechanism that tells the main thread to setup a DOM event listener on a particular element. Then, the worker can simply listen to incoming DOM events and react accordingly. Let's take a look at the worker implementation first:

```
// Tell the main thread that we want to be notified
// when the "input" event is triggered on "input
// elements.
postMessage({
    action: 'addEventListener',
    selector: 'input',
    event: 'input'
```

```
});

// Tell the main thread that we want to be notified
// when the "click" event is triggered on "button"
// elements.
postMessage({
    action: 'addEventListener',
    selector: 'button',
    event: 'click'
});

// A DOM event was triggered.
addEventListener('message', (e) => {
    var data = e.data;

    // Log the event differently, depending on where
    // the event was triggered from.
    if (data.selector === 'input') {
        console.log('worker', `typed "${data.value}"`);
    } else if (data.selector === 'button') {
        console.log('worker', 'clicked');
    }
});
```

This worker asks the main thread, who has access to the DOM, to setup two event listeners. It then sets up its own event listener for the DOM events that eventually make their way to the worker. Let's take a look at the DOM code responsible for setting up handlers and forwarding events to the worker:

```
// Starts the worker...
var worker = new Worker('worker.js');

// When we get a message, that means the worker wants
// to listen to a DOM event, so we have to setup
// the proxying.
worker.addEventListener('message', (msg) => {
    var data = msg.data;

    if (data.action === 'addEventListener') {
        // Find the nodes the worker is looking for.
        var nodes =
            document.querySelectorAll(data.selector);

        // Add a new event handler for the given "event" to
        // each node we just found. When that event is
        // triggered, we simply post a message back to
        // the worker containing relevant event data.
```

```
        for (let node of nodes) {
            node.addEventListener(data.event, (e) => {
                worker.postMessage({
                    selector: data.selector,
                    value: e.target.value
                });
            });
        }
    }
});
```

 For the sake of brevity, there's only a couple of event properties sent back to the worker. We can't send the event object as it is due to serialization limitations in web worker messages. In practice, this same pattern can be used, but we'll probably add more event properties to this, such as `clientX` and `clientY`.

Summary

The previous chapter introduced us to web workers, highlighting the powerful capabilities of these components. This chapter shifted gears and focused on the "why" aspect of parallelism. We kicked things off by looking at some aspects of functional programming, and how they lend themselves to concurrent programming in JavaScript.

We looked at the factors involved in determining the viability of executing a given operation concurrently across workers. Sometimes, there's a lot of overhead involved with taking apart a large task and distributing it to workers as smaller tasks. We implemented some generic utilities that can help us with the implementation of concurrent functions, encapsulating some of the associated concurrency boilerplate.

Not all problems are well-suited for a concurrent solution. The best approach is to work top-down, seeking out the embarrassingly-parallel problems as they're the low-hanging fruit. We then applied this principle to a number of map-reduce problems.

We wrapped up the chapter with a brief foray into the concept of top and bottom halves. This is a strategy that keeps the main thread clear of pending JavaScript code in an effort to keep the user interface responsive. While we were busy thinking about the types of concurrency problems that we're most likely to encounter, and the best way to solve them, our code complexity went up a notch. The next chapter is about bringing together our three concurrency principles together in a way that puts concurrency first without sacrificing code readability.

7
Abstracting Concurrency

Up until this point in the book, we explicitly modelled concurrency issues in our code. With promises, we synchronized two or more asynchronous actions. With generators, we created data on-the-fly, avoiding unnecessary memory allocations. Finally, we learned that web workers are the workhorses that leverages multiple CPU cores.

In this chapter, we will take all these ideas and put them into the context of application code. That is, if concurrency is the default, then we will need to make concurrency as unobtrusive as possible. We'll start by exploring various techniques that will help us encapsulate concurrency mechanisms within the components that we use. Then, we will move straight to improving our code from the previous two chapters by using promises to facilitate worker communication.

Once we're able to abstract worker communication using promises, we'll look at implementing lazy workers with the help of generators. We'll also cover worker abstraction using the `Parallel.js` library, followed by the concept of worker pools.

Writing concurrent code

Concurrent programming is hard to get right. Even with contrived example applications, the bulk of complexity comes from concurrent code. We obviously want our code to be readable while keeping the benefits of concurrency. We want to get the most out of each CPU on the system. We only want to compute what we need, when we need it. We don't want spaghetti code that joins together several asynchronous operations. Focusing on all these aspects of concurrent programming while developing applications detracts from what we should really be focusing on—the features that give our application value.

In this section, we'll look at the approaches that we might use to insulate the rest of our application from tricky concurrency bits. This generally means making concurrency the default mode — even when there's no real concurrency happening under the hood. In the end, we don't want our code to contain 90% concurrency acrobatics and 10% functionality.

Hiding the concurrency mechanism

The difficulty with exposing concurrency mechanisms all throughout our code is that they're all slightly different from one another. This magnifies the callback hell that we may already find ourselves in. For example, not all concurrent operations are network requests that fetch data from some remote resource. Asynchronous data might come from a worker or some another callback that's asynchronous in itself. Picture a scenario where we have three disparate data sources used to compute a value that we need — all of which are asynchronous. Here's an illustration of the problem:

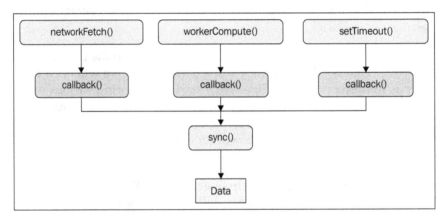

The data in this diagram is the thing we care about in our application code. From the perspective of the feature that we're building we don't care about anything above it. So, our front-end architecture needs to encapsulate the complexities associated with concurrency. This means each of our components should be able to access data in the same way. There's another complication to consider here in addition to all our asynchronous data sources — what about when the data isn't asynchronous and originates from a local source? What about synchronizing a local data source and an HTTP request? We'll cover this in the following section.

Without concurrency

Just because we're writing a concurrent JavaScript application, not every operation is inherently concurrent. For example, if one component asks another component for data that it already has in memory, then it's not an asynchronous operation and is returned immediately. Our application is likely filled with operations these, where concurrency simply doesn't make sense. And therein lies the challenge—how do we mix asynchronous operations seamlessly with synchronous operations?

The simple answer is that we make the default assumption of concurrency everywhere. Promises make this problem tractable. Here's an illustration of using a promise to encapsulate both asynchronous and synchronous operations:

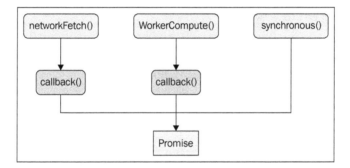

This looks a lot like the previous diagram with two important differences. We've added a synchronous() operation; this doesn't have a callback function because it doesn't need one. It's not waiting for anything else, so it returns without delay. The other two functions are just as they were in the previous diagram; both rely on callback functions to feed their data into our application. The second important difference is that there's a promise object. This replaces both the sync() operation and the data concept. Or rather, it melds them into the same concept.

This is the key aspect of promises—their general ability to abstract synchronization problems away for us. This is applicable not just with network requests, but also web worker messages, or any other asynchronous operation that relies on callbacks. It requires a bit of an adjustment to think about our data as we promise that it'll get here eventually. But, once we close this mental gap, concurrency is enabled by default. Concurrency is the default as far as our features are concerned, and what we do behind the operating curtain isn't disruptive in the slightest.

Let's turn our attention to some code now. We'll create two functions: one asynchronous and the other a plain old function that simply returns a value. The goal here is to make the code that uses these functions the same, despite the major differences in how the value is generated:

```javascript
// An asynchronous "fetch" function. We use "setTimeout()"
// to pass "callback()" some data after 1 second.
function fetchAsync(callback) {
    setTimeout(() => {
        callback({ hello: 'world' });
    }, 1000);
}

// The synchronous fetch simply returns the data.
function fetchSync() {
    return { hello: 'world' };
}

// A promise for the "fetchAsync()" call. We pass the
// "resolve" function as the callback.
var asyncPromise = new Promise((resolve, reject) => {
    fetchAsync(resolve);
});

// A promise for the "fetchSync()" call. This promise
// is resolved immediately with the return value.
var syncPromise = new Promise((resolve, reject) => {
    resolve(fetchSync());
});

// Creates a promise that'll wait for two promises
// to complete before resolving. This allows us
// to seamlessly mix synchronous and asynchronous
// values.
Promise.all([
    asyncPromise,
    syncPromise
]).then((results) => {
    var [ asyncResult, syncResult ] = results;

    console.log('async', asyncResult);
    // → async { hello: 'world' }

    console.log('sync', syncResult);
    // → sync { hello: 'world' }
});
```

The trade-off here is the added promise complexity, wrapped around what would otherwise be a simple value returned from a function. But in reality, the complexity is encapsulated within the promise, and if we weren't writing a concurrent application, we obviously would need to concern ourselves with issues such as these. The benefit is huge. When everything is a promised value, we can safely rule out the inconsistencies that lead to nasty concurrency bugs.

Worker communication with promises

We now have a handle on why treating primitive values as promises benefits our code. It's time to apply this concept to web workers. In the preceding two chapters, our code that synchronized responses coming from web workers started to look a little intractable. This was because we were essentially trying to emulate many boilerplate chores that promises are good at handling. We'll first attempt to solve these problems by creating helper functions that wrap the worker communications for us, returning promises. Then we'll try another approach that involves extending the web worker interface at a lower level. Lastly, we'll look at some more complex synchronization scenarios that involve multiple workers, such as those from the last chapter.

Helper functions

It would be ideal if we could get web worker responses back in the form of a promise resolution. But, we need to create the promise in the first place—how do we do this? Well, we could manually create the promise, where the message that's sent to the worker is sent from within the promise executor function. But, if we take this approach, we're not much better off than we were before introducing promises.

The trick is to encapsulate both the message posted to the worker and any message received from the worker, within a single helper function as is illustrated here:

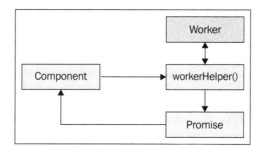

Let's take a look at an example helper function that implements this pattern. First, we'll need a worker that carries out some task—we'll start with this:

```
// Eat some CPU cycles...
// Taken from http://adambom.github.io/parallel.js/
function work(n) {
    var i = 0;
    while (++i < n * n) {}
    return i;
}


// When we receive a message, we post a message with the
// id, and the result of performing "work()" on "number".
addEventListener('message', (e) => {
    postMessage({
        id: e.data.id,
        result: work(e.data.number)
    });
});
```

Here we have a worker that will square any number we pass it. This `work()` function is intentionally slow so that we can see how our application, as a whole, performs when web workers take longer than usual to complete a task. It also uses an ID as we've seen with our previous web worker examples, so it can reconcile with the code that sent the message. Let's implement the helper function that uses this worker now:

```
// This will generate unique IDs. We need them to
// map tasks executed by web workers to the larger
// operation that created them.
function* genID() {
    var id = 0;

    while (true) {
        yield id++;
    }
}

// Creates the global "id" generator.
var id = genID();

// This object holds the resolver functions from promises,
// as results comeback from workers, we look them up here,
// based on ID.
```

```
var resolvers = {};

// Starts our worker...
var worker = new Worker('worker.js');

worker.addEventListener('message', (e) => {
    // Finds the appropriate resolver function.
    var resolver = resolvers[e.data.id];

    // Deletes it from the "resolvers" object.
    delete resolvers[e.data.id];

    // Pass the worker data to the promise by calling
    // the resolver function.
    resolver(e.data.result);
});

// This is our helper function. It handles the posting of
// messages to the worker, and tying the promise to the
// worker responses.
function square(number) {
    return new Promise((resolve, reject) => {
        // The ID that's used to tie together a web
        // worker response, and a resolver function.
        var msgId = id.next().value;

        // Stores the resolver so in can be used later, in
        // the web worker message callback.
        resolvers[msgId] = resolve;

        // Posts the message - the ID and the number
        // argument.
        worker.postMessage({
            id: msgId,
            number: number
        });
    });
}

square(10).then((result) => {
    console.log('square(10)', result);
    // → square(10) 100
});

square(100).then((result) => {
```

```
        console.log('square(100)', result);
        // → square(100) 10000
});

square(1000).then((result) => {
        console.log('square(1000)', result);
        // → square(1000) 1000000
});
```

If we focus on the way that the `square()` function is used, passing a number argument and getting a promise as a return value, we can see that this fits in with our earlier discussion on making code concurrent by default. For example, we can completely remove workers from this scenario and simply change the way the helper function resolves the promise that it returns, and the rest of our code will continue to function unaltered.

The helper function tactic is just one approach to simplify worker communication using promises. Perhaps we can decide that we don't necessarily want to maintain a bunch of helper functions. Next, we'll look at a more granular approach than helper functions.

Extending postMessage()

Rather than amassing vast quantities of helper functions, we can take a more generic route. There's nothing wrong with helper functions; they're direct and to the point. If we reach a point where there are literally hundreds of them, their value would start to depreciate very quickly. The more generic approach is to keep using `worker.postMessage()`.

So let's see if we can make this method return a promise just like our helper function from the previous section. This way, we keep using the granular `postMessage()` method, but improve our synchronization semantics. First, here's the worker code:

```
addEventListener('message', (e) => {

    // The result we're posting back to the main
    // thread - it should always contain the
    // message ID.
    var result = { id: e.data.id };

    // Based on the "action", compute the response
    // "value". The options are leave the text alone,
    // convert it to upper case, or convert it to
    // lower case.
```

```
    if (e.data.action === 'echo') {
        result.value = e.data.value
    } else if (e.data.action === 'upper') {
        result.value = e.data.value.toUpperCase();
    } else if (e.data.action === 'lower') {
        result.value = e.data.value.toLowerCase();
    }

    // Simulate a longer-running worker by waiting
    // 1 second before posting the response back.
    setTimeout(() => {
        postMessage(result);
    }, 1000);
});
```

This is nothing radically different from what we've seen so far in our web worker code. Now, in the main thread, we have to figure out how to alter the interface of `Worker`. Let's do this now. Then, we'll try posting some messages to this worker and resolving promises as a response:

```
// This object holds the resolver functions from promises,
// as results comeback from workers, we look them up here,
// based on ID.
var resolvers = {};

// Keep the original implementation of "postMessage()"
// so we can call it later on, in our custom "postMessage()"
// implementation.
var postMessage = Worker.prototype.postMessage;

// Replace "postMessage()" with our custom implementation.
Worker.prototype.postMessage = function(data) {
    return new Promise((resolve, reject) => {

        // The ID that's used to tie together a web worker
        // response, and a resolver function.
        var msgId = id.next().value;

        // Stores the resolver so in can be used later, in
        // the web worker message callback.
        resolvers[msgId] = resolve;

        // Run the original "Worker.postMessage()"
        // implementation, which takes care of actually
        // posting the message to the worker thread.
```

```
            postMessage.call(this, Object.assign({
                id: msgId
            }, data));
        });
};

// Starts our worker...
var worker = new Worker('worker.js');

worker.addEventListener('message', (e) => {

    // Finds the appropriate resolver function.
    var resolver = resolvers[e.data.id];

    // Deletes it from the "resolvers" object.
    delete resolvers[e.data.id];

    // Pass the worker data to the promise by calling
    // the resolver function.
    resolver(e.data.value);
});

worker.postMessage({
    action: 'echo',
    value: 'Hello World'
}).then((value) => {
    console.log('echo', `"${value}"`);
    // → echo "Hello World"
});

worker.postMessage({
    action: 'upper',
    value: 'Hello World'
}).then((value) => {
    console.log('upper', `"${value}"`);
    // → upper "HELLO WORLD"
});

worker.postMessage({
    action: 'lower',
    value: 'Hello World'
}).then((value) => {
    console.log('lower', `"${value}"`);
    // → lower "hello world"
});
```

Well, this is exactly what we need, right? We can post message data directly to the worker, and the response data is sent back to us through the promise resolution. As an added bonus, we can actually wrap helper functions around this new `postMessage()` function implementation if we're so inclined. The main trick involved with making this work is storing a reference to the original `postMessage()`. Then, we override the web worker property `postMessage`, not the function itself. Finally, we can reuse it to add the necessary reconciliation and promise goodness.

Synchronizing worker results

The code in the last two sections has adequately reduced our web worker callback hell to a more tolerable level. In fact, now that we've got a handle on how to encapsulate web worker communication by having `postMessage()` return a promise, we're ready to start simplifying any messy worker code that isn't using this approach. The examples that we've looked at, so far, have benefited greatly from promises, they are simple; not having these abstractions wouldn't be the end of the world.

What about the scenario where we map a collection of data and then reduce the mapped collection? We may recall the map reduce code got a little hairy in *Chapter 6, Practical Parallelism*. This is mostly due to all the worker communication boilerplate code entangled with the code that's trying to execute a map/reduce operation. Let's see if we fair any better using our promise technique. First, we'll create a very basic worker:

```
// Returns a map of the input array, by squaring
// each number in the array.
addEventListener('message', (e) => {
    postMessage({
        id: e.data.id,
        value: e.data.value.map(v => v * v)
    });
});
```

We can use this worker to pass arrays for mapping. So we'll create two of them and split the workload between the two workers, shown as follows:

```
function onMessage(e) {

    // Finds the appropriate resolver function.
    var resolver = resolvers[e.data.id];

    // Deletes it from the "resolvers" object.
    delete resolvers[e.data.id];
```

```
        // Pass the worker data to the promise by calling
        // the resolver function.
        resolver(e.data.value);
    }

    // Starts our workers...
    var worker1 = new Worker('worker.js'),
        worker2 = new Worker('worker.js');

    // Create some data to process.
    var array = new Array(50000)
        .fill(null)
        .map((v, i) => i);

    // Finds the appropriate resolver function to call,
    // when the worker responds with data.
    worker1.addEventListener('message', onMessage);
    worker2.addEventListener('message', onMessage);

    // Splits our input data in 2, giving the first half
    // to the first worker, and the second half to the
    // second worker. At this point, we have two promises.
    var promise1 = worker1.postMessage({
        value: array.slice(0, Math.floor(array.length / 2))
    });

    var promise2 = worker2.postMessage({
        value: array.slice(Math.floor(array.length / 2))
    });

    // Using "Promise.all()" to synchronize workers is
    // much easier than manually trying to reconcile
    // through worker callback functions.
    Promise.all([ promise1, promise2 ]).then((values) => {
        console.log('reduced', [].concat(...values)
            .reduce((r, v) => r + v));
        // → reduced 41665416675000

    });
```

When this is all we need to post data to workers, and to synchronize data from two or more workers, we're actually motivated to write concurrent code – it looks the same as the rest of our application code now.

Lazy workers

It's time for us to look at web workers from a different angle. The fundamental reason we're using workers in the first place is that we want to compute more than we have in the past in the same amount of time. Doing this, as we now know, involves messaging intricacies, divide and conquer strategies so to speak. We have to get data into and out of the worker, usually as an array.

Generators help us compute lazily. That is, we don't want to compute something or allocate data in memory until we really need it. Do web workers make this difficult or impossible to achieve? Or can we leverage generators to compute lazily and in parallel?

In this section, we'll explore ideas related to using generators in web workers. First, we'll look at the overhead issues associated with web workers. Then, we'll write some code that uses generators to pass data in and out of workers. Finally, we'll see if we can lazily pass data through a chain of generators, all residing in web workers.

Reducing overhead

The main thread can offload expensive operations web workers, running them in another thread. This means the DOM is able to paint pending updates and process pending user events. However, we still face the overhead of allocating large arrays and the time taken to update the UI. Despite parallel processing with web workers, our users could still face a slowdown because there's no update to the UI until the entire data set has been processed. Here is a visualization of the general pattern:

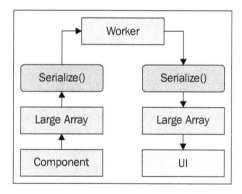

This is a generic path taken by data with a single worker; the same approach applies when there are multiple workers. With this approach, we can't escape the fact that we need to serialize the data twice, and we have to allocate it twice. These overheads are merely to facilitate the worker communication and have very little to do with the application functionality that we're trying to implement.

The overhead with arrays and serialization, required for worker communication, generally isn't a big deal. However, with larger collections, we could be faced with real performance issues, stemming from the very mechanism that we use to improve performance. So looking at worker communication from another perspective doesn't hurt, even if it's not necessary at first.

Here's a variation of the generic path taken by most workers. Instead of allocating and serializing lots of data upfront, individual items are passed in and out of workers. This gives the UI a chance to update using the data that's been processed, before all of the processed data arrives.

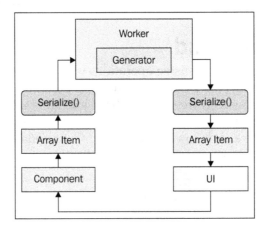

Generating values in workers

If we want to update the UI as our workers generate results, then they can't package the result set as an array to send back to the main thread after all the computations are done. While this happens, the UI sits there without responding to the user. We want a lazier approach where values are generated one at a time so that the UI can be updated sooner. Let's build an example that sends input to the web worker and sends results back at a much more granular level than what we've seen so far in this book:

First, we'll create a worker; the code for it is as follows:

```
// Eat some CPU cycles...
// Taken from http://adambom.github.io/parallel.js/
function work(n) {
    var i = 0;
    while (++i < n * n) {}
    return i;
}


// Post the result of calling "work()" back to the
// main thread.
addEventListener('message', (e) => {
    postMessage(work(e.data));
});
```

There's nothing earth-shattering here. It's the same work() function that we've already used to intentionally slow-down our code by inefficiently squaring a number. There's no actual generator used inside the worker. This is because we really don't need one, we'll see why in a moment:

```
// Creates an "update()" coroutine that continuously
// updates the UI as results are generated from the
// worker.
var update = coroutine(function* () {
    var input;

    while (true) {
        input = yield;
        console.log('result', input.data);
    }
});

// Creates the worker, and assigns the "update()"
// coroutine as the "message" callback handler.
var worker = new Worker('worker.js');
worker.addEventListener('message', update);

// An array of progressively larger numbers.
var array = new Array(10)
    .fill(null)
    .map((v, i) => i * 10000);

// Iterate over the array, passing each number to the
```

```
// worker as an individual message.
for (let item of array) {
    worker.postMessage(item);
}
// →
// result 1
// result 100000000
// result 400000000
// result 900000000
// result 1600000000
// result 2500000000
// result 3600000000
// result 4900000000
// result 6400000000
// result 8100000000
```

Each number that's passed to our worker is more expensive to process than the previous number. So overall, processing the entire input array before showing anything to the user would feel as if the application is hanging or broken. But, this is not the case here because although each number is expensive to process, we're posting the results back as they become available.

We perform the same amount of work as we would perform by passing in an array and getting back an array as output. However, this approach simply changes the order in which things happen. We've introduced cooperative multi-tasking into the picture—compute some data in one task and update the UI in another. The aggregate time taken to complete the work is the same, but to the user, it feels much faster. At the end of the day, the user perceivable performance of our application is the only performance metric that counts.

> We passed in the input as individual messages. We could have passed in the input as an array, posted the results individually, and gotten the same effect. However, this would probably amount to nothing more than an unneeded complexity. There's a natural correspondence to the pattern as it is—item in, item out. Don't change it if you don't have to.

Lazy worker chains

As we saw in *Chapter 4, Lazy Evaluation with Generators* we can assemble chains of generators. This is how we implement complex functionality lazily; an item flows through a chain of generator functions that transform the item before yielding to the next generator until it reaches the caller. Without generators, we would have to allocate a lot of intermediary data structures just for the sake of passing data from one function to the next.

In the section prior to this one, we saw that a pattern similar to generators was possible with web workers. Since we face a similar problem here, we don't want to allocate large data structures. We can avoid doing this by passing in items at a more granular level. This has the added benefit of keeping the UI responsive because we're able to update it before the last item arrives from the worker. Given that we can do this much with workers, could we not build on this idea and assemble more complex chains of worker processing nodes?

For instance, let's say we have a collection of numbers and several transformations. We need to make these transformations in a specific order before we can display them in our UI. Ideally, we would setup a chain of workers where each worker is responsible for performing its designated transformation, then passing the output on to the next worker. Eventually, the main thread gets a value back that it can display in the DOM.

The problem with this goal is the tricky communication that it involves. Since dedicated workers only communicate with the main thread that created them, it's hardly advantageous to send the results back to the main thread, then onto the next worker in the chain, and so on. Well, it turns out that dedicated workers can directly communicate without involving the main thread. We can use something called channel messaging here. The idea is simple; it involves creating a channel, which has two ports—messages posted on one port and received on the other.

We've been using messaging channels and ports all along. They're baked into web workers. This is where the message event and `postMessage()` method pattern comes from.

The following is a visualization of how we would go about connecting our web workers using channels and ports:

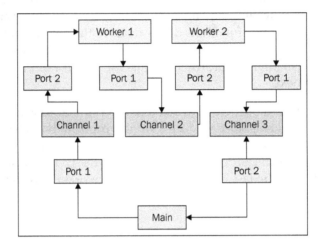

As we can see, each channel uses two messaging ports. The first port is used to post messages, whereas the second is used to receive message events. The only time the main thread is used is when the processing chain is first kicked off by posting a message to the first channel and when the message is received from the third channel.

Instead of letting the six ports required for worker communication intimidate us, let's write some code; maybe, it'll look a little more approachable there. First we'll create the workers used in the chain. Actually, they're two instances of the same worker. Here's the code:

```
addEventListener('message', (e) => {

    // Get the ports used to send and receive messages.
    var [ port1, port2 ] = e.ports;

    // Listen for incoming messages of the first port.
    port1.addEventListener('message', (e) => {

        // Respond on the second port with the result of
        // calling "work()".
        port2.postMessage(work(e.data));
    });

    // Starts both ports.
```

```
        port1.start();
        port2.start();
});
```

This is interesting. In this worker, we have message ports to work with. The first port is used to receive input, and the second port is used to send output. The `work()` function simply squares the given number using our now familiar approach of wasting CPU cycles to see how workers behave. What we want to do in our main thread is to create two instances of this worker so that we can pass the first instance a number to square. Then, without passing the result back to the main thread, it passes the result to the next worker, and the number is squared again. The communication paths should closely mimic the previous diagram. Let's look at some code that connects workers using messaging channels:

```
// Starts our workers...
var worker1 = new Worker('worker.js');
var worker2 = new Worker('worker.js');

// Creates the message channels necessary to communicate
// between the 2 workers.
var channel1 = new MessageChannel();
var channel2 = new MessageChannel();
var channel3 = new MessageChannel();

// Our "update()" coroutine logs worker responses as they're
// delivered.
var update = coroutine(function* () {
    var input;

    while (true) {
        input = yield;
        console.log('result', input.data);
    }
});

// Connects "channel1" and "channel2" using "worker1".
worker1.postMessage(null, [
    channel1.port2,
    channel2.port1
]);

// Connects "channel2" and "channel3" using "worker2".
worker2.postMessage(null, [
    channel2.port2,
    channel3.port1
```

```
]);

// Connects our coroutine "update()" to any messages
// received on "channel3".
channel3.port2.addEventListener('message', update);
channel3.port2.start();

// Our input data - an array of numbers.
var array = new Array(25)
    .fill(null)
    .map((v, i) => i * 10);

// Posts each array item to "channel1".
for (let item of array) {
    channel1.port1.postMessage(item);
}
```

In addition to the data that we want to send to the worker, we can also send a list
of message ports that we want to transfer to the worker context. This is what we do
with the first two messages sent to the worker. The message data is `null` because
we're not doing anything with it. In fact, these are the only messages we're sending
directly to the worker. The rest of the communication happens through the message
channels that we've created. The expensive computation happens on the worker
because that's where the message handler resides.

Using Parallel.js

The aim of the `Parallel.js` library is to make interacting with web workers as
seamless as possible. In fact, it handles one of the key goals of this book — it hides the
concurrency mechanism and allows us to focus on the application that we're building.

In this section, we'll look at the approach taken by `Parallel.js` for worker
communication and the general approach of passing code to workers. Then, we'll
walk through some code that uses `Parallel.js` to spawn new worker processes.
Lastly, we'll explore the built-in map/reduce capabilities that the library has to offer.

How it works

All the workers that we've used so far in this book have been our own creation. We
implemented message event handling in our workers that computed some value,
then posted a response. With `Parallel.js`, we don't implement workers. Instead,
we implement functions, which are then passed to workers that are managed by
the library.

This takes care of a few headaches for us. All our code is implemented in the main thread, meaning that it's easier to use the functions that we've implemented in the main thread because we don't need to import them into web workers using `importScripts()`. We also don't need to manually start web workers by creating them with a script path. Instead, we let `Parallel.js` spawn new workers for us, and then, we can tell the workers what to do by passing functions and data to them. So, how does this work, exactly?

Workers need a script argument. Without a valid script, workers simply do not work. `Parallel.js` has a straightforward `eval` script. This is what's passed to any worker that the library creates. Then, the API within the main thread assembles code that's to be evaluated within the worker and sends it over whenever we need to communicate with workers.

This is feasible because `Parallel.js` doesn't aim to expose a plethora of functionality backed by workers. Instead, the aim is to make the worker communication mechanism as seamless as possible while providing minimal functionality. This makes it easy to build only the concurrency functionality that's relevant to our application and not a host of other functions that we'll never use.

Here is an illustration of how we pass data and code into a worker using `Parallel.js` and its `eval` script:

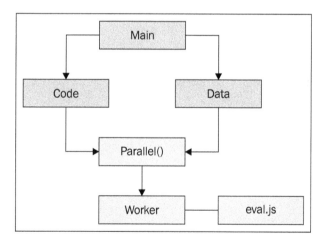

Spawning workers

The `Parallel.js` library has the notion of a job. The primary input to a job is the data that the job is going to process. The creation of a job isn't directly tied to the creation of a background worker. Workers are distinct from `Parallel.js` jobs; we don't interact directly with workers when using the library. Once we have our job instance, and it's supplied with our data, we use a job method to invoke workers.

The most basic method is `spawn()`, which takes a function as an argument and runs it in a web worker. The function that we pass to it can return results, and these are then resolved as a thenable object that's returned by `spawn()`. Let's look at some code that uses `Parallel.js` to spawn new job backed by a web worker:

```javascript
// An input array of numbers.
var array = new Array(2500)
    .fill(null)
    .map((v, i) => i);

// Creates a new parallel job. No workers have been
// created at this point - we only pass the constructor
// the data we're working with.
var job = new Parallel(array);

// Start a timer for our "spawn()" job.
console.time(`${array.length} items`);

// Creates a new web worker, passing it our data and
// this function. We're slowly mapping each number in
// the array to it's square.
job.spawn((coll) => {
    return coll.map((n) => {
        var i = 0;
        while (++i < n * n) {}
        return i;
    });

// The return value of "spawn()" is a thenable. Meaning
// we can assign a "then()" callback function, just as
// though a promise were returned.
}).then((results) => {
    console.timeEnd(`${array.length} items`);
    // → 2500 items: 3408.078ms
});
```

Well now, that's pretty cool; we don't have to worry about any of the monotonous web worker life-cycle tasks. We have some data and some function that we want to apply to the data, and we want to run it in parallel with other work taking place on the page. The cherry on the top is the familiar thenable that's returned from the spawn() method. It fits right into our concurrent application, where everything else is treated as a promise.

We log how long it takes for our function to process the input data we give it. We only spawn a single web worker for this task, so the result is reached in the same amount of time as it would have been, were it computed in the main thread. Aside from freeing up the main thread to handle DOM events and repainting, there's no objective performance gain. We'll see if we can use a different method to up the concurrency level.

 The worker created by spawn() is immediately terminated when we're done with it. This frees up memory for us. However, there's no concurrency level governing the use of spawn(), we can call it 100 times in a row if we like.

Mapping and reducing

In the last section, we spawned a worker thread using the spawn() method. Parallel.js also has a map() method and a reduce() method. The idea is to make things easier for us. By passing map() a function, the library will automatically apply it to each item in the job data. Similar semantics apply with the reduce() method. Let's take a look at how this works by writing some code:

```
// An input array of numbers.
var array = new Array(2500)
    .fill(null)
    .map((v, i) => i);

// Creates a new parallel job. No workers have been
// created at this point - we only pass the constructor
// the data we're working with.
var job1 = new Parallel(array);

// Start a timer for our "spawn()" job.
console.time('job1');

// The problem here is that Parallel.js will
// create a new worker for every array element, resulting
```

```
// in parallel slowdown.
job1.map((n) => {
    var i = 0;
    while (++i < n * n) {}
    return i;
}).reduce((pair) => {

    // Reduces the array items to a sum.
    return pair[0] + pair[1];
}).then((data) => {
    console.log('job1 reduced', data);
    // → job1 reduced 5205208751

    console.timeEnd('job1');
    // → job1: 59443.863ms
});
```

Ouch! This is quite the performance hit—what's going on here? What we're seeing here is a phenomenon called parallel slowdown. This slowdown takes place when there's too much parallel communication overhead. The reason this is happening in this particular example is due to the way `Parallel.js` processes arrays in `map()`. Each array item goes through a worker. This doesn't mean that 'there are 2500 workers created—one for each element in the array. The number of created workers maxes out at four or the `navigator.hardwareConcurrency` value—similar semantics we looked at earlier in this book.

The real overhead comes from messages sent to and received from the workers—5000 messages! This is obviously not optimal, as evidenced by the timer in the code. Let's see if we can make a drastic improvement on these numbers while keeping roughly the same code structure:

```
// A faster implementation.
var job2 = new Parallel(array);

console.time('job2');

// Before mapping the array, split the array into chunks
// of smaller arrays. This way, each Parallel.js worker is
// processing an array instead of an array item. This avoids
// sending thousands of web worker messages.
job2.spawn((data) => {
    var index = 0,
        size = 1000,
```

```
        results = [];

    while (true) {
        let chunk = data.slice(index, index + size);

        if (chunk.length) {
            results.push(chunk);
            index += size;
        } else {
            return results;
        }
    }
}).map((array) => {

    // Returns a mapping of the array chunk.
    return array.map((n) => {
        var i = 0;
        while (++i < n * n) {}
        return i;
    });
}).reduce((pair) => {

    // Reduces array chunks, or numbers, to a sum.
    return (Array.isArray(pair[0]) ?
            pair[0].reduce((r, v) => r + v) : pair[0]) +
        (Array.isArray(pair[1]) ?
            pair[1].reduce((r, v) => r + v) : pair[1]);
}).then((data) => {
    console.log('job2 reduced', data);
    // → job2 reduced 5205208751

    console.timeEnd('job2');
    // → job2: 2723.661ms
});
```

Here, we can see that the same results are generated, and much faster. The difference is that we start things off by slicing the array into chunks of smaller arrays. These arrays are the items that get passed to the workers, instead of individual numbers. So the mapping job has to change slightly as well, instead of squaring a number, it's mapping a smaller array to an array of squares. The reduce logic is slightly more complex, but overall, our approach is still the same. Most importantly, we've removed the heavy message-passing bottleneck that was causing unacceptable performance flaws in the first implementation.

Just like the spawn() method cleans up the worker when it returns, so too do the map() and reduce() Parallel.js methods. The downside to freeing workers is that they need to be recreated whenever these methods are called. We'll address this challenge in the next section.

Worker pools

The final section of this chapter covers the concept of worker pools. In the preceding section on Parallel.js, we ran up against an issue where workers were frequently created and terminated. This is a lot of overhead. If we know the level of concurrency we're capable of operating at, then why not allocate a statically-sized pool of workers that can take on work?

The first design task for creating a worker pool is to allocate the workers. The next step is to schedule the jobs as they come in by distributing them to available workers in the pool. Lastly, we'll need to account for busy states when all the workers are busy. Let's do this.

Allocating pools

Before we think about allocating pools of worker threads, we need to look at the overarching worker pool abstraction. How do we want it to look and behave? Ideally, we want the pool abstraction to look and behave like a plain dedicated worker. We can post a message to the pool and get a promise in response. So while we can't directly extend the Worker prototype, we can create a new abstraction that closely resembles the Worker API.

Let's look at some code now. Here's the initial abstraction that we'll use:

```
// Represents a "pool" of web worker threads, hidden behind
// the interface of a single web worker interface.
function WorkerPool(script) {

    // The level of concurrency, or, the number of web
    // workers to create. This uses the
    // "hardwareConcurrency" property if it exists.
    // Otherwise, it defaults to 4, since this is
    // a reasonable guess at the most common CPU topology.
    var concurrency = navigator.hardwareConcurrency || 4;

    // The worker instances themselves are stored in a Map,
    // as keys. We'll see why in a moment.
```

```
var workers = this.workers = new Map();

// The queue exists for messages that are posted while,
// all workers are busy. So this may never actually be
// used.
var queue = this.queue = [];

// Used below for creating the worker instances, and
// adding event listeners.
var worker;

for (var i = 0; i < concurrency; i++) {
    worker = new Worker(script);
    worker.addEventListener('message', function(e) {

        // We use the "get()" method to lookup the
        // "resolve()" function of the promise. The
        // worker is the key. We call the resolver with
        // the data returned from the worker, and
        // can now reset this to null. This is important
        // because it signifies that the worker is free
        // to take on more work.
        workers.get(this)(e.data);
        workers.set(this, null);

        // If there's queued data, we get the first
        // "data" and "resolver" from the queue. Before
        // we call "postMessage()" with the data, we
        // update the "workers" map with the new
        // "resolve()" function.
        if (queue.length) {
            var [ data, resolver ] = queue.shift();
            workers.set(this, resolver);
            this.postMessage(data);
        }
    }.bind(worker));

    // This is the initial setting of the worker, as a
    // key, in the "workers" map. It's value is null,
    // meaning there's no resolve function, and it can
    // take on work.
    this.workers.set(worker, null);
}
}
```

When a new `WorkerPool` is created, the given script is used to spawn all the workers within the pool. The `workers` property is a `Map` instance, and the worker instances themselves are the keys. The reason we store the workers as map keys is so that we can easily lookup the appropriate resolver function to call.

When a given worker responds, the `message` event handler that we've added to each worker is called, and this is where we find the resolver function that's waiting to be called. There's no chance of us calling the wrong resolver because a given worker doesn't take on new work until it's finished with its current task.

Scheduling jobs

Now we'll implement the `postMessage()` method. This is what the caller will use to post a message to one of the workers in the pool. The caller doesn't know which worker fulfills their request, nor do they care. They get a promise as a return value, and it's resolved with the worker response as the value:

```
WorkerPool.prototype.postMessage = function(data) {

    // The "workers" Map instance, where all the web workers
    // are stored.
    var workers = this.workers;

    // The "queue" where messages are placed when all the
    // workers are busy.
    var queue = this.queue;

    // Try finding an available worker.
    var worker = this.getWorker();

    // The promise is immediately passed back to the caller,
    // even if there's no worker available.
    return new Promise(function(resolve) {

        // If a worker is found, we can update the map,
        // using the worker as the key, and the "resolve()"
        // function as the value. If there's no worker, then
        // the message data, along with the "resolve()"
        // function get pushed to the "queue".
        if (worker) {
            workers.set(worker, resolve);
            worker.postMessage(data);
        } else {
```

```
        queue.push([ data, resolve ]);
    }
  });
};
```

It's the promise executor function that takes care of actually finding the first available worker and posting our message there. When an available worker is found, we also set the worker's resolver function in our `workers` map. If there are no available `workers` in the pool, the posted message goes into the `queue`. This queue is emptied in the `message` event handler. This is because when a worker comes back with a message, it means the worker is free to take on more work, and it checks if there's anything queued before returning to an idle state.

The `getWorker()` method is a simple helper that finds the next available worker for us. We know a worker is available to take on a task if its `resolver` function is set to null in the `workers` map. Lastly, let's see this worker pool in action:

```
// Create a new pool, and a workload counter.
var pool = new WorkerPool('worker.js');
var workload = 0;

document.getElementById('work')
    .addEventListener('click', function(e) {

        // Get the data we're going to pass to the
        // worker, and create a timer for this workload.
        var amount = +document.getElementById('amount').value,
            timer = 'Workload ' + (++workload);

        console.time(timer);

        // Pass the message to the pool, and when the promise
        // resolves, stop the timer.
        pool.postMessage(amount).then(function(result) {
            console.timeEnd(timer);
        });

        // If messages are getting queued, our pool is
        // overworked display a warning.
        if (pool.queue.length) {
            console.warn('Worker pool is getting busy...');
        }
    });
```

In this usage scenario, we have a couple of form controls that send parameterized work to the worker. The larger the number, the longer the work will take; it uses our standard work() function that slowly squares numbers. If we use a large number and frequently click the button that posts the message to the pool, then eventually, we'll exhaust the pool. If 'this is the case, we will display a warning. However, this is just for troubleshooting purposes—the posted messages aren't lost when the pool is busy, they're simply queued.

Summary

The focus of this chapter has been removing obtrusive concurrency semantics from our code. It simply raises the likelihood of our application's success because we'll have code that's easy to maintain and build upon. The first issue that we tackled was writing concurrent code by making everything concurrent. When there's no guesswork involved, our code is consistent and less susceptible to concurrency bugs.

Then, we looked at various approaches we can take to abstract web worker communication. Helper functions are one option and so is extending the postMessage() method. We then addressed some of the limitations of web workers when we need our UI to be responsive. Even though our large dataset is processed faster, we still have the issue of updating the UI. This is done by treating web workers as generators.

We don't have to write all these JavaScript parallelization tools ourselves. We spent some time looking at the various capabilities and limitations of the Parallel.js library. We wrapped up the chapter with a look at web worker pools. These remove a lot of overhead related to worker creation and termination, and they drastically simplify how tasks are distributed and results are reconciled.

That does it for our concurrency topics in the front-end. Now it's time to shift gears and look at JavaScript concurrency in the back-end with NodeJS.

8
Evented IO with NodeJS

NodeJS leverages V8, the Chrome JavaScript engine, to provide a high-performance server environment. Node isn't limited in scope to just web servers—this is just the original problem space in which it was conceived. In fact, it was created to solve some tough concurrency problems faced by web programmers everywhere.

The aim of this chapter is to explain how Node handles concurrency, and how we need to program our NodeJS code to take full advantage of this environment. The most obvious difference between Node and other web server environments is that it uses a single thread to handle processing requests and relies on evented IO for high levels of concurrency. We'll then dig into why the evented IO approach to concurrency makes sense in a web context.

Since the IO event loop is grounded in network and file operations, we'll spend the remainder of the chapter looking at various network and file IO examples.

Single threaded IO

A common misconception of NodeJS is that it's actually restricted to one CPU and can't achieve true parallelism. The fact is that Node often does use multiple threads of control. We'll explore these concepts later on in the chapter. Perhaps it's the IO event loop that's misleading because it does run in a single thread, on a single CPU.

The goal of this section is to introduce the concept of an IO loop, why it's a good idea for most web application back-ends, and how it overcomes challenges faced multithreading approaches to concurrency.

 The following chapter covers more advanced Node concurrency topics, including the ways in which the event loop can bite us. While the event loop is a novel idea, it's not perfect; every solution to a given concurrency problem has negative trade-offs.

IO is slow

The slowest parts of a given web application infrastructure are the network IO and the storage IO. These operations are reasonably fast, mostly thanks to physical hardware improvements over the past several years, but compared to the software tasks taking place on the CPU, IO is a turtle. What makes web applications so challenging in terms of performance is that there's a lot of IO happening. We constantly read and write from databases and transfer data to a client browser. IO performance is a major headache in the web application arena.

The fundamental breakthrough with evented IO is that it actually takes advantage of the fact that IO is slow. For example, let's say that we have 10 CPU tasks queued, but first, we need to write something to disk. If we had to wait for the write operation to complete before starting on our tasks, they would take much longer than they need to. With evented IO, we issue the write command, but we don't wait for the low-level operating system IO write operation to complete. Instead, we continue executing our 10 CPU tasks while the IO is taking place.

Here's an illustration of CPU tasks running in a single thread, while the IO tasks happen in the background:

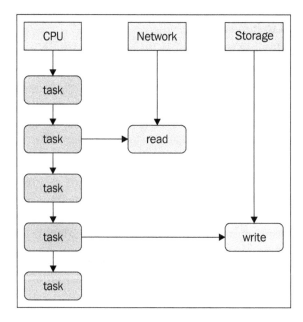

It doesn't matter what type of IO operating a given task needs to perform; it will not block other tasks from running. This is how evented IO architectures can get away with running in a single thread. NodeJS excels at this type of concurrency—performing lots of IO work in parallel. However, we do need to know about the state of these IO operations taking place at the operating system level. Up next, we'll look at how Node uses these events to reconcile the state of a given file descriptor.

IO events

Our application code needs some way of knowing that an IO operation has completed. This is where the IO events come into play. For example, if an asynchronous read operation is started somewhere in our JavaScript code, the operating system handles the actual reading of the file. When it's done reading, and the contents are in memory, the operating system triggers an IO event that indicates the IO operation has completed.

All major operating systems support these types of IO events in one form or another. NodeJS uses low-level c libraries to manage these events, and it also accounts for the various platform differences. Here's an illustration of the node IO event loop, sending various IO tasks to the operating system and listening to the corresponding IO events:

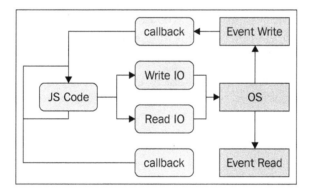

As this diagram shows, anything that's IO is handled outside of the event loop. The event loop itself is just a queue with JavaScript code tasks to run. These are generally IO-related tasks. As we can see, the result of an IO event is a callback function that gets pushed onto the queue. In Node, JavaScript doesn't wait for IO to complete. The front-end analog is the rendering engine not waiting for the slower computational tasks to complete in a web worker.

Most of this happens transparently to us, within the NodeJS modules that are used to perform IO. We just need to concern ourselves with the callback functions. If callbacks don't sound appealing, it's a good thing that we just spent several chapters addressing concurrency issues related to callback hell. These ideas are mostly applicable in Node; additionally, we'll address some synchronization techniques that are unique to Node in the next chapter.

Multi-threading challenges

For many years, if the predominant approach to serving web requests has been multithreading, then what's all the fuss about evented IO? Besides, running all our JavaScript code on a single CPU hardly takes advantage of the multi-core systems that we're likely running on. Even if we are running in a virtualized environment, we're likely to have parallelized virtual hardware. The short answer is that there's nothing wrong with either approach as they both solve similar problems using different tactics. We would want to rethink our approach when we move to the extreme in either direction; for example, we start handling a lot more IO or a lot more compute.

In a web environment, the common case is to spend more time performing IO than expensive CPU-burning activities. When the users of our application interact with it, we generally need to make API calls over a network, and then we need to read or write to or from the file system. Then, we need to respond over the network. Unless these requests are doing some heavy number crunching in their computations, the majority of the time is spent doing IO operations.

So, what makes IO-intensive applications not well-suited for the multithreaded approach? Well, if we want to spawn new threads or use a pool of threads for that matter, there will be a lot of memory overhead involved. Think of a thread that serves a request as a process with it's own chunk of memory. If we have lots of incoming requests, then we can handle them in parallel. However, we still have to perform IO. It's a little trickier to do the IO synchronization without an event loop because we have to hold the thread open for the current request that we're servicing while we wait for the IO operation to complete.

This model is very difficult to scale once we start getting into very large volumes of IO. But, for the average application, there's no need to abandon it. Likewise, if our application morphs into something that requires a ton of CPU power for any given request, a single-threaded event loop probably isn't going to cut it. Now that we have a basic understanding of what makes the IO event loop a powerful concept for IO-heavy web applications, it's time to look at some other characteristics of the event loop.

More connections, more problems

In this section, we'll address the challenges posed by building applications that run in an Internet-connected world. In this turbulent environment, unexpected things can happen; mainly, lots of user uptake translating to a lot of simultaneous user connections. In this section, we'll look at the types of things we need to be worried about when deploying to an Internet-facing environment. Then we'll look at the C10K problem—10,000 users connecting to an application with limited hardware resources. We'll close the section with a closer look at the event handlers that actually run within the NodeJS event loop.

Deploying to the Internet

The Internet is a rewarding and ruthless environment in which to deploy our applications. Our users need only a browser and a URL. If we deliver something people want, and the demand for this something continues to grow, we'll soon face a connectivity challenge. This could be a gradual increase in popularity, or a sudden spike. In either case, the onus on us to handle these scalability challenges.

Since our application faces the public, there's a strong likelihood that we have socially-focused features that are computationally remiss. On the other hand, this usually means that 'there are a high number of connections, each performing their own IO-intensive operations. This sounds like a good fit for an IO event loop, like the one found in NodeJS.

The Internet is actually the perfect environment to test the versatility of our application. If ever there were an audience that wanted more for less, you'd find it here. Assuming our application is something useful and in-demand, we can see for ourselves how well we stand up to tens of thousands of connections. We probably don't have a gigantic infrastructure backing us either, so we have to be responsible with our hardware resources.

Can NodeJS concurrency efficiently cope with such an environment? It certainly can, but beware; this audience has zero-tolerance for failed requests or even sub-optimal performance.

The C10K problem

Dan Kegel first started thinking about the C10K problem back in 1999 (`http://www.kegel.com/c10k.html`). So the initial idea is fast approaching 20 years of age; hardware has come a long way since then. However, the idea of connecting 10,000 concurrent users to an application is still relevant today. In fact, maybe the modern version of the problem should be C25K because for what most would consider affordable server hardware or virtual hardware, we can squeeze out a lot more performance than we could have in 1999.

The second reason that the scope of the problem has grown is due to the growing population of the Internet. There's an order of magnitude more connected people and devices than there were in 1999. One thing that hasn't changed is the nature of C10K—fast performance for a large number of connections without a vast infrastructure needed to support it. For example, here's a diagram showing incoming requests being mapped to threads on the system:

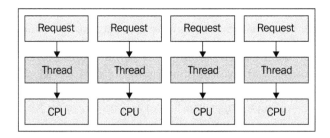

As the numbers of connected users grows, the numbers of requests also grow. We'll need to scale out our physical infrastructure fairly soon using this approach because it inherently relies on processing requests in parallel. The evented IO loop also processes requests in parallel, but using a different tactic, as is illustrated here:

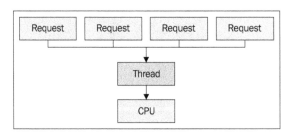

The point at which our application can't handle the number of connections due to the number of CPUs is much different here. This is because our JavaScript code runs linearly in one thread, on one CPU. However, the type of JavaScript code we write that runs within this IO loop plays an important role, as we'll see next.

Lightweight event handlers

The assumption with NodeJS is that we don't spend much time, relatively speaking, executing JavaScript code. Put differently, when a request arrives at a Node application, the JavaScript code that handles the request is short-lived. It figures out the IO it needs to perform, perhaps by reading something from the file system and exits, yielding control back to the IO loop.

However, there's nothing to enforce that our JavaScript code be small and efficient. And sometimes, CPU-intensive code is unavoidable due to changes in how our application functions, or the introduction of a new feature that takes the product in another direction. If this does happen, it's imperative that we take the necessary corrective design steps because a runaway JavaScript handler can wreak havoc on all our connections.

Let's take a look at the Node event loop, the types of JavaScript tasks that work well, and the ones that can cause problems:

```
// Eat some CPU cycles...
// Taken from http://adambom.github.io/parallel.js/
function work(n) {
    var i = 0;
    while (++i < n * n) {}
    return i;
}


// There's no handlers in the queue, so this is
// executed immediately.
process.nextTick(() => {
    console.log('first handler');
});


// The previous handler was quick to exit, so this
// handler is executed without delay.
process.nextTick(() => {
    console.log('second handler');
});


// Starts immediately because the previous handler
```

```
    // exited quickly. However, this handler executes
    // some CPU intensive code.
    process.nextTick(() => {
        console.log('hogging the CPU...');
        work(100000);
    });

    // This handler isn't run immediately, because the
    // handler before this one takes a while to complete.
    process.nextTick(() => {
        console.log('blocked handler');
    });
```

The `process.nextTick()` function is an entry point into the Node IO event loop. In fact, this function is used all over the place by the core Node modules. Each and every event loop iteration is called a tick. So all we're doing by calling this function with a callback is saying — add this function to the queue of functions to be called in the next loop iteration.

There could be hundreds or even thousands of callbacks to process in a given loop iteration. This doesn't matter because there's no waiting on IO in any of these callbacks. So, a single thread is sufficient to handle web requests, except for when we start a task that eats a lot of CPU cycles. One of the handlers in the previous example does exactly this. It takes several seconds to return and while this is going on, the event loop is stuck. The handler that we added after the CPU-expensive handler doesn't run. The consequences are disastrous when there are thousands of connected clients waiting for a response.

 We'll tackle this issue in depth in the next chapter when we look at creating clusters of Node processes, each with their own event loops.

Evented network IO

NodeJS excels at serving HTTP requests. This is because a given request life-cycle spends much time in transit between the client and the server. During this time, Node processes other requests. In this section, we'll look at some of Node's HTTP networking capabilities, and how they fit into the IO event loop.

We'll start with a look at basic HTTP requests, and how they serve as the foundation for many Node modules and projects. Then, we'll move onto streaming responses to the client, instead of sending a giant blob of data all at once. Finally, we'll look at how Node servers can proxy requests to other services.

Handling HTTP requests

The `http` module in NodeJS takes care of all the nitty-gritty details with regard to creating and setting up HTTP servers. It should be no surprise that this module is heavily utilized by many Node projects that create web servers. It even has a helper function that will create the server for us, and setup the callback function that's used to respond to incoming requests. These callbacks get a `request` argument and a `response` argument. The request contains information that's sent from the client, and we generally read from this object. The response contains information that's sent back to the client, and we generally write to this object. Here's a visualization that puts these two concepts into the context of the IO event loop:

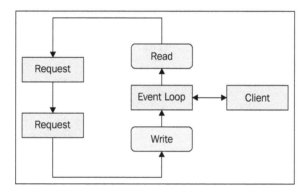

It may seem counter-intuitive at first, that the client communicates directly with the event loop. Well, this is actually a close approximation of what's really going on. The `request` and `response` objects are simply abstractions accessible to us in our JavaScript code. They exist to help us read and write the correct socket data. These abstractions hand off the correct data to the socket or read the correct socket data. In both cases, our code deferrers to the event loop where the real client communication happens:

Let's take a look at some basic HTTP server code now.

```
// We need the "http" module for HTTP-related
// code.
var http = require('http');

// Creates the server instance, and sets of the
// callback function that's called on every request
// event for us.
var server = http.createServer((req, res) => {

    // The response header is always going to be plain
```

```
    // text.
    res.setHeader('Content-Type', 'text/plain');

    // If the request URL is "hello" or "world", we
    // respond with some text immediately. Otherwise,
    // if the request URL is "/", we simulate a slow
    // response by using "setTimeout()" to finish the
    // request after 5 seconds.
    if (req.url === '/hello') {
        res.end('Hello');
    } else if (req.url === '/world') {
        res.end('World');
    } else {
        setTimeout(() => {
            res.end('Hello World');
        }, 5000);
    }
});

// Starts the server.
server.listen(8081);
console.log('listening at http://localhost:8081');
```

In this example, we send back plain text to the browser. We run a quick check on the URL and adjust the content accordingly. There's something interesting in the default path though, we're using setTimeout() to delay the response by 5 seconds. So if we were to visit http://localhost/, the page would spin for 5 seconds before displaying any content. The idea here is to demonstrate the asynchronous nature of the event loop. While this request waits for something to happen, all other requests get serviced immediately. We can test this by loading the /hello URL or the /world URL in another tab while this loads.

Streaming responses

The previous example, we wrote the entire HTTP response content with one call. This is generally fine, especially in our case because we were only writing a handful of characters to the connected socket. With some applications, the response to a given request is going to be much larger than this. For example, what if we implement an API call, and the client has asked for a collection of entities, and each entity has several properties?

When we transfer large amounts of data to the client from our request handler, we can get ourselves into trouble. Even though we're not performing CPU-intensive computations, we're still going to consume the CPU and block other request handlers while we write huge pieces of data to our responses. Here's an illustration of the problem:

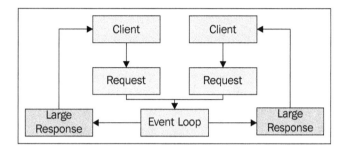

The problem isn't necessarily responding with one of these large responses, but when there are lots of them. Earlier in the chapter, we discussed the problem of establishing and maintaining a large number of connected users because this is a very likely scenario for our application. So, the problem with returning relatively large amounts of data in each response is the performance degradation of the application overall. Each user will experience non-optimal performance, and this isn't what we want at all.

We can tackle this issue using streaming techniques. Rather than writing the whole response at once, we can write it in chunks. As a chunk of data is written to the response stream, the event loop is free to process queued requests. Overall, we can avoid any one request handler from taking more time from the event loop than what is absolutely necessary. Let's take a look at an example:

```
// We need the "http" module.
var http = require('http');

// Creates some sample data, an array of
// numbers.
var array = new Array(1000)
    .fill(null)
    .map((v, i) => i);

// Creates the HTTP server, and the request
// callback function.
```

```javascript
var server = http.createServer((req, res) => {
    var size = 25,
        i = 0;

    // This function is called when we need to
    // schedule a chunk of data to be written to
    // the response.
    function schedule() {

        // Here's the actual scheduling,
        // "process.nextTick()" let's other handlers,
        // if any, run while we're streaming our writes
        // to the response.
        process.nextTick(() => {
            let chunk = array.slice(i, i + size);

            // If there's a chunk of data to write,
            // write it, then schedule the next round by
            // calling "schedule()". Otherwise, we can
            // "end()" the response.
            if (chunk.length) {
                res.write(chunk.toString() + '\n');
                i += size;
                schedule();
            } else {
                res.end();
            }
        });
    }

    // Kicks off the stream writing scheduler.
    schedule();
});

// Starts the server.
server.listen(8081);
console.log('listening at http://localhost:8081');
```

This example responds to the client request by returning a list of numbers in plain text. If we look at this page in a browser, we can actually see how the numbers are chunked because they're separated by new lines. This is only there for illustrative purposes; in practice, we would probably use the response as one big list. The important thing is that our request handler is no longer greedy, as by using the streaming approach, we're sharing the event loop with other request handlers.

Proxy network requests

Our main NodeJS web server doesn't need to fulfill every single aspect of every request. Instead, our handlers can reach out to other systems that form the backbone of our application and ask them for data. This is a form of microservices, and it's a topic that exceeds the scope of this discussion. Let's just think of these services as independent parts that help us compose a larger application whole.

Within a Node request handler, we can create other HTTP requests that talk to these external services. These requests utilize the same event loop as the handler that creates them. For example, when the service responds with data, it triggers an IO event, and a corresponding piece of JavaScript code runs. The following illustration shows how this type of setup works:

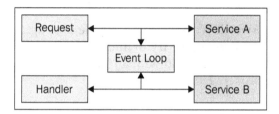

Let's see if we can write a request handler that's really a composition of other services that live on different servers. We'll first implement a users service, which allows us to retrieve specific user information. Then, we'll implement a preference service, which allows us to fetch preferences set by a specific user. Here's the user service code:

```
var http = require('http');

// Our sample user data.
var users = [
    { name: 'User 1' },
    { name: 'User 2' },
    { name: 'User 3' },
    { name: 'User 4' }
];

var server = http.createServer((req, res) => {

    // We'll be returning JSON data.
    res.setHeader('Content-Type', 'application/json');

    var id = /\/(\d+)/.exec(req.url),
        user;
```

```
        // If a user is found from the ID in the URL, return
        // a JSON string of it. Otherwise, respond with a 404.
        if (id && (user = users[+id[1]])) {
            res.end(JSON.stringify(user));
        } else {
            res.statusCode = 404;
            res.statusReason = http.STATUS_CODES[404];
            res.end();
        }

});

server.listen(8082);
console.log('Users service at http://localhost:8082');
```

This is pretty straightforward. We have some sample user data stored in an array, and when a request arrives, we try to find a specific user object based on ID (the array index). Then, we respond with a JSON string. The preference service uses the exact same approach. Here's the code:

 Note that each of these servers is started on different ports. If you're following along by running the code in this book, this example requires starting three web servers on the command line. It's probably easiest to open three terminal tabs (if supported, on OSX for instance) or open three terminal windows.

```
// Our sample preference data.
var preferences = [
    { spam: false },
    { spam: true },
    { spam: false },
    { spam: true }
];

var server = http.createServer((req, res) => {

    // We'll be returning JSON data.
    res.setHeader('Content-Type', 'application/json');

    var id = /\/(\d+)/.exec(req.url),
        preference;

    // If the ID in the URL finds a sample preference,
```

```
    // return the JSON string for it. Otherwise,
    // respond with a 404.
    if (id && (preference = preferences[+id[1]])) {
        res.end(JSON.stringify(preference));
    } else {
        res.statusCode = 404;
        res.statusMessage = http.STATUS_CODES[404];
        res.end();
    }
});

server.listen(8083);
console.log('Preference service: http://localhost:8083');
```

Now we can write our main server with request handlers that reach out to these services. Here's what the code looks like:

```
var http = require('http');

var server = http.createServer((req, res) => {

    // Looks for a user ID in the URL.
    var id = /\/(\d+)/.exec(req.url);

    // If there's no ID in the URL, don't
    // even try handling the request.
    if (!id) {
        res.end();
        return;
    }

    // This promise is resolved when the call to
    // the "users" service responds with data. This
    // service is another server, running on port
    // 8082.
    var user = new Promise((resolve, reject) => {
        http.get({
            hostname: 'localhost',
            port: 8082,
            path: `/${id[1]}`
        }, (res) => {
            res.on('data', (data) => {
                resolve(JSON.parse(data.toString()));
            });
```

```
        });
    });

    // This promise is resolved when the call to
    // the "preference" service responds with data. This
    // service is just another web server, running
    // on port 8082.
    var preference = new Promise((resolve, reject) => {
        http.get({
            hostname: 'localhost',
            port: 8083,
            path: `/${id[1]}`
        }, (res) => {
            res.on('data', (data) => {
                resolve(JSON.parse(data.toString()));
            });
        });
    });

    // Once both the user and the preference services have
    // responded, we have all the data we need to render
    // the page.
    Promise.all([ user, preference ]).then((results) => {
        let user = results[0],
            preference = results[1];

        res.end(`
            <p><strong>Name:</strong> ${user.name}</p>
            <p><strong>Spam:</strong> ${preference.spam}</p>
        `);
    });
});

server.listen(8081);
console.log('Listening at http://localhost:8081');
```

Now, we need to make sure that all three services are running—the users service, the preference service, and the main service that users interact with directly. They're all on different ports because they're all running as a web server on the same machine. In practice, these services could be running anywhere—that's part of their appeal.

Evented file IO

Now that we have a fairly good handle on network IO in NodeJS, it's time to focus our attention on file system IO. After this section, we'll see how files and network sockets are treated the same inside the event loop. Node takes care of the subtle differences for us, which means we can write consistent code.

First, we'll look at reading form files, followed by writing to files. We'll close the section with a look at streaming from one file to another, performing data transformations in between.

Reading from files

Let's start with a simple example that reads the entire contents of a file into memory. This will help us get a feel for doing asynchronous file IO:

```
// We need the "fs" module to read files.
var fs = require('fs');
var path = require('path');

// The file path we're working with.
var filePath = path.join(__dirname, 'words');

// Starts the timer for reading our "words" file.
console.time('reading words');

// Reads the entire file into memory, then fires
// a callback with the data.
fs.readFile(filePath, (err, data) => {
    console.timeEnd('reading words');
    // → reading words: 5ms

    console.log('size',
        `${(data.length / 1024 / 1024).toFixed(2)}MB`);
    // →   size 2.38MB
});
```

In the callback function that we passed to `fs.readFile()`, we have access to the `Buffer` object that holds the file contents in memory. While the operating system does the actual file reading, and the buffer is populated with the result, other handlers in the IO event loop continue to run. This is just like reading from a network socket, and also why there's a callback that's added to the event queue, which gets called once the data has been read.

The problem with reading files in one shot like this is that there could be ramifications outside of node at the OS level. The file that we will use here as an example is fairly modest in size, but what if we try to read from a much larger file? What if several request handlers try to read the same file? Maybe instead of reading the entire file at once, we only read chunks of data at a time? This would ease the resource contention if there were any. Let's look at an alternative approach:

```
// Creates a promise that's resolved once all the
// file chunks have been read into memory.
var contents = new Promise((resolve, reject) => {

    // Opens the "filePath" for reading. The file
    // descriptor, like a file identifier, is needed
    // when we call "fs.read()" later on.
    fs.open(filePath, 'r', (err, fd) => {

        // Set up some variables needed for reading
        // a file one chunk at a time. We need to know
        // how big the file is, that does in "size". The
        // "buffer" is where the chunks go as they're
        // read. And we have the "chunk" size, and the
        // number of "bytes" read so far.
        var size = fs.fstatSync(fd).size,
            buffer = new Buffer(size),
            chunk = 1024,
            read = 0;

        // We wrap this reading iteration in a named
        // function because it's recursive.
        function schedule() {

            // The reading of a chunk always happens in
            // the next tick of the IO loop. This gives
            // other queued handlers a chance to run while
            // we're reading this file.
            // process.nextTick(() => {

                // Makes sure the last chunk fits evenly
                // into the buffer.
                if ((read + chunk) > size) {
                    chunk = size - read;
                }

                // Reads the chunk of data into the buffer,
```

```
                    // and increments the "read" counter.
                    fs.read(fd, buffer, read, chunk, read);
                    read += chunk;

                    // Check if there's still data to read. If
                    // yes, "schedule()" the next "read()". If
                    // no, resolve the promise with the "buffer".
                    if (read < size) {
                        schedule();
                    } else {
                        resolve(buffer);
                    }
                });
            }

            // Kicks off the reading and scheduling process.
            schedule();
        });
    });

    // When the promise is resolved, show how many words
    // were read into the buffer by splitting them by
    // newlines.
    contents.then((buffer) => {
        console.log('words read',
            buffer.toString().split('\n').length);
        // → words read 235887
    });
```

Here, we get the exact same result, except that we've broken the single `fs.readFile()` call into several smaller `fs.read()`. We also use a promise here to make the callback handling a little more straightforward.

You may be wondering why we're not using a loop to iterate over the chunks and issue the `fs.read()` calls. Instead, we're scheduling the read calls using `process.nextTick()`. If we loop over the chunks, each `read()` call gets added to the event queue in order. So we end up with a bunch of `read()` calls in succession without any other handlers being called. This defeats the purpose of breaking up `fs.readFile()`. Instead, `process.nextTick()` allows other handlers to run in between our `read()` calls.

Writing to files

Writing to files works a lot like reading from files. Actually, writing is slightly easier since we don't have to maintain any data in memory; we just have to worry about writing data that's already in memory to disk. Let's start by looking at some code that writes a blob of data to a file with one call. This would be the equivalent of reading the entire file at once only in reverse:

```
// We need the "fs" and the "path" modules for
// working with files.
var fs = require('fs');
var path = require('path');

// The two files we'll be working with.
var filePath1 = path.join(__dirname, 'output1'),
    filePath2 = path.join(__dirname, 'output2');

// The sample array we'll be writing to files.
var array = new Array(1000)
    .fill(null)
    .map((v, i) => i);

// Starts a timer for writing the entire array to
// the file in one shot.
console.time('output1');

// Performs the file write and stops the timer when
// it's complete.
fs.writeFile(filePath1, array.toString(), (err) => {
    console.timeEnd('output1');
});
```

See, nothing to it. We write the string representation of our array to the file using `fs.writeFile()`. However, this has potential to block other things from happening at the OS level; especially if we're writing a lot of data all at once. Let's try breaking up the write operation into several smaller calls just like we did with the read example prior to this one:

```
// Creates a promise that's resolved when all chunks
// have been written to file.
var written = new Promise((resolve, reject) => {

    // Opens the file for writing, and the callback
    // starts writing chunks.
```

```
    fs.open(filePath2, 'w', (err, fd) => {
        var chunk = 50,
            i = 0;

        // The recursive scheduler places the call
        // to perform the write into the IO event loop
        // queue.
        function schedule() {
            process.nextTick(() => {

                // The chunk of data from "array" to
                // write.
                let slice = array.slice(i, i + chunk);

                // If there's a chunk to write, write it.
                // If not, close the file and resolve the
                // promise.
                if (slice.length) {
                    fs.write(fd, slice.toString(), i);
                    i += chunk;
                    schedule();
                } else {
                    fs.close(fd);
                    resolve();
                }
            });
        }

        // Kicks of the chunk/write scheduler.
        schedule();
    });
});

// When the promise is resolved, it means the file has been
// written.
written.then(() => {
    console.log('finished writing');
});
```

This works the same as the approach we took with the chunked read. The main difference is that we write a file instead and that there's less moving parts. Also, the promise is resolved without a value, which is fine, because callers can treat this value as a `null` and still know that the file has been successfully written to disk. In the next section, we'll look at a more streamlined version of reading and writing files.

Streaming reads and writes

So far, we've addressed reading files in chunks, as well as splitting data into chunks, and writing them to disk one at a time. The advantage is that we yield control to other code, perhaps, other operating system calls during the time that we read or write. The advantage is that when we're working with large amounts of data, one hardware resource is never monopolized by a read or write operation.

In effect, we were implementing streaming reads and writes. In this section, we'll look at the streaming interface that NodeJS implements for various components, including files. The code that we wrote in the preceding sections for streaming reads and writes got a little verbose in places. As we know by now, we don't want boilerplate concurrency code where it can be avoided. We especially don't want it sprinkled throughout our code base. Let's look at a different approach to stream file reads and writes:

```javascript
// All the modules we need.
var fs = require('fs');
var path = require('path');
var stream = require('stream');

// Creates a simple upper-case transformation
// stream. Each chunk that's passed in is
// "pushed" to the next stream in upper-case.
var transform = new stream.Transform({
    transform: function(chunk) {
        this.push(chunk.toString().toUpperCase());
    }
});

// The file names we're using.
var inputFile = path.join(__dirname, 'words'),
    outputFile = path.join(__dirname, 'output');

// Creates an "input" stream that reads from
// "inputFile" and an "output" stream that writes
// to "outputFile".
var input = fs.createReadStream(inputFile),
    output = fs.createWriteStream(outputFile);

// Starts the IO by building the following
// pipeline: input -> transform -> output.
input.pipe(transform);
transform.pipe(output);
```

We basically copy one file into another, making a small modification to the data along the way. Thankfully, NodeJS streaming facilities make performing this transformation easy without the need to write a lot of boilerplate code that reads input than writes to the output again. Almost all of this is abstracted away in the Transform class. Here's an illustration of the pipeline that our previous code just created:

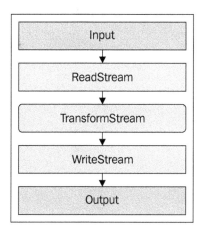

Summary

This chapter introduced you to concurrency in NodeJS. The premise is that Node applications will perform a lot of IO, and that IO is slow, relative to other computations that take place in memory. Node implements an IO loop, a mechanism that notifies our code when a given IO resource is ready for input or output.

We saw some of the advantages and disadvantages to this model. The alternative approach involves relying on parallelism at the CPU level, which can pose challenges when there's lots of slow IO taking place. Conversely, the IO loop approach isn't impacted the same when there's lots of IO, but suffers greatly when there are expensive CPU tasks to perform.

We spent the remainder of the chapter looking at various network and file IO examples. In the following chapter, we'll continue our exploration of NodeJS by looking at some more advanced topics, some of which can help us scale as our applications grow more computationally expensive.

9
Advanced NodeJS Concurrency

In *Chapter 8, Evented IO with NodeJS*, you learned about the concurrency mechanism that's central to NodeJS applications — the IO event loop. In this chapter, we'll dig into some more advanced topics that are both — complimentary to the event loop and contrary to the event loop.

Kicking us off is a discussion on implementing coroutines in Node using the `Co` library. Next, we'll look at creating subprocesses and communicating with these processes. After this, we'll dig into Node's built-in capability to create a process cluster, each with their own event loop. We'll close this chapter with a look at creating clusters at large-scale clusters of Node servers.

Coroutines with Co

We've already seen one approach to implement coroutines in the front-end using generators, in *Chapter 4, Lazy Evaluation with Generators*. In this section, we'll use the `Co` library (`https://github.com/tj/co`) to implement coroutines. This library also relies on generators and promises.

We'll start by walking through the general premise of `Co`, and then, we'll write some code that waits for asynchronous values using promises. We'll then look into the mechanics of transferring resolved values from a promise to our coroutine function, asynchronous dependencies, and creating coroutine utility functions.

Generating promises

At its core, the Co library uses a co() function to create a coroutine. In fact, its basic usage looks familiar to the coroutine function that we created earlier in this book. Here's what it looks like:

```
co(function* () {
    // TODO: co-routine amazeballs.
});
```

Another similarity between the Co library and our earlier coroutine implementation is that values are passed in through the yield statement. However, instead of calling the returned function to pass in the values, this coroutine uses promises to pass in values. The effect is the same—asynchronous values being passed into synchronous code, as this diagram shows:

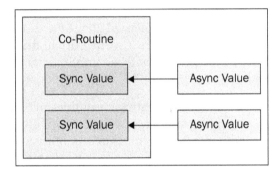

The asynchronous value actually comes from a promise. The resolved value makes its way into the coroutine. We'll dig deeper into the mechanics of how this works shortly. Even if we don't yield promises, say we yielded a string for instance, the Co library will wrap this into a promise for us. But, doing this defeats the purpose of using asynchronous values in synchronous code.

>
> It cannot be understated how valuable it is for us, as programmers, when we find a tool such as Co, that encapsulates messy synchronization semantics. Our code inside the coroutine is synchronous and maintainable.

Awaiting values

Coroutines created by the `co()` function work a lot like ES7 asynchronous functions. The `async` keyword marks a function as asynchronous—meaning that it uses asynchronous values within. The `await` keyword, used in conjunction with a promise, pauses the execution of the function till the value resolves. If this feels a lot like what a generator does, it's because it's exactly what a generator does. Here's what the ES7 syntax looks like:

```
// This is the ES7 syntax, where the function is
// marked as "async". Then, the "await" calls
// pause execution till their operands resolve.
(async function() {
    var result;
    result = await Promise.resolve('hello');
    console.log('async result', `"${result}"`);
    // → async result "hello"

    result = await Promise.resolve('world');
    console.log('async result', `"${result}"`);
    // → async result "world"

}());
```

In this example, the promises are resolved immediately, so there's no real need to pause the execution. However, it waits even if the promise resolves a network request that takes several seconds. We'll go into more depth on resolving promises in the next section. Given that this is ES7 syntax, it'd be nice if we could use the same approach today. Here's how we would implement the same thing with Co:

```
// We need the "co()" function.
var co = require('co');

// The differences between the ES7 and "co()" are
// subtle, the overall structure is the same. The
// function is a generator, and we pause execution
// by yielding generators.
co(function*() {
    var result;
    result = yield Promise.resolve('hello');
    console.log('co result', `"${result}"`);
    // → co result "hello"

    result = yield Promise.resolve('world');
```

```
        console.log('co result', `"${result}"`);
        // → co result "world"
    });
```

It should be no surprise that the Co library is moving in the direction of ES7; nice move Co authors.

Resolving values

There are at least two places in a given Co coroutine where a promise is resolved. First, there's one or more promises yielded from within the generator function that we'll pass to co(). If there weren't any promises yielded within this function, there wouldn't be much point in using Co. The return value when calling co() is another promise, which is kind of cool because it means that coroutines can have other coroutines as dependencies. We'll explore this idea in more depth momentarily. For now, let's look at resolving the promises, and how it's done. Here's an illustration of the promise resolution order of a coroutine:

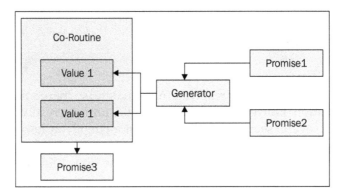

The promises are resolved in the same order that they're named. For instance, the first promise causes the execution of the code within the coroutine to pause execution until it's value is resolved. Then, the execution is paused again while waiting for the second promise. The final promise that's returned from co() is resolved with the return value of the generator function. Let's look at some code now:

```
var co = require('co');

co(function* () {

    // The promise that's yielded here isn't resolved
```

```
    // till 1 second later. That's when the yield statement
    // returns the resolved value.
    var first = yield new Promise((resolve, reject) => {
        setTimeout(() => {
            resolve([ 'First1', 'First2', 'First3' ]);
        }, 1000);
    });

    // Same idea here, except we're waiting 2 seconds
    // before the "second" variable gets it's value.
    var second = yield new Promise((resolve, reject) => {
        setTimeout(() => {
            resolve([ 'Second1', 'Second2', 'Second3' ]);
        }, 2000);
    });

    // Both "first" and "second" are resolved at this
    // point, so we can use both to map a new array.
    return first.map((v, i) => [ v, second[i] ]);

}).then((value) => {
    console.log('zipped', value);
    // →
    // [
    //    [ 'First1', 'Second1' ],
    //    [ 'First2', 'Second2' ],
    //    [ 'First3', 'Second3' ]
    // ]
});
```

As we can see, the return value from the generator ends up as the resolved promise value. Recall that returning from a generator will return the same object as yielding does with the value and done properties. Co knows to resolve the promise with the value property.

Asynchronous dependencies

Coroutines made with Co really shine when an action depends on an earlier asynchronous value later on in the coroutine. What would otherwise be a tangled mess of callbacks and state is instead just placing the assignments in the correct order. The dependent action is never called until the value is resolved. Here's an illustration of the idea:

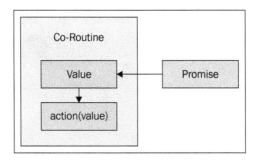

Now let's write some code that has two asynchronous actions, where the second action depends on the result of the first. This can be tricky, even with the use of promises:

```
var co = require('co');

// A simple user collection.
var users = [
    { name: 'User1' },
    { name: 'User2' },
    { name: 'User3' },
    { name: 'User4' }
];

co(function* () {

    // The "userID" value is asynchronous, and execution
    // pause at this yield statement till the promise
    // resolves.
    var userID = yield new Promise((resolve, reject) => {
        setTimeout(() => {
            resolve(1);
        }, 1000);
    });

    // At this point, we have a "userID" value. This
```

```
    // nested co-routine will look up the user based
    // on this ID. We nest coroutines like this because
    // "co()" returns a promise.
    var user = yield co(function* (id) {
        let user = yield new Promise((resolve, reject) => {
            setTimeout(() => {
                resolve(users[id]);
            }, 1000);
        });

        // The "co()" promise is resolved with the
        // "user" value.
        return user;
    }, userID);

    console.log(user);
    // → { name: 'User2' }
});
```

We used a nested coroutine in this example, but it could have been any type of function that required a parameter and returned a promise. This example, if nothing else, serves to highlight the versatility of promises in a concurrent environment.

Wrapping coroutines

The last Co example that we'll look at uses the `wrap()` utility to make a plain coroutine function into a reusable function that we can call over and over. As the name suggests, the coroutine is simply wrapped in a function. This is especially useful when we pass arguments to coroutines. Let's take a look at a modified version of the code example that we built:

```
var co = require('co');

// A simple user collection.
var users = [
    { name: 'User1' },
    { name: 'User2' },
    { name: 'User3' },
    { name: 'User4' }
];

// The "getUser()" function will create a new
// co-routine whenever it's called, forwarding
// any arguments as well.
```

```
var getUser = co.wrap(function* (id) {
    let user = yield new Promise((resolve, reject) => {
        setTimeout(() => {
            resolve(users[id]);
        }, 1000);
    });

    // The "co()" promise is resolved with the
    // "user" value.
    return user;
});

co(function* () {

    // The "userID" value is asynchronous, and execution
    // pause at this yield statement till the promise
    // resolves.
    var userID = yield new Promise((resolve, reject) => {
        setTimeout(() => {
            resolve(1);
        }, 1000);
    });

    // Instead of a nested co-routine, we have a function
    // that can now be used elsewhere.
    var user = yield getUser(userID);

    console.log(user);
    // → { name: 'User2' }
});
```

So, instead of a nested coroutine, we used `co.wrap()` to create a reusable coroutine function. That is, it'll create a new coroutine every time it's called, passing it all the arguments that the function gets. There really isn't much more to it than this, but the gains are noticeable and worthwhile. Instead of a nested coroutine function, we have something that can potentially be shared across components.

Child Processes

We know that NodeJS uses an evented IO loop as its main concurrency mechanism. This is based on the assumption that our application does a lot of IO and very little CPU-intensive work. This is probably true for the majority of handlers in our code. However, there's always a particular edge case that requires more CPU time than usual.

In this section, we'll discuss how handlers can block the IO loop, and why all it takes is one bad handler to ruin the experience for everyone else. Then, we'll look at ways to get around this limitation by forking new Node child processes. We'll also look at how to spawn other non-Node processes in order to get the data that we need.

Blocking the event loop

In *Chapter 8, Evented IO with NodeJS*, we saw an example that demonstrated how one handler can block the entire IO event loop while performing expensive CPU operations. We're going to reiterate this point here to highlight the full scope of the problem. It's not just one handler that we're blocking, but all handlers. This could be hundreds, or it could be thousands, depending on the application, and how it's used.

Since we're not processing requests in parallel at the hardware level, which is the case with the multithreaded approach—it only takes one expensive handler to block all handlers. If there's one request that's able to cause this expensive handler to run, then we're likely to receive several of these expensive requests, bringing our application to a standstill. Let's look at a handler that blocks every other handler that comes in after it:

```
// Eat some CPU cycles...
// Taken from http://adambom.github.io/parallel.js/
function work(n) {
    var i = 0;
    while (++i < n * n) {}
    return i;
}

// Adds some functions to the event loop queue.
process.nextTick(() => {
    var promises = [];

    // Creates 500 promises in the "promises"
    // array. They're each resolved after 1 second.
    for (let i = 0; i < 500; i++) {
        promises.push(new Promise((resolve) => {
            setTimeout(resolve, 1000);
        }));
    }

    // When they're all resolved, log that
    // we're done handling them.
    Promise.all(promises).then(() => {
        console.log('handled requests');
```

```
        });
    });

    // This takes a lot longer than the 1 second
    // it takes to resolve all the promises that
    // get added to the queue. So this handler blocks
    // 500 user requests till it finishes..
    process.nextTick(() => {
        console.log('hogging the CPU...');
        work(100000);
    });
```

The first call to `process.nextTick()` simulates actual client requests by scheduling functions to run after one second. All these lead to a single promise being resolved; and this logs the fact that all the requests have been handled. The next call to `process.nextTick()` is expensive and completely blocks these 500 requests. This definitely isn't good for our application. The only way around scenarios where we run CPU-intensive code inside of NodeJS is to break out of the single-process approach. This topic is covered next.

Forking processes

We've reached the point in our application where there's simply no way around it. We have some relatively expensive requests to process. We need to utilize parallelism at the hardware layer. In Node, this means only one thing—forking a child process to handle the CPU-intensive work outside of the main process so that normal requests may continue on uninterrupted. Here's an illustration of what this tactic looks like:

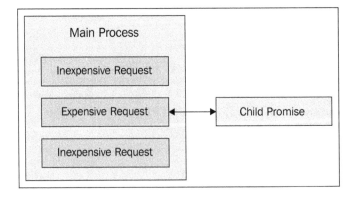

Now, let's write some code that uses the `child_process.fork()` function to spawn a new Node process, when we need to process a request that's CPU-hungry. First, the main module:

```
// We need the "child_process" to fork new
// node processes.
var child_process = require('child_process');

// Forks our worker process.
var child = child_process.fork(`${__dirname}/child`);

// This event is emitted when the child process
// responds with data.
child.on('message', (message) => {

    // Displays the result, and kills the child
    // process since we're done with it.
    console.log('work result', message);
    child.kill();
});

// Sends a message to the child process. We're
// sending a number on this end, and the
// "child_process" ensures that it arrives as a
// number on the other end.
child.send(100000);
console.log('work sent...');

// Since the expensive computation is happening in
// another process, normal requests flow through
// the event loop like normal.
process.nextTick(() => {
    console.log('look ma, no blocking!');
});
```

The only overhead we face now is that of actually spawning the new process, which pales in comparison to the actual work that we need to perform. We can clearly see that the main IO loop isn't blocked because the main process isn't hogging the CPU. The child process, on the other hand, hammers the CPU, but this is okay because it's probably happening on a different core. Here's what our child process code looks like:

```
// Eat some CPU cycles...
// Taken from http://adambom.github.io/parallel.js/
```

```
function work(n) {
    var i = 0;
    while (++i < n * n) {}
    return i;
}


// The "message" event is emitted when the parent
// process sends a message. We then respond with
// the result of performing expensive CPU operations.
process.on('message', (message) => {
    process.send(work(message));
});
```

Spawning external processes

Sometimes, our Node applications need to talk to other programs that aren't Node processes. These could be other applications we write, but using a different platform or basic system commands. We can spawn these types of processes and talk to them, but they don't work the same as forking another node process. Here's a visualization of the difference:

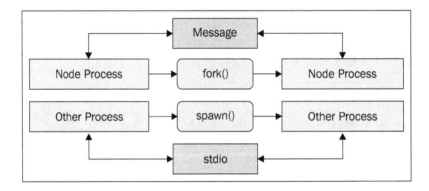

We could use spawn() to create a child Node process if we're so inclined, but this puts us at a disadvantage in some cases. For example, we don't get the message-passing infrastructure that's setup automatically for us by fork(). However, the best communication path depends on what we're trying to achieve, and most of the time, we don't actually need message-passing.

Let's look at some code that spawns a process and reads the output of that process:

```javascript
// Our required modules...
var child_process = require('child_process');
var os = require('os');

// Spawns our child process - the "ls" system
// command. The command line flags are passed
// as an array.
var child = child_process.spawn('ls', [
    '-lha',
    __dirname
]);

// Our output accumulator is an empty string
// initially.
var output = '';

// Adds output as it arrives from process.
child.stdout.on('data', (data) => {
    output += data;
});

// We're done getting output from the child
// process - so log the output and kill it.
child.stdout.on('end', () => {
    output = output.split(os.EOL);
    console.log(output.slice(1, output.length - 2));
    child.kill();
});
```

 The ls command that we spawn doesn't exist on Windows systems. I have no other consolatory words of wisdom here—it's just a fact.

Inter-process communication

In the example that we just looked at, the child process was spawned, and our main process collected the output, killing the process; but, what about when we write servers and other types of long-lived programs? Under these circumstances, we probably don't want to constantly spawn and kill child processes. Instead, it's probably better to keep the process alive alongside the main program and keep feeding it messages, as is illustrated here:

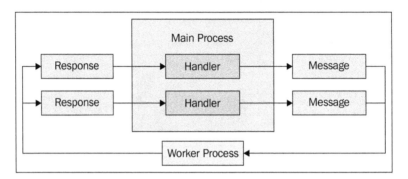

Even if the worker is synchronously processing requests, it still serves as an advantage to our main application because nothing blocks it from serving requests. For instance, requests that don't require any heavy-lifting on behalf of the CPU can continue to deliver fast responses. Let's turn our attention to a code example now:

```
var child_process = require('child_process');

// Forks our "worker" process and creates a "resolvers"
// object to store our promise resolvers.
var worker = child_process.fork(`${__dirname}/worker`),
    resolvers = {};

// When the worker responds with a message, pass
// the message output to the appropriate resolver.
worker.on('message', (message) => {
    resolvers[message.id](message.output);
    delete resolvers[message.id];
});

// IDs are used to map responses from the worker process
// to the promise resolver functions.
```

```
function* genID() {
    var id = 0;

    while (true) {
        yield id++;
    }
}

var id = genID();

// This function sends the given "input" to the worker,
// and returns a promise. The promise is resolved with
// the return value of the worker.
function send(input) {
    return new Promise((resolve, reject) => {
        var messageID = id.next().value;

        // Store the resolver function in the "resolvers"
        // map.
        resolvers[messageID] = resolve;

        // Sends the "messageID" and the "input" to the
        // worker.
        worker.send({
            id: messageID,
            input: input
        });
    });
}

var array;

// Builds an array of numbers to send to the worker
// individually for processing.
array = new Array(100)
    .fill(null)
    .map((v, i) => (i + 1) * 100);

// Sends each number in "array" to the worker process
// as a message. When each promise is resolved, we can
// reduce the results.
```

```
var first = Promise.all(array.map(send)).then((results) => {
    console.log('first result',
        results.reduce((r, v) => r + v));
    // → first result 3383500000
});


// Creates a smaller array, with smaller numbers - it
// should take less time to process than the previous
// array.
array = new Array(50)
    .fill(null)
    .map((v, i) => (i + 1) * 10);


// Process the second array, log the reduced result.
var second = Promise.all(array.map(send))
    .then((results) => {
        console.log('second result',
            results.reduce((r, v) => r + v));
        // → second result 4292500
});


// When both arrays have finished being processed, we need
// to kill the worker in order to exit our program.
Promise.all([ first, second ]).then(() => {
    worker.kill();
});
```

Now let's take a look at the `worker` module that we fork from the main module:

```
// Eat some CPU cycles...
// Taken from http://adambom.github.io/parallel.js/
function work(n) {
    var i = 0;
    while (++i < n * n) {}
    return i;
}


// Respond to the main process with the result of
// calling "work()" and the message ID.
process.on('message', (message) => {
    process.send({
        id: message.id,
        output: work(message.input)
    });
});
```

Each number in the arrays that we create is passed to the worker process where the CPU-heavy work is performed. The result is passed back to the main process, and is used to resolve a promise. This technique is very similar to the promise approach that we took with web workers in *Chapter 7, Abstracting Concurrency*.

There are two results we're trying to compute here—one for the first array, and one for the second. The first one has more array items than the second one, and the numbers are larger. This means that this will take longer to compute, and, in fact, it does. But, if we run this code, we don't see the output from the second array until the first has completed.

This is because despite requiring less CPU time, the second job is still blocked because the order of the messages sent to the worker is preserved. In other words, all 100 messages from the first array are processed before even starting on the second array. At first glance, this may seem like a bad thing because it doesn't actually solve anything for us. Well, this simply not true.

The only thing that's blocked are the queued messages that arrive at the worker process. Because the worker is busy with the CPU, it can't process messages immediately as they arrive. However, the purpose of this worker is to remove the heavy processing from web request handlers that require it. Not every request handler has this type of heavy load, and guess what? They can continue to run normally because there's nothing in the process that hogs the CPU.

However, as our applications continue to grow larger and more complex due to added features and the ways in which they interact with other features, we'll need a better approach to handling expensive request handlers because we'll have more of them. This is what we're going to cover in the next section.

Process Clusters

In the preceding section, we introduced child process creation in NodeJS. This is a necessary measure for web applications when request handlers start consuming more and more CPU, because of the way that this can block every other handler in the system. In this section, we'll build on this idea, but instead of forking a single general-purpose worker process, we'll maintain a pool of general-purpose processes, which is capable of handling any request.

We'll start by reiterating the challenges posed by manually managing these processes that help us with concurrency scenarios in Node. Then, we'll look at the built-in process clustering capabilities of Node.

Challenges with process management

The obvious problem with manually orchestrating processes within our application is that the concurrent code is right there, out in the open, intermingling with the rest of our application code. We actually experienced the exact same problem earlier in this book when implementing web workers. Without encapsulating the synchronization and the general management of the workers, our code consists mostly of concurrency boilerplate. Once this happens, it's tough to separate the concurrency mechanisms from the code that's essential to the features that make our product unique.

One solution with web workers is to create a pool of workers and hide them behind a unified API. This way, our feature code that needs to do things in parallel can do so without littering our editors with concurrency synchronization semantics.

It turns out that NodeJS solves the problem of leveraging the hardware parallelism available on most systems, which is similar to what we did with web workers. Next, we'll jump into how this works.

Abstracting process pools

We're able to use the `child_process` module to manually fork our Node process to enable true parallelism. This is important when doing CPU-intensive work that could block the main process, and hence, the main IO event loop that services incoming requests. We could increase the level of parallelism beyond just a single worker process, but that would require a lot of manual synchronization logic on our part.

The `cluster` module requires a little bit of setup code, but the actual communication orchestration between worker processes and the main process is entirely transparent to our code. In other words, it looks like we're just running a single Node process to handle our incoming web requests, but in reality, there are several cloned processes that handle them. It's up to the `cluster` module to distribute these requests to the worker nodes, and by default, this uses the round-robin approach, which is good enough for most cases.

On Windows, the default isn't round-robin. We can manually change the approach we want to use, but the round-robin approach keeps things simple and balanced. The only challenge is when we have request handlers that are substantially more expensive to run than the majority. Then, we can end up distributing requests to an overloaded worker process. This is just something to be aware of when troubleshooting this module.

Here's a visualization showing worker Node processes relative to the main Node process:

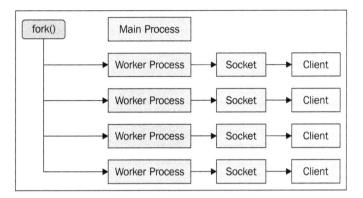

The main process has two responsibilities in a clustering scenario. First, it needs to establish communication channels with worker processes. Second, it needs to accept incoming connections and distribute them to the worker processes. This is actually trickier to draw and so isn't represented in the diagram. Let's look at some code before I try to explain this any further:

```
// The modules we need...
var http = require('http');
var cluster = require('cluster');
var os = require('os');

// Eat some CPU cycles...
// Taken from http://adambom.github.io/parallel.js/
function work(n) {
    var i = 0;
    while (++i < n * n) {}
    return i;
}

// Check which type of process this is. It's either
// a master or a worker.
if (cluster.isMaster) {

    // The level of parallelism that goes into
    // "workers".
```

```
        var workers = os.cpus().length;

        // Forks our worker processes.
        for (let i = 0; i < workers; i++) {
            cluster.fork();
        }

        console.log('listening at http://localhost:8081');
        console.log(`worker processes: ${workers}`);

    // If this process isn't the master, then it's
    // a worker. So we create the same HTTP server as
    // every other worker.
    } else {
        http.createServer((req, res) => {
            res.setHeader('Content-Type', 'text/plain');
            res.end(`worker ${cluster.worker.id}: ${work(100000)}`);
        }).listen(8081);
    }
```

What's really nice about this approach to parallelizing our request handlers is that the concurrent code is unobtrusive. There' are about 10 lines of it in total. At a glance, we can easily see what this code does. If we want to see this application in action, we can open several browser windows and point them to the server at the same time. Since the request handler is expensive in terms of CPU cycles, we should be able to see that each page responds with the value that was computed as well as the worker ID that computed it. If we hadn't forked these worker processes, then we'd probably still be waiting for each of our browser tabs to load.

The only part that's a little tricky is the part where we actually create the HTTP server. Because this same code is run by each of the workers, the same host and port are used on the same computer—how can this be? Well, this is not actually what's happening. The net module, the low-level networking library that the http module uses, is actually cluster-aware. This means that when we ask the net module to listen to a socket for incoming requests, it first checks if it's a worker node. If it is, then it actually shares the same socket handle used by the main process. This is pretty neat. There's a lot of ugly logistics required to distribute requests to worker processes and actually hand off the request, all of which is handled for us by the cluster module.

Server clusters

It's one thing to scale up a single machine that's running our NodeJS application by enabling parallelism through process management. This is a great way to get the most of our physical hardware or our virtual hardware — they both cost money. However, there's an inherent limitation to scaling up just one machine — it can only go so far. At some threshold in some dimension of our scaling problems, we'll hit a wall. Before this happens, we need to think about scaling our Node application to several machines.

In this section, we'll introduce the idea of proxying our web requests to other machines instead of handling them all on the machine where they arrive. Then, we'll look at implementing microservices, and how they can help compose a sound application architecture. Finally, we'll implement some load balancing code that's tailored to our application; and how it handles requests.

Proxying requests

A request proxy in NodeJS is exactly what it sounds like. The request arrives at a server where it's handled by a Node process. However, the request isn't fulfilled here — it's proxied to another machine. So the question is, why bother with the proxy at all? Why not go straight to the target machine that actually responds to our requests?

The problem with this idea is that Node applications typically respond to HTTP requests coming from a browser. This means that we generally need a single entry point into the back-end. On the other hand, we don't necessarily want this single entry point to be a single Node server. This gets kind of limiting when our application grows larger. Instead, we want the ability to spread our application or scale it horizontally as they say. Proxy servers remove geographic restrictions; different parts of our application can be deployed in different parts of the world, different parts of the same data center, or even as different virtual machines. The point is that we have the flexibility to change where our application components reside, and how they're configured without impacting other parts of the application.

Another cool aspect of distributing web requests via proxy is that we can actually program our proxy handlers to modify requests and responses. So while the individual services that our proxy depends on can implement one specific aspect of our application, the proxy can implement the generic parts that apply to every request. Here is a visualization of a proxy server and the API endpoints that actually fulfill each request:

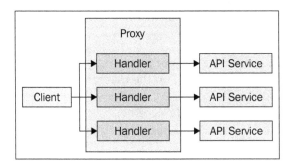

Facilitating micro-services

Depending on the type of application that we're building, our API can be one monolithic service, or it can be composed of several microservices. On the one hand, monolithic APIs tend to be easier to maintain for smaller applications that don't have a large breadth of features and data. On the other hand, APIs for larger applications tend to grow outrageously complex to the point that it's impossible to maintain because there are so many areas that are all intertwined with one another. If we split them out into microservices, it's much easier to deploy them to specific environments suited to their needs and have a dedicated team focus on one service that's working well.

 Microservice architecture is a huge topic that obviously goes well beyond the scope of this book. The focus here is on microservice enablement—the mechanism more so than the design.

We're going to use the node-http-proxy (`https://github.com/nodejitsu/node-http-proxy`) module to implement our proxy servers. This isn't a core Node module, so our applications need to include it as an npm dependency. Let's look at a basic example that proxies requests to the appropriate service:

 This example starts three web servers, each running on different ports.

```
// The modules we need...
var http = require('http'),
    httpProxy = require('http-proxy');

// The "proxy" server is how we send
// requests to other hosts.
var proxy = httpProxy.createProxyServer();

http.createServer((req, res) => {

    // If the request is for the site root, we
    // return some HTML with some links'.
    if (req.url === '/') {
        res.setHeader('Content-Type', 'text/html');
        res.end(`
            <html>
                <body>
                    <p><a href="hello">Hello</a></p>
                    <p><a href="world">World</a></p>
                </body>
            </html>
        `);

    // If the URL is "hello" or "world", we proxy
    // the request to the appropriate micro-service
    // using "proxy.web()".
    } else if (req.url === '/hello') {
        proxy.web(req, res, {
            target: 'http://localhost:8082'
        });
    } else if (req.url === '/world') {
        proxy.web(req, res, {
            target: 'http://localhost:8083'
        });
    } else {
        res.statusCode = 404;
        res.end();
    }
}).listen(8081);
console.log('listening at http://localhost:8081');
```

The two services hello and world aren't actually listed here because all they do is return a single line of plain text for any request. They' listen on ports 8082 and 8083 respectively. The http-proxy module makes it easy for us to simply forward the request to the appropriate service using the minimal amount of logic.

Informed load balancing

Earlier in this chapter, we looked at process clustering. This is where we use the `cluster` module to create a pool of processes, each capable of handling requests from clients. The main process acts as a proxy in this scenario, and by default, distributes requests to the worker processes in a round-robin fashion. We can do something similar using the `http-proxy` module, but using a less naive approach than round-robin one.

For example, let's say we have two instances of the same micro service running. Well, one of these services could become busier than the other, which knocks the service off balance because the busy node will continue to receive requests even though it can't get to them right away. It makes sense to hold onto the requests until the service can handle them. First, we'll implement a service that randomly takes a while to complete:

```js
var http = require('http');

// Get the port as a command line argument,
// so we can run multiple instances of the
// service.
var port = process.argv[2];

// Eat some CPU cycles...
// Taken from http://adambom.github.io/parallel.js/
function work() {
    var i = 0,
        min = 10000,
        max = 100000,
        n = Math.floor(Math.random() * (max - min)) + min;
    while (++i < n * n) {}
    return i;
}

// Responds with plain text, after blocking
// the CPU for a random interval.
http.createServer((req, res) => {
    res.setHeader('Content-Type', 'text/plain');
    res.end(work().toString());
}).listen(port);

console.log(`listening at http://localhost:${port}`);
```

Now we can start two instances of these processes, listening on different ports. In practice, these will be running on two different machines, but we're just testing the idea at this point. Now we'll implement the proxy server that needs to figure out which service worker a given request goes to:

```
var http = require('http'),
    httpProxy = require('http-proxy');

var proxy = httpProxy.createProxyServer();

// These are the service targets. They have a "host",
// and a "busy" property. Initially they're
// not busy because we haven't sent any work.
var targets = [
    {
        host: 'http://localhost:8082',
        busy: false
    }
    {
        host: 'http://localhost:8083',
        busy: false
    }
];

// Every request gets queued here, in case all
// our targets are busy.
var queue = [];

// Process the request queue, by proxying requests
// to targets that aren't busy.
function processQueue() {

    // Iterates over the queue of messages.
    for (let i = 0; i < queue.length; i++) {

        // Iterates over the targets.
        for (let target of targets) {

            // If the target is busy, skip it.
            if (target.busy) {
                continue;
            }
```

```
            // Marks the target as busy - from this
            // point forward, the target won't accept
            // any requests untill it's unmarked.
            target.busy = true;

            // Gets the current item out of the queue.
            let item = queue.splice(i, 1)[0];

            // Mark the response, so we know which service
            // worker the request went to when it comes
            // back.
            item.res.setHeader('X-Target', i);

            // Sends the proxy request and exits the
            // loop.
            proxy.web(item.req, item.res, {
                target: target.host
            });

            break;
        }
    }
}

// Emitted by the http-proxy module when a response
// arrives from a service worker.
proxy.on('proxyRes', function(proxyRes, req, res) {

    // This is the value we set earlier, the index
    // of the "targets" array.
    var target = res.getHeader('X-Target');

    // We use this index to unmark it. Now it'll
    // except new proxy requests.
    targets[target].busy = false;

    // The client doesn't need this internal
    // information, so remove it.
    res.removeHeader('X-Target');

    // Since a service worker just became available,
    // process the queue again, in case there's pending
    // requests.
```

```
        processQueue();
    });

    http.createServer((req, res) => {

        // All incoming requests are pushed onto the queue.
        queue.push({
            req: req,
            res: res
        });

        // Reprocess the queue, leaving the request there
        // if all the service workers are busy.
        processQueue();
    }).listen(8081);

    console.log('listening at http://localhost:8081');
```

The key thing to note about the way this proxy works is that requests are only proxied to services that aren't already busy handling a request. This is the informed part—the proxy knows when the server is available because it responds with the last request that it was busy with. When we know which servers are busy, we know not to overload them with yet more work.

Summary

In this chapter, we looked beyond the event loop as a concurrency mechanism in NodeJS. We started out by implementing coroutines using the Co library. From there, we learned about launching new processes, including the difference between forking another Node process and spawning other non-Node processes. Then, we looked at another approach to managing concurrency using the cluster module, which makes handling web requests in parallel processes as transparent as possible. Finally, we wrapped up the chapter with a look at using the node-http-proxy module to parallelize our web requests at the machine level.

That does it for JavaScript concurrency topics. We've covered a lot of ground, both in the browser and in Node. But, how do these ideas and components all come together to form a concurrent application? In the final chapter of this book, we'll walk through the implementation of a concurrent app.

10
Building a Concurrent Application

We've now covered all the major areas that JavaScript has to offer in terms of concurrency. We've seen the browser and how the JavaScript interpreter fits into this environment. We've looked at the few language mechanisms that assist with writing concurrent code, and we've learned how to write concurrent JavaScript in the back-end. In this chapter, we're going to try and put this all together by building a simple chat application.

It's worth noting upfront that this isn't a basic rehash of individual topics covered in earlier chapters, which would serve no real purpose. Instead, we're going to focus more on the concurrency decisions that we have to make during the initial implementation of the app, adapting earlier ideas learned in this book wherever appropriate. It's the design of concurrency semantics we put to use in our code that matters much more so than the actual mechanism that's used to do so.

We'll start with a brief foray into the pre-implementation activities. Then, we'll look at the more detailed requirements of the application that we're building. Finally, we'll walk through the actual implementation, which is divided into two parts, the front-end and back-end.

Getting started

Looking at examples with code snippets is a good avenue for introducing a given topic. This is more or less what we've done so far throughout this book while going through concurrency in JavaScript. In the first chapter, we introduced a few concurrency principles. We should parallelize our code to take advantage of concurrent hardware. We should synchronize concurrent actions unobtrusively. We should conserve the CPU and memory by deferring computations and allocations wherever possible. Throughout the chapters, we've seen how these principles apply to different areas of JavaScript concurrency. They're also applicable in the first stages of development when we don't have an application or we're trying to fix an application.

We'll start this section with another look at the idea that concurrency is the default mode. When concurrency is the default, everything is concurrent. We'll go over again, why this is such an important system trait. Then, we'll look at whether or not the same principles apply to applications that already exist. Lastly, we'll look at the types of applications we might be building, and how they influence our approach to concurrency.

Concurrency first

As we're well aware by now, concurrency is difficult. No matter how we dress it up or how solid our abstractions are, it's simply counter-intuitive to how our brains work. This sounds impossible, doesn't it? This definitely isn't the case. As with any difficult problem, the right approach is almost always a variation of divide and conquer. In the case of JavaScript concurrency, we want to divide the problem into no more than a few really small, easy-to-solve problems. An easy way to do this is to heavily scrutinize potential concurrency issues before we actually sit down to write any code.

For example, let's say we work under the assumption that we're likely to encounter concurrency issues frequently, all throughout our code. This would mean that we'd have to spend a lot of time doing upfront concurrency design. Things like generators and promises make sense from the early stages of development, and they get us closer to our end goal. But other ideas, like functional programming, map/reduce, and web workers solve larger concurrency problems. Does this mean that we want to spend a lot of design time on issues like these that we have yet to actually experience in our application?

The other approach is to spend less time on upfront concurrency design. This is not to say that we ignore concurrency; that would defeat the whole premise of this book. Rather, we work under the assumptions that we don't yet have any concurrency issues, but there's a strong possibility that we will have them later on. Put differently, we continue to write code that's concurrent by default, without investing in solutions to concurrency problems that don't exist yet. The principles we've used throughout this book, again, help us solve the important problems first.

For instance, we want to parallelize our code where we can get the most out of multiple CPUs on the system. Thinking about this principle forces the question — do we really care about leveraging eight CPUs for something that's easily handled by one? With little effort, we can build our application in such a way that we don't end up paralyzing ourselves by bikeshedding on concurrency issues that aren't real. Think about how to facilitate concurrency in the early stages in development. Think, how does this implementation make future concurrency issues difficult to deal with, and what's a better approach? Later in the chapter, our demo application will aim to implement code in this fashion.

Retrofitting concurrency

Given that it's ill-advised to spend much time upfront thinking about concurrency issues, how do we go about fixing these issues once they happen? In some circumstances, the issues can be serious problems that render the interface unusable. For example, if we try to process a large amount of data, we could crash the browser tab by trying to allocate too much memory, or the UI could simply freeze. These are tough problems that require immediate attention, and they often don't come with the luxury of time.

The other circumstance that we're likely to find ourselves in is less-critical cases, where a concurrent implementation could objectively improve the user experience, but the application isn't going to fail if we don't fix it right away. For example, let's say that our application makes three API calls on the initial page load. Each call waits for the previous call to complete. But, it turns out that there's no actual dependency between the calls; they don't require response data from each other. Fixing these calls so that they all happen in parallel is relatively low-risk and improves the load time, possibly by more than a second.

The ultimate deciding factor on how easy or difficult these changes are to retrofit into our application depends on how the application was written. As mentioned in the preceding section, we don't want to spend a lot of time thinking about concurrency problems that don't exist. Instead, our initial focus should be on facilitating concurrency by default. So, when these circumstances arise, and we need to implement a concurrent solution that solves a tangible problem, it's not so difficult. We're already thinking concurrently because that's the way the code was written.

We're just as likely to find ourselves fixing an application that paid no mind to concurrency. These are trickier to handle when trying to fix issues that call for a concurrent solution. We'll often find that we need to refactor a lot of code just to fix something basic. This gets tough when we're under-the-gun time-wise, but generally-speaking, this can be a good thing. If a legacy application starts getting refactored for better concurrency facilitation one piece at a time, then we're better off. This just makes the next concurrency issue easier to fix, and it promotes a good style of coding—concurrency by default.

Application types

One thing you can and should pay close attention to during the initial phases of implementation is the type of application that we're building. There's no generic approach to writing code that facilitates concurrency. The reason for this is that every application is concurrent in its own unique way. There's obviously some overlap between concurrency scenarios, but in general, it's a good bet that our application is going to require its own special treatment.

For example, does it make sense to devote a lot of time and effort to designing abstractions around web workers? It wouldn't make sense to think about making API responses promised values if our application hardly makes any web requests at all. Finally, do we really want to think about inter-process communication design in our Node components if we don't have a high request/connectivity rate?

The trick isn't to ignore these lower-priority items, because as soon as we ignore some dimension of concurrency in our application, next week is when everything changes, and we'll be completely unprepared to handle the situation. Instead of completely ignoring these dimensions of our application in a concurrency context, we need to optimize for the common case. The most effective way to do this is to profoundly think about the nature of our application. By doing this, we can easily spot the best candidate problems to work on in our code as far as concurrency is concerned.

Requirements

Now it's time to turn our attention to actually building a concurrent application. In this section, we'll go through a brief overview of the chat application that we're going to build, starting with the overall goal of the application. Then, we'll break down the other requirements into the "API" and the "UI". We'll drive into some code momentarily, don't worry.

The overall goal

First things first, why yet another chat application? Well, for two reasons; first, it's not a real application, and we're not building it for the sake of reinventing the wheel; we're building it to learn about concurrent JavaScript in the context of an application. Second, a chat application has a lot of moving parts that help you demonstrate some of the concurrency mechanisms that you've learned about in this book. That being said, it will be a very simply chat application—we only have so much space in a chapter.

The chat concept that we'll implement is the same as with most other familiar chat applications out there. There's the chat itself, labeled with a topic, and there are the users and messages within. We'll implement these and not much else. Even the UI itself will be a stripped-down version of a typical chat window. Again, this is an effort to keep the code samples down to what's pertinent in a concurrency context.

To further simplify things, we won't actually persist the chats to disk; we'll just hold everything in memory. This way, we can keep our focus on other concurrency issues in the app, and it's easy to run without setting up storage or dealing with disk space. We'll also skip on the other common features of chats, such as typing notifications, emoji, etc. They're just not relevant to what we're trying to learn here. Even with all these functions removed, we'll see how involved concurrency design and implementation can get; larger projects are all the more challenging.

Finally, instead of using authentication, this chat app will serve more of a transient usage scenario, where users want to throw up a quick chat that doesn't require registration. So, the chat creator will create a chat, and this creates a unique URL that can be shared with participants.

The API

The API for our chat app will be implemented using a simple Node HTTP server. It doesn't use any web frameworks, only a couple small libraries. There's no reason for this other than the application is simple enough that using a framework doesn't enhance the examples in this chapter in any way. In the real world, by all means, use a Node web framework that simplifies your code—the lessons from this book—including this chapter—are still applicable.

The responses will be JSON strings of our chat data. Only the most basic API endpoints that are fundamental to the application will be implemented. Here's what we need in terms of API endpoints:

- Create a new chat
- Join an existing chat

- Post a new message to an existing chat
- Fetch an existing chat

Pretty simple, right? It's deceptively simple. Since there are no filtering capabilities, this needs to be handled in the front-end. This is on purpose; an API that's missing features is common, and a concurrent solution in the front-end is the likely outcome. We'll revisit this topic again when we start building the UI.

> The NodeJS code implemented for this sample application also includes handlers for serving static files. This is really a convenience measure more than a reflection on what should be happening in production. It's more important that you be able to easily run this application and play around with it, than replicate how static files are served in a production environment.

The UI

The user interface of our chat application will consist of a single HTML file and some accompanying JavaScript code. There are three pages within the HTML document—just simple `div` elements, and they are as follows:

- **Create chat**: user provides a topic and their name.
- **Join chat**: user provides their name and is redirected to the chat.
- **View chat**: user can view chat messages and send new messages.

The role of these pages is fairly self-explanatory. The most complex page is view chat, and even this isn't too bad. It displays a list of all messages sent from any participant, including ourselves, along with the list of users. We'll have to implement a polling mechanism to keep the content of this page synchronized with chat data. Style-wise, we're not doing much beyond some very basic layout and font adjustments.

Lastly, since users are likely to join chats frequently, they're transient and ad-hoc in nature. After all, it'd be nice if we didn't always have to enter our user name every time we create or join a chat. We'll add functionality that keeps the name of the user in browser local storage.

Alright, time to write some code, ready?

Building the API

We'll begin the implementation with the NodeJS back-end. This is where we'll build the necessary API endpoints. We don't necessarily have to start with building the back-end first. In fact, a lot of the time, the UI design drives the API design. Different development shops have different approaches; we're doing the back-end first for no particular reason.

We'll start by implementing the basic HTTP serving and request routing mechanisms. Then, we'll look at using coroutines as handler functions. We'll wrap up the section with a look at how each of our handler functions are implemented.

The HTTP server and routing

We're not going to use anything more than the core `http` Node module for handling HTTP requests. In a real application, where we're more likely to use a web framework that takes care of a lot of boilerplate code for us, we would probably have a router component at our disposal. Our requirements are very similar to what we'd find in these routers, so we'll just roll our own here for the sake of simplicity.

We'll use the `commander` library for parsing command line options but this is actually not so straightforward to do. The library is tiny and introducing it early on in our project just means it's easier to add new configuration options to our server. Let's look at a diagram that shows how our main program fits into the environment:

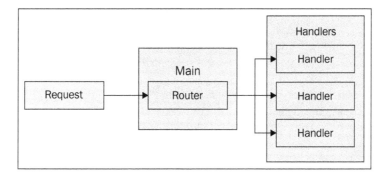

The job of our main module is to launch the HTTP server and set up a handler function that does the routing. The routes themselves are a static mapping of regular expression to handler function. As we can see, the handler functions are stored in a separate module. So let's take a look at our main program now:

```javascript
// The core Node modules we'll need.
var http = require('http');

// Commander is an "npm" package, and is very helpful
// with parsing command line arguments.
var commander = require('commander');

// Our request handler functions that respond to
// requests.
var handlers = require('./handlers');

// The routes array contains route-handler parings. That
// is, when a given route RegExp matches against the
// request URL, the associated handler function is
// called.
var routes = [
    [ /^\/api\/chat\/(.+)\/message/i,
        handlers.sendMessage ],
    [ /^\/api\/chat\/(.+)\/join$/i, handlers.joinChat ],
    [ /^\/api\/chat\/(.+)$/i, handlers.loadChat ],
    [ /^\/api\/chat$/i, handlers.createChat ],
    [ /^\/(.+)\.js$/i, handlers.staticFile ],
    [ /^\/(.*)$/i, handlers.index ]
];

// Adds command line options using the "commander" library,
// and parses them. We're only interested in the "host" and
// the "port" values right now. Both options have default
// values.
commander
    .option('-p, --port <port>',
        'The port to listen on', 8081)
    .option('-H --host <host>',
        'The host to serve from', 'localhost')
    .parse(process.argv);

// Creates an HTTP server. This handler will iterate over
// our "routes" array, and test for a match. If found, the
// handler is called with the request, the response, and
```

```
// the regular expression result.
http.createServer((req, res) => {
    for (let route of routes) {
        let result = route[0].exec(req.url);

        if (result) {
            route[1](req, res, result);
            break;
        }
    }
}).listen(commander.port, commander.host);

console.log(`listening

at http://${commander.host}:${commander.port}`);
```

This is the extent of our handler routing mechanism. We have all our routes defined in the `routes` variable, and as our application changes over time, this is where the route changes happen. We can also see that getting options from the command line using `commander` is pretty straightforward. Adding new options here is easy.

The request handler function that we've given to our HTTP server will probably never need to change, because it doesn't actually fulfill any requests. All it does is iterate over the routes until the route regular expression matches the request URL. When this happens, the request is handed off to the handler function. So, let's turn our attention to the actual handler implementation.

Co-routines as handlers

As we saw in earlier chapters of this book, it doesn't take much to introduce callback hell in our front-end JavaScript code. This is where promises come in handy, because they allow us to encapsulate nasty synchronization semantics. The result is clean and readable code in our components, where we try to implement product features. Do we have the same problem with Node HTTP request handlers?

In simpler handlers, no, we don't face this challenge. All we have to do is look at the request, figure out what to do about it, do it, and then update the response before sending it. In more complex scenarios, we have to do all kinds of asynchronous activities within our request handler before we're able to respond. In other words, callback hell is inevitable if we're not careful. For example, our handler might reach out to other web services for some data, it could issue a database query, or it could write to disk. In all these cases, we need to execute callbacks when the asynchronous action completes; otherwise, we'd never finish our responses.

In *Chapter 9, Advanced NodeJS Concurrency,* we looked at implementing coroutines in Node using the Co library. What if we could do something similar with our request handler functions? That is, make them coroutines instead of plain callable functions. The ultimate goal would be to produce something that looks like the following:

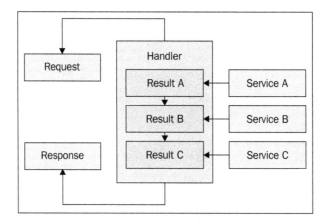

Here, we can see that the values we get from these services behave as simple variables in our code. They don't have to be services; however, they could be any asynchronous action. For example, our chat application needs to parse form data that's posted from the UI. It's going to use the formidable library to do this, which is an asynchronous action. The parsed form fields are passed to a callback function. Let's wrap this action in a promise, and see what it looks like:

```
// This function returns a promise, which is resolved
// with parsed form data as an object.
function formFields(req) {
    return new Promise((resolve, reject) => {

        // Use the "IncomingForm" class from the
        // "formidable" lib to parse the data. This
        // "parse()" method is async, so we resolve or
        // reject the promise in the callback.
        new formidable.IncomingForm()
            .parse(req, (err, fields) => {
                if (err) {
                    reject(err);
                } else {
                    resolve(fields);
                }
            });
    });
}
```

When we want form fields, we have a promise to work with, which is good. But now, we need to use the function in the context of a coroutine. Let's walk through each of our request handlers, and see how to use the `formFields()` function to treat the promised value as a synchronous value.

The create chat handler

The create chat handler is responsible for creating a new chat. It expects a topic and a user. It's going to use the `formFields()` function to parse the form data that's posted to this handler. After it stores the new chat in the global `chat` object (remember, this application stores everything in memory), the handler responds with the chat data as a JSON string. Let's take a look at the handler code:

```
// The "create chat" API. This endpoint
// creates a new chat object and stores it in memory.
exports.createChat = co.wrap(function* (req, res) {
    if (!ensureMethod(req, res, 'POST')) {
        return;
    }

    // Yield the promise returned by "formFields()".
    // This pauses the execution of this handler because
    // it's a co-routine, created using "co.wrap()".
    var fields = yield formFields(req);

    // The ID for the new chat.
    var chatId = id();

    // The timestamp used for both the chat, and the
    // added user.
    var timestamp = new Date().getTime();

    // Creates the new chat object and stores it. The
    // "users" array is populated with the user that
    // created the chat. The "messages" array is empty
    // by default.
    var chat = chats[chatId] = {
        timestamp: timestamp,
        topic: fields.topic,
        users: [{
            timestamp: timestamp,
            name: fields.user
        }],
```

```
        messages: []
    };

    // The response is the JSON encoded version of the
    // chat object. The chat ID is added to the response
    // since it's stored as a key, not a chat property.
    res.setHeader('Content-Type', 'application/json');
    res.end(JSON.stringify(Object.assign({
        id: chatId
    }, chat)));
});
```

We can see that the `createChat()` function is exported from this module, because it's used by our router in the main application module. We can also see that the handler function is a generator, and it's wrapped with `co.wrap()`. This is because we want it to be a coroutine instead of a regular function. The call to `formFields()` illustrates the ideas that we covered in the previous section. Notice that we yield the promise, and we get the resolved value in return. The function blocks while this is happening, and this is of key importance because it's how we're able to keep our code clean and free of excessive callbacks.

> There are a few utility functions used by each of our handlers. These functions aren't covered here in the interest of page space. However, they're in the code that ships with this book, and they're documented in the comments.

The join chat handler

The join chat chandler is how a user is able to join a chat created by another user. The user first needs the URL of the chat shared with them. Then, they can provide their name and post to this endpoint, which has the chat ID encoded as part of the URL. The job of this handler is to push the new user onto the users array of the chat. Let's take a look at handler code now:

```
// This endpoint allows a user to join an existing
// chat that's been shared with them (a URL).
exports.joinChat = co.wrap(function* (req, res, id) {
    if (!ensureMethod(req, res, 'POST')) {
        return;
    }

    // Load the chat from the memory - the "chats"
```

```
    // object.
    var chat = chats[id[1]];

    if (!ensureFound(req, res, chat)) {
        return;
    }

    // Yield to get the parsed form fields. This
    // function is a co-routine created using "co.wrap()".
    var fields = yield formFields(req);

    chat.timestamp = new Date().getTime();

    // Adds the new user to the chat.
    chat.users.push({
        timestamp: chat.timestamp,
        name: fields.user
    });

    // Responds with the JSON encoded chat string. We
    // need to add the ID separately as it's not a
    // chat property.
    res.setHeader('Content-Type', 'application/json');
    res.end(JSON.stringify(Object.assign({
        id: id[1],
    }, chat)));
});
```

We can probably notice many similarities between this handler and the create chat handler. We check for the correct HTTP method, return a JSON response, and wrap the handler function as a coroutine so that we can parse the form in a way that completely avoids callback functions. The main difference is that we update an existing chat, instead of creating a new one.

> The code where we push the new user object to the users array would be considered storing the chat. In a real application, this would mean writing the data to disk somehow — likely a call to a database library. This would mean making an asynchronous request. Luckily, we can follow the same technique used with our form parsing — have it return a promise and leverage the coroutine that's already in place.

The load chat handler

The job of the load chat handler is exactly what it sounds like—load the given chat using an ID found in the URL and respond with the JSON string of this chat. Here's the code to do this:

```
// This endpoint loads a chat. This function
// isn't wrapped as a co-routine because there's
// no asynchronous actions to wait for.
exports.loadChat = function(req, res, id) {

    // Lookup the chat, using the "id" from the URL
    // as the key.
    var chat = chats[id[1]];

    if (!ensureFound(req, res, chat)) {
        return;
    }

    // Respond with the JSON encoded string version
    // of the chat.
    res.setHeader('Content-Type', 'application/json');
    res.end(JSON.stringify(chat));
};
```

There's no `co.wrap()` call for this function, nor a generator. This is because it's not needed. It's not that it's harmful to have this function be a generator that's wrapped as a coroutine, it's just wasteful.

 This is actually an example of us, the developers, making a conscious decision to avoid concurrency where it isn't justified. This might change down the road with this handler, and if it does, we'll have work to do. However, the trade-off is the fact that we now have less code, and it runs faster. It's beneficial to others who read it as it doesn't look like an asynchronous function, and it shouldn't be treated as such.

The send message handler.

The last major API endpoint that we need to implement is send message. This is how any user in a given chat is able to post a message that's available for all other chat participants to consume. This is similar to the join chat handler, except we're pushing a new message object onto the messages array. Let's take a look at the handler code; this pattern should start to look familiar by now:

```
// This handler posts a new message to a given chat. It's
// also a co-routine function since it needs to wait for
// asynchronous actions to complete.
exports.sendMessage = co.wrap(function* (req, res, id) {
    if (!ensureMethod(req, res, 'POST')) {
        return;
    }

    // Load the chat and ensures that it's found.
    var chat = chats[id[1]];

    if (!ensureFound(req, res, chat)) {
        return;
    }

    // Get's the parsed form fields by yielding the
    // promise returned from "formFields()".
    var fields = yield formFields(req);

    chat.timestamp = new Date().getTime();

    // Pushes the new message object to the "messages"
    // property.
    chat.messages.push({
        timestamp: chat.timestamp,
        user: fields.user,
        message: fields.message
    });

    res.setHeader('Content-Type', 'application/json');
    res.end(JSON.stringify(chat));
});
```

The same idea applies when joining a chat. Modifying the chat object is likely an asynchronous action in a real application, and now, our coroutine handler pattern is all set up for us to make this change when the time is right. That's the key with these coroutine handlers, making it easy to add new asynchronous actions to handlers instead of overwhelmingly difficult.

Static handlers

The last group of handlers that make up our chat application are the static content handlers. These have the job of serving static files from the file system to the browser, such as the index.html document and our JavaScript source. Typically, this is handled outside of the node application, but we'll include them here because there are times where it's just easier to go batteries included:

```javascript
// Helper function used to serve static files.
function serveFile(req, res, file) {

    // Creates a stream to read the file.
    var stream = fs.createReadStream(file);

    // End the response when there's no more input.
    stream.on('end', () => {
        res.end();
    });

    // Pipe the input file to the HTTP response,
    // which is a writable stream.
    stream.pipe(res);
}

// Serves the requested path as a static file.
exports.staticFile = function(req, res) {
    serveFile(req, res,
        path.join(__dirname, req.url));
};

// By default, we want to serve the "index.html" file.
exports.index = function index(req, res) {
    res.setHeader('ContentType', 'text/html');

    serveFile(req, res,
        path.join(__dirname, 'index.html'));
};
```

Building the UI

We now have an API to target; it's time to start building the user interface for our chat. We'll start by thinking about talking to the API that we've just built, then implementing that piece. Next, we'll build the actual HTML we need to render the three pages used by this application. From here, we'll move onto perhaps the most challenging part of the front end – building the DOM event handlers and manipulators. Finally, we'll see if we can enhance the responsiveness of the application by throwing a web worker into the mix.

Talking to the API

The API communication paths in our UI are inherently concurrent – they send and receive data over a network connection. Therefore, it's in the best interest of our application architecture that we take time to hide the synchronization mechanisms from the rest of the system as best as we can. To communicate with our API, we'll use instances of the XMLHttpRequest class. However, as we've seen in earlier chapters of this book, this class can lead us toward callback hell.

The solution, as we know, is to use a promise to support a consistent interface to all our API data. This doesn't mean we need to abstract the XMLHttpRequest class over and over again. We create a simple utility function that handles the concurrency encapsulation for us, and then we create several smaller functions that are specific to a corresponding API endpoint. Here's a diagram that illustrates the idea:

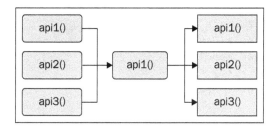

This approach to talking with asynchronous API endpoints scales well, because adding new capabilities involves simply adding a small function. All the synchronization semantics are encapsulated within one api() function. Let's take a look at the code now:

```
// A generic function used to send HTTP requests to the
// API. The "method" is the HTTP method, the "path" is
// the request path, and the "data" is the optional
// request payload.
```

```
function api(method, path, data) {

    // Returns a promise to the called, resolved with
    // the API response, or failure.
    return new Promise((resolve, reject) => {
        var request = new XMLHttpRequest();

        // Resolves the promise using the parsed JSON
        // object - usually a chat.
        request.addEventListener('load', (e) => {
            resolve(JSON.parse(e.target.responseText));
        });

        // Rejects the promise when there's a problem with
        // the API.
        request.addEventListener('error', (e) => {
            reject(e.target.statusText || 'unknown error');
        });

        request.addEventListener('abort', resolve);

        request.open(method, path);

        // If there's no "data", we can simply "send()"
        // the request. Otherwise, we have to create a
        // new "FormData" instance to properly encode
        // the form data for the request.
        if (Object.is(data, undefined)) {
            request.send();
        } else {
            var form = new FormData();

            Object.keys(data).forEach((key) => {
                form.append(key, data[key]);
            });

            request.send(form);
        }
    });
}
```

This function is pretty easy to use and supports all our API usage scenarios. The smaller API functions that we'll implement shortly can simply return the promise that's returned by this `api()` function. There's no need to do anything fancier than this.

However, there is another thing we'll want to consider here. If we recall from the requirements of this application, the API doesn't have any filtering capabilities. This is a problem for the UI because we're not going to re-render the entire chat object. Messages can be posted frequently, and if we re-render a lot of messages, there's a good chance that the screen will flicker as we render the DOM elements. So, we obviously need to filter the chat messages and users in the browser; but where should this happen?

Let's think about this in the context of concurrency. Say we decide to perform the filtering in a component that directly manipulates the DOM. This is good in a sense because it means that we can have several independent components using the same data yet filtering it differently. It's also difficult to make any kind of adjustments for concurrency when the data transformations are this close to the DOM. For example, our application doesn't need flexibility. There's only one component that renders filtered data. But, it might benefit from concurrency. The following diagram illustrates another approach, where the API functionality that we implement performs the filtering:

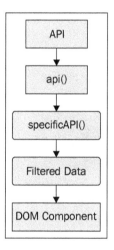

With this approach, the API functions are isolated enough from the DOM. We can introduce concurrency later on if we want. Let's look at some specific API functions now in addition to a filtering mechanism we can attach to the given API calls as needed:

```
// Filters the "chat" object to include only new users
// and new messages. That is, data with a newer
// "timestamp" than when we last checked.
```

```
function filterChat(chat) {
    Object.assign(chat, {

        // Assigns the filtered arrays to the
        // corresponding "chat" properties.
        users: chat.users.filter(
            user => user.timestamp > timestamp
        ),
        messages: chat.messages.filter(
            message => message.timestamp > timestamp
        )
    });

    // Reset the "timestamp" so we can look for newer
    // data next time around. We return the modified
    // chat instance.
    timestamp = chat.timestamp;
    return chat;
}


// Creates a chat using the given "topic" and "user".
// The returned promise is resolved with the created
// chat data.
function createChat(topic, user) {
    return api('post', 'api/chat', {
        topic: topic,
        user: user
    });
}


// Joins the given "user" to the given chat "id".
// The returned promise is resolved with the
// joined chat data.
function joinChat(id, user) {
    return api('post', `api/chat/${id}/join`, {
        user: user
    }).then(filterChat);
}


// Loads the given chat "id". The returned promise
// is resolved with filtered chat data.
function loadChat(id) {
    return api('get', `api/chat/${id}`)
        .then(filterChat);
};


// Posts a "message" from the given "user" to the given
```

```
// chat "id". The returned promise is resolved with
// filtered chat data.
function sendMessage(id, user, message) {
    return api('post', `api/chat/${id}/message`, {
        user: user,
        message: message
    }).then(filterChat);
}
```

The `filterChat()` function is straightforward enough. It just modifies the given `chat` object to include only new users and messages. New messages are those that have a timestamp greater than the `timestamp` variable used here. After the filtering is done, `timestamp` is updated based on the chat's `timestamp` property. This could be the same value if nothing has changed, but if something has changed, this value is updated so that duplicate values aren't returned.

We can see that in our specific API functions, the `filterChat()` function is passed to the promise as a resolver. So we do retain a level of flexibility here. For example, if a different component needs to filter the chat differently, we can introduce a new function that uses the same approach, and add a different promise resolver function that filters accordingly.

Implementing the HTML

Our UI needs some HTML in order to render. The chat application is simple enough to get away with just a single HTML page. We can organize the DOM structure into three `div` elements, each of which represents our page. The elements on each page are simple in themselves, because there aren't many moving parts at this stage in development. Our first priority is functionality—building features that work. At the same time, we should be thinking about concurrency design. These items are definitely more pertinent to building a resilient architecture than thinking about, say, widgets and virtual DOM rendering libraries. These are important considerations, but they're also easier to work around than a faulty concurrency design.

Let's take a look at the HTML source used with our UI. There are a few CSS styles defined for these elements. However, they're trivial and aren't covered here. For example, the hide class is used to toggle the visibility of a given page. By default, everything is hidden. It's up to our event handlers to handle the display of these elements—we'll cover these next:

```
<div id="create" class="hide">
    <h1>Create Chat</h1>
    <p>
        <label for="topic">Topic:</label>
```

```
        <input name="topic" id="topic" autofocus/>
    </p>
    <p>
        <label for="create-user">Your Name:</label>
        <input name="create-user" id="create-user"/>
    </p>
    <button>Create</button>
</div>
<div id="join" class="hide">
    <h1>Join Chat</h1>
    <p>
        <label for="join-user">Your Name:</label>
        <input name="join-user" id="join-user" autofocus/>
    </p>
    <button>Join</button>
</div>
<div id="view" class="hide">
    <h1></h1>
    <div>
        <div>
            <ul id="messages"></ul>
            <input placeholder="message" autofocus/>
        </div>
        <ul id="users"></ul>
    </div>
</div>
```

DOM events and manipulation

We now have some API communication mechanisms and DOM elements in place. Let's turn our attention to the event handlers of our application, and how they interact with the DOM. The most involved DOM manipulation activity for us to tackle is drawing the chat. That is, displaying messages and users participating in the chat. Let's start here. We'll implement a drawChat() function because it's likely going to be used in more than one place:

```
// Updates the given "chat" in the DOM.
function drawChat(chat) {

    // Our main DOM components. "$users" is the
    // list of users in the chat. "$messages" is the
    // list of messages in the chat. "$view" is the
    // container element for both lists.
```

```
var $users = document.getElementById('users'),
$messages = document.getElementById('messages'),
$view = document.getElementById('view');

// Update the document title to reflect the chat
// "topic", display the chat container by removing
// the "hide" class, and update the title of the
// chat in bold heading.
document.querySelector('title')
    .textContent = chat.topic;
$view.classList.remove('hide');
$view.querySelector('h1')
    .textContent = chat.topic;

// Iterates over the messages, making no assumptions
// about filtering or anything like that.
for (var message of chat.messages) {

    // Constructs the DOM elements we'll need for
    // the user portion of the message.
    var $user = document.createElement('li'),
        $strong = document.createElement('strong'),
        $em = document.createElement('em');

    // Assemble the DOM structure...
    $user.appendChild($strong);
    $user.appendChild($em);
    $user.classList.add('user');

    // Add content - the user name, and time the message
    // was posted.
    $strong.textContent = message.user + ' ';
    $em.textContent = new Date(message.timestamp)
        .toLocaleString();

    // The message itself...
    var $message = document.createElement('li');
    $message.textContent = message.message;

    // Attach the user portion and the message portion,
    // to the DOM.
    $messages.appendChild($user);
```

```
        $messages.appendChild($message);
    }


    // Iterates over the users in the chat, making no
    // assumptions about the data, only displaying it.
    for (var user of chat.users) {
        var $user = document.createElement('li');
        $user.textContent = user.name;

        $users.appendChild($user);
    }


    // Make sure that the user can see the newly-rendered
    // content.
    $messages.scrollTop = $messages.scrollHeight;


    // Return the chat so that this function can be used
    // as a resolver in a promise resolution chain.
    return chat;
}
```

There are two important things to note about the drawChat() function. First, there's no chat filtering done here. It assumes that any message and user are new, and it simply appends them to the DOM. Second, we actually return the chat object after we've rendered the DOM. This may seem unnecessary at first, but we're actually going to use this function as a promise resolver. This means that if we want to add more resolvers to the then() chain, we have to pass the data along by returning it.

Let's take a look at the load event to highlight the previous point. After the chat has been rendered, we need to perform some more work. To do this, we can just chain the next function with another then() call:

```
// When the page loads...
window.addEventListener('load', (e) => {

    // The "chatId" comes from the page URL. The "user"
    // might already exist in localStorage.
    var chatId = location.pathname.slice(1),
        user = localStorage.getItem('user'),
        $create = document.getElementById('create'),
        $join = document.getElementById('join');

    // If there's no chat ID in the URL, then we display
    // the create chat screen, populating the user
    // input if it was found in localStorage.
```

```
    if (!chatId) {
        $create.classList.remove('hide');

        if (user) {
            document.getElementById('create-user')
                .value = user;
        }

        return;
    }

    // If there's no user name found in localStorage,
    // we display the join screen which allows them
    // to enter their name before joining the chat.
    if (!user) {
        $join.classList.remove('hide');
        return;
    }

    // We load the chat, draw it using drawChat(), and
    // start the chat polling process.
    api.postMessage({
        action: 'loadChat',
        chatId: chatId
    }).then(drawChat).then((chat) => {

        // If the user isn't part of the chat already,
        // we join it. This happens when the user name
        // is cached in localStorage. If the user creates
        // a chat, then loads it, they'll already belong
        // to the chat.
        if (chat.users.map(u => u.name).indexOf(user) < 0) {
            api.postMessage({
                action: 'joinChat',
                chatId: chatId,
                user: user
            }).then(drawChat).then(() => {
                poll(chatId);
            });
        } else {
            poll(chatId);
        }
    });
});
```

This handler is called when the page first loads, and it first needs to check if there's a chat to load based on the current URL. If there is, then we make an API call to load the chat using `drawChat()` as the resolver. But, we also need to perform some additional functionality, and this is added to the next `then()` resolver in the chain. It's job is to make sure the user is actually part of the chat, and for this, it needs the chat we just loaded from the API, which is passed along from `drawChat()`. After we make further API calls to add the user to the chat, if necessary, we start the polling mechanism. This is how we keep the UI up-to-date with new messages and new users joining the chat:

```
// Starts polling the API for the given chat "id".
function poll(chatId) {
    setInterval(() => {
        api.postMessage({
            action: 'loadChat',
            chatId: chatId
        }).then(drawChat);
    }, 3000);
}
```

You may have noticed that we're using strange call almost like a web worker — `api.postMessage()`. This is because it is a web worker, and this is what we'll cover next.

 In the interest of space, we're leaving out three other DOM event handlers related to creating chats, joining chats, and sending messages. There's nothing different about them in terms of concurrency compared to the load handler that we just covered.

Adding an API worker

Earlier, when we were implementing the API communication functions, we decided that having filtering components coupled with the API rather than the DOM made more sense from a concurrency perspective. It's now time to benefit from this decision and encapsulate our API code within a web worker. The main reason we want to do this is because the `filterChat()` function has the potential to lock up responsiveness. In other words, for larger chats, this would take longer to complete, and text inputs would stop responding to user input. For instance, there's no reason to prevent a user from sending a message while we try to render the updated list of messages.

First, we need to extend the worker API to have `postMessage()` return a promise. This is just as we did in *Chapter 7, Abstracting Concurrency*. Take a look at the following code:

```
// This will generate unique IDs. We need them to
// map tasks executed by web workers to the larger
// operation that created them.
function* genID() {
    var id = 0;

    while (true) {
        yield id++;
    }
}

// Creates the global "id" generator.
var id = genID();

// This object holds the resolver functions from promises,
// as results come back from workers, we look them up here,
// based on ID.
var resolvers = {};

var rejectors = {};

// Keep the original implementation of "postMessage()"
// so we can call it later on, in our custom "postMessage()"
// implementation.
var postMessage = Worker.prototype.postMessage;

// Replace "postMessage()" with our custom implementation.
Worker.prototype.postMessage = function(data) {
    return new Promise((resolve, reject) => {

        // The ID that's used to tie together a web worker
        // response, and a resolver function.
        var msgId = id.next().value;

        // Stores the resolver so in can be used later, in
        // the web worker message callback.
        resolvers[msgId] = resolve;

        rejectors[msgId] = reject;

        // Run the original "Worker.postMessage()"
        // implementation, which takes care of
        // actually posting the message to the
```

```
            // worker thread.
            postMessage.call(this, Object.assign({
                msgId: msgId,
            }, data));
        });
    };


    // Starts our worker...
    var api = new Worker('ui-api.js');


    // Resolves the promise that was returned by
    // "postMessage()" when the worker responds.
    api.addEventListener('message', (e) => {

        // If the data is in an error state, then
        // we want the rejector function, and we call
        // that with the error. Otherwise, call the
        // regular resolver function with the data returned
        // from the worker.
        var source = e.data.error ? rejectors : resolvers,
            callback = source[e.data.msgId],
            data = e.data.error ? e.data.error : e.data;


        callback(data);


        // Don't need'em, delete'em.
        delete resolvers[e.data.msgId];
        delete rejectors[e.data.msgId];
    });
```

There's one minor detail that we didn't cover in *Chapter 7, Abstracting Concurrency*, with this technique of rejecting promises. For example, if the API call for some reason fails, we have to make sure that the promise in the main thread that's waiting on the worker is rejected; otherwise, strange bugs will start popping up.

Now, we need to make an addition to our ui-api.js module, where all our API functions are defined to accommodate for the fact that it's running inside a web worker. We just need to add the following event handler:

```
    // Listens for messages coming from the main thread.
    addEventListener('message', (e) => {

        // The generic promise resolver function. It's
        // job is to post data back to the main thread
        // using "postMessage()". It also returns the
        // data so that it may be used further down in
```

```
// the promise resolution chain.
function resolve(data) {
    postMessage(Object.assign({
        msgId: e.data.msgId
    }, data));

    return data;
}


// The generic rejector function posts data back
// to the main thread. The difference here is that
// it marks the data as an error. This allows the
// promise on the other end to be rejected.
function reject(error) {
    postMessage({
        msgId: e.data.msgId,
        error: error.toString()
    });

    return error;
}


// This switch decides which function to call based
// on the "action" message property. The "resolve()"
// function is passed as the resolver to each returned
// promise.
switch (e.data.action) {
    case 'createChat':
        createChat(e.data.topic, e.data.user)
            .then(resolve, reject);
        break;
    case 'joinChat':
        joinChat(e.data.chatId, e.data.user)
            .then(resolve, reject);
        break;
    case 'loadChat':
        loadChat(e.data.chatId)
            .then(resolve, reject)
        break;
    case 'sendMessage':
        sendMessage(
            e.data.chatId,
            e.data.user,
```

```
                    e.data.message
          ).then(resolve, reject);
          break;
    }

});
```

This `message` event handler is how we're able to communicate with the main thread. The `action` property is how we're able to determine which API endpoint to call. So now, whenever we perform any expensive filtering on our chat messages, it's in a separate thread.

Another consequence of introducing this worker is that it encapsulates the API functionality into a cohesive whole. The API web worker component can now be thought of as a smaller application within the larger UI as a whole.

Additions and improvements

And that's the extent of coverage we'll have on the development of our chat application. We didn't walk through every bit of code, but this is why the code is made available as a companion to this book to look through it in it's entirety. The focus of the preceding sections has been through the lens of writing concurrent JavaScript code. We didn't utilize every last example from the chapters before this one, which would defeat the whole purpose of concurrency to fix issues that lead to a suboptimal user experience.

The focus of the chat application example was the facilitation of concurrency. This means making it possible to implement concurrent code when there's a need to do so as opposed to the implementing concurrent code for the sake of it. The latter doesn't make our application any better than it is right now, nor does it leave us in a better position to fix concurrency issues that happen later on.

We'll wrap up the chapter with a few areas that might be worth considering for our chat application. You, the reader, are encouraged to work with the chat application code and see if any of these points that follow are applicable. How would you go about supporting them? Do we need to alter our design? The point is that concurrency design in our JavaScript applications isn't a one-time occurrence, it's an ever evolving design task that changes alongside our application.

Clustering the API

In *Chapter 9, Advanced NodeJS Concurrency*, you were introduced to the cluster module in NodeJS. This transparently scales the request handling ability of our HTTP servers. This module works by forking the node process into several child processes. Since they're each they're own process, they have their own even loop. Furthermore, there's no additional communication synchronization code required.

It wouldn't take much effort on our behalf to add in these clustering capabilities to our `app.js` module. But here's the question—at what point do we decide that clustering is worthwhile? Do we wait until we actually have performance issues, or we just have it turned on automatically? These are the things that are difficult to know in advance. The reality is that it depends on how CPU-intensive our request handlers get. And these changes usually come about as a result of new features being added to the software.

Will our chat app ever need clustering? Perhaps, someday. But there's really no work being performed by the handlers. This can always change. Maybe we could go ahead and implement the clustering capabilities, but also add an option that let's us turn it off.

Cleaning up chats

Our chat application doesn't have any persistent storage; it holds all the chat data in memory. This is fine for our particular use case, because it's meant for users that want to spin up a transient chat so that they can share a link with people and not have to go through a registration process. The problem here is that long after the chat is no longer being used, its data still occupies memory. Eventually, this will be fatal to our Node process.

What if we decided to implement a cleanup service, whose job would be to periodically iterate over the chat data and chats that hadn't been modified in a given amount of time would be deleted? This would keep only active chats in memory.

Asynchronous entry points

We made the early decision to use coroutines for most of our request handlers. The only asynchronous action used by these handlers is the form parsing behavior. However, the likelihood of this remaining the only asynchronous action in any given handler is small. Especially as our application grows, we're going to start depending on more core NodeJS functionality, which means we're going to want to wrap in promises more asynchronous callback-style code. We'll probably start depending on external services too either our own or third-party software.

Can we take our asynchronous architecture a step further and provide entry points into these handlers for those that wish to extend the system? For example, if the request is a create chat request, send requests to any before create chat extensions that have been provided. Something like this is quite the undertaking and is error prone. But for larger systems that have many moving parts, all of them being asynchronous, it's best to look at standardizing on asynchronous entry points into the system.

Who's typing?

Something we left out of our chat application is the typing state for a given user. This is the mechanism that informs all other members of the chat that a particular user is typing a message and is present on just about every modern chat system.

What would it take for us to implement such a feature, given our current design? Is the polling mechanism enough to deal with such a constantly-changing state? Would the data model have to change much, and would such a change bring about problems with our request handlers?

Leaving chats

Another feature missing from our chat application is removing users that are no longer participating in the chat. For example, does it really make sense for other chat participants to see users in the chat that aren't really there? Would listening to a unload event and implementing a new leave chat API endpoint suffice, or is there a lot more to it than this?

Polling timeouts

The chat application that we've just built does little to no error handling. One case in particular that's worth fixing is killing the polling mechanism when it times out. By this, we're talking about preventing the client from repeating failed request attempts. Let's say the server is down, or the handler is simply failing because of a bug introduced; do we want the poller to just spin indefinitely? We don't want it to do this, and there's probably something that can be done about it.

For example, we would need to cancel the interval that's set up when the polling starts with the call to `setInterval()`. Likewise, we would need a means to track the number of successive failed attempts, so we would know when to shut it off.

Summary

Hopefully, this walk-through of a silly chat application has given you a new appreciation of what's involved with designing concurrent JavaScript applications end-to-end. This book started off with a high-level overview of what concurrency is, especially in the context of a JavaScript application, because it is different from other programming language environments. Then, we introduced some guiding principles to help us along the way.

The chapters where we took a disciplined look at the various language and environment concurrency mechanisms are really just a means to an end. The ultimate end game for us—the JavaScript programmers and architects—is an application that's free of concurrency issues. This is a broad statement, but at the end of the day, many issues that we face in our web applications are a direct result of inadequate concurrency design.

So use these principles. Use the awesome concurrency features available in JavaScript. Combine these two things to make great applications that exceed the expectations of our users. When we write code that's concurrent by default, many JavaScript programming challenges simply vanish.

Index

A

API
  building 235
API communication 245-249
API worker
  adding 254-258
applications
  deploying, to Internet 181
application state
  sharing 104
application types 232
array
  iterating over 65
  using 64
asynchronous browsers 4
asynchronous JavaScript 3

B

bottom-halves 141

C

C10K problem
  about 182, 183
  reference link 182
callback chains
  building 48
call stacks 63
communicating, with workers
  about 100
  message serialization 101, 102
  messages, posting 101

messages, receiving from workers 103
concurrency
  about 1, 230
  retrofitting 231
concurrency challenges, execution model
  about 30
  limited opportunity for parallelism 31
  synchronization through callbacks 31
concurrency mechanism
  downsides 114
  hiding 148
concurrency principles, JavaScript
  about 8
  conserve 11-13
  parallelize 9
  synchronize 10
concurrent actions, JavaScript code
  about 5
  asynchronous actions 5, 6
  parallel actions 6-8
concurrent application, requisites
  about 232
  API 233
  overall goal 233
  UI 234
concurrent code
  writing 147
concurrent programming 3, 147
conserve principle, JavaScript
  about 11, 12
  checklist 13
coroutine functions
  creating 86-88

co-routines
about 85
DOM events, handling 88
functions, creating 86-88
promised values, handling 90, 91
using, as handlers 237-239
create chat handler 239, 240

D

data
passing, to generators 79
debouncing 24
dedicated workers 96, 97
Document Object Model (DOM) 2
DOM events
about 250-254
handling 88
responding to 24
translating 143-145
DOM manipulation
about 250-254
translating 141-143
DOM responsive, for users
bottom halves 141

E

empty promises 39, 40
error callbacks 43, 44
error handling, in web workers
about 115
error condition checking 115, 116
exception handling 116, 117
evented file IO 193
evented network IO
about 184
HTTP requests, handling 185, 186
HTTP response, streaming 186-188
event frequency
managing 26, 27
event loop 16-18
EventTarget interface 24-26
execution contexts 19
execution environment 16, 17

execution state
maintaining 20
executor 34

F

file reads
streaming 198, 199
files
reading from 193-195
writing to 196, 197
file writes
streaming 198, 199
first in first out (FIFO) 141
function contexts
bookmarking 64

G

generators
about 1, 63
creating 66
data, passing to 79
function syntax 66
interweaving 76
iterating over 68, 69
lightweight map/reduce,
performing 81-84
reusing 79-81
values, yielding 66-68

H

handlers
co-routines, using as 237-239
HTTP requests
handling 185, 186
HTTP response
streaming 186-188
HTTP server 235-237

I

immutable promises 50, 51
improvements
about 258

API, clustering 259
asynchronous entry points 259
chats, cleaning up 259
chats, leaving 260
timeouts, polling 260
typing state 260
infinite sequences
about 69
alternating 70-72
items, allocating 69, 70
informed load balancing 224-227
Internet
applications, deploying to 181
IO events 179
IO loop 177

J

JavaScript
about 1
concurrency principles 8
JavaScript application
writing, without concurrency 149-151
JavaScript code
concurrent actions 5
JavaScript interpreter 16
job queues 20, 21
join chat handler 240, 241

L

lazy evaluation 63
lazy worker chains 163-166
lazy workers
about 159
overhead, reducing 159, 160
lightweight event handlers 183, 184
load chat handler 242

M

memory allocation 63
mesh of generators
creating 72
messages
receiving, from workers 103

multiple connections
challenges 181
multi-threading
challenges 180
multi-threading environments 3

N

node-http-proxy
reference link 222

P

parallelize principle, JavaScript
about 9
checklist 9
Parallel.js
mapping 169-171
reducing 169-171
using 166
workers, spawning 168, 169
working 166, 167
parallel slowdown 170
pools
allocating, of worker threads 172-174
promise
about 33
cancelling 57-59
passing, around 53-55
reacting to 41, 45, 46
rejecting 35-39
resolving 35-47
state, changing 48-50
waiting on 56
without executors 59-62
Promise API 10, 11
promise chain example 52
promised data
using 42, 43
promised values
handling 90, 91
Promise.resolve() method 47
promise, states
fulfilled 34
pending 34
rejected 34

promise terminology
  about 33
  executor 34
  promise 33
  rejector 34
  resolver 34
  state 34
  thenable 34
proxy network requests 189-192

R

rejector 34
request routing mechanisms 235-237
resolution job queues 41
resolver 34
responding, to network events
  about 28
  requests, coordinating 29, 30
  requests, making 28, 29
run-to-completion (RTC) 2

S

send message handler 242, 243
sequences
  about 64, 65
  infinite sequences 69
  iterating over 66
server clusters
  informed load balancing 224-227
  micro-services, facilitating 222, 223
setInterval() function
  using 23
setTimeout() function
  using 22
several promises
  synchronizing 56
shared workers 98, 99
single threaded IO
  about 177
  IO events 179
  slow IO 178, 179
static handlers 244

strategy
  selecting 73-75
sub-tasks
  performing, with sub-workers 110
sub-workers
  about 114
  sub-tasks, performing with 110
synchronize principle, JavaScript
  about 10
  checklist 11
synchronous JavaScript
  about 2
  easy to understand 2, 3

T

task queues 18, 19
tasks
  creating, timers used 21
  work, dividing into 110-114
thenable 34
thread 3
timers
  used, for creating tasks 21

U

UI
  building 245
  HTML, implementing 249

V

values
  generating, in workers 160-162
  yielding, to generator 66-68

W

web worker execution environments
  reference link 99
web workers
  about 1
  communicating, between pages 108, 109
  memory, sharing 104-106
  resources, fetching 106, 107

work
  dividing, into tasks 110-114
worker communication, with promises
  about 151
  helper functions 151-154
  postMessage(), extending 154-157
  worker results, synchronizing 157, 158
worker environments
  about 99
  scripts, loading 100
worker pools
  about 172
  jobs, scheduling 174-176

workers
  about 93
  event targets 94, 95
  messages, receiving from 103
  OS threads 94
  true parallelism 95
  values, generating in 160-162
workers, types
  about 96
  dedicated workers 96, 97
  shared workers 98, 99
  sub workers 97
worker threads
  pools, allocating of 172-174
World Wide Web Consortium (W3C) 16

X

XMLHttpRequest (XHR) 2

Thank you for buying
JavaScript Concurrency

About Packt Publishing

Packt, pronounced 'packed', published its first book, *Mastering phpMyAdmin for Effective MySQL Management*, in April 2004, and subsequently continued to specialize in publishing highly focused books on specific technologies and solutions.

Our books and publications share the experiences of your fellow IT professionals in adapting and customizing today's systems, applications, and frameworks. Our solution-based books give you the knowledge and power to customize the software and technologies you're using to get the job done. Packt books are more specific and less general than the IT books you have seen in the past. Our unique business model allows us to bring you more focused information, giving you more of what you need to know, and less of what you don't.

Packt is a modern yet unique publishing company that focuses on producing quality, cutting-edge books for communities of developers, administrators, and newbies alike. For more information, please visit our website at www.packtpub.com.

About Packt Open Source

In 2010, Packt launched two new brands, Packt Open Source and Packt Enterprise, in order to continue its focus on specialization. This book is part of the Packt Open Source brand, home to books published on software built around open source licenses, and offering information to anybody from advanced developers to budding web designers. The Open Source brand also runs Packt's Open Source Royalty Scheme, by which Packt gives a royalty to each open source project about whose software a book is sold.

Writing for Packt

We welcome all inquiries from people who are interested in authoring. Book proposals should be sent to author@packtpub.com. If your book idea is still at an early stage and you would like to discuss it first before writing a formal book proposal, then please contact us; one of our commissioning editors will get in touch with you.

We're not just looking for published authors; if you have strong technical skills but no writing experience, our experienced editors can help you develop a writing career, or simply get some additional reward for your expertise.

JavaScript at Scale

JavaScript at Scale

Build enduring JavaScript applications with scaling insights from the front-line of JavaScript development

Adam Boduch

PACKT open source *

ISBN: 978-1-78528-215-7   Paperback: 266 pages

Build enduring JavaScript applications with scaling insights from the front-line of JavaScript development

1. Design and implement JavaScript application architectures that scale from a number of perspectives, such as addressability, configurability, and performance.

2. Understand common JavaScript scaling pitfalls and how to tackle them through practical, real-world, solutions and strategies.

3. Learn techniques to deliver reusable architectures that stand the test of time.

KnockoutJS By Example

KnockoutJS By Example

Develop rich, interactive, and real-world web applications using knockout.js

Adnan Jaswal

PACKT open source *

ISBN: 978-1-78528-854-8   Paperback: 268 pages

Develop rich, interactive, and real-world web applications using knockout.js

1. Master the full range of features provided by knockout.js such as declarative binding, automatic refresh, dependency tracking, and templating using this project based guide.

2. Tackle real-world problems such as page navigation, forms, composite UI components, maps integration, server interaction for CRUD operations, and application security.

3. Discover the power of knockout.js as you build applications with complexity ranging from beginner to advanced.

Please check **www.PacktPub.com** for information on our titles

www.ingramcontent.com/pod-product-compliance
Lightning Source LLC
Chambersburg PA
CBHW060520060326
40690CB00017B/3333